Makuliert!
entwidmet aus den Beständen
der Stadtbibliothek Mitte

D1717283

Building Better

Sustainable Architecture for Family Homes

gestalten

Content

Preface

A Homeowner's Guide to Sustainable Interventions	4

Building Better! — 6
Hans Drexler

What is Sustainability?	6
Four Dimensions of Sustainable Architecture	8
A Methodological Discourse	18

Projects

Ábaton Arquitectura — 28
Off Grid Home

Bercy Chen Studio — 34
Edgeland House

Juri Troy Architects — 40
Sunlighthouse

BLAF Architecten — 46
Passive House with Textile Skin

Pitman Tozer Architects — 52
Gap House

Acme — 56
Hunsett Mill

Architecten de Vylder Vinck Taillieu — 62
House Rot-Ellen-Berg

Aray Architecture — 68
Shirasu House

Barton Myers Associates — 76
Montecito Residence

Carl Turner Architects — 82
Slip House

Desai Chia Architecture PC — 88
LM Guest House

FRPO Rodriguez & Oriol — 94
MO House

John Wardle Architects — 100
The Shearers Quarters

Institute for Advanced Architecture of Catalonia — 106
Endesa Pavilion

Rural Urban Framework — 112
A House for All Seasons

Jun Igarashi Architects — 118
House O

Arcgency — 124
WFH House—Sustainable Prefab House

Renzo Piano Building Workshop 132	
"Diogene" Basic Shelter	

Studio 1984 138	
The Nest	

H & P Architects 142	
Blooming Bamboo Home	

Tegnestuen Vandkunsten a/s 148	
The Modern Seaweed House	

Kraus Schönberg 154	
Haus W	

—

Lifethings 160
Sosoljip, Net-Zero Energy House

Paul Archer Design 166
Green Orchard

Powerhouse Company 172
Village House

Kjellgren Kaminsky Architecture AB 178
Villa Nyberg

Tham & Videgård Arkitekter 182
Garden House

Djuric Tardio Architectes 188
Eco Sustainable House

—

UUfie 194
Lake Cottage

Kengo Kuma & Associates 200
Meme Meadows Experimental House

Lode Architecture 206
G House

BME-Odooproject 212
Odooproject

Parsonson Architects 218
Shoal Bay Bach

Ryall Porter Sheridan Architects 222
Orient House IV and Artist Studio

Unsangdong Architects Cooperation 228
Kolon e+ Green Home

—

Guilhem Eustache 234
Fobe House

Andrea Oliva 240
House on "Morella"

Vo Trong Nghia Architects 246
Stacking Green

Appendix

—

Index 253

—

Imprint 256

A Homeowner's Guide to Sustainable Interventions

by Sofia Borges

There are many ways to live and build sustainably. While some forms of ecological design involve state-of-the-art technologies, solar panels, and a green roof, others engage with time-tested methods that have existed for centuries. The now widespread conversation on sustainability opens the door to a broad array of ecological approaches. From homes built using local seaweed and bamboo to residences made from prefabricated components in order to minimize their impact on the environment, the contemporary sustainable house proves as diverse as it is beautiful.

The countless methods available to achieve an energy-efficient home demonstrate that sustainability is not a unifying label, but in fact a local condition that changes in accordance with its natural environment. Local factors influence everything from the home's layout and orientation to overall material choices that are subject to availability, context, and climate. Not only concerned with efficiency, the sustainable home stays in sync with its surroundings. Seasonal changes, the path of the sun, and a family's day-to-day activities all play important roles in generating comprehensive sustainable strategies. Closing the gap between construction, production, and reuse, these holistic and site-specific approaches account for both macro and micro considerations that respond to the ecosystem of a given place.

Ecology and aesthetics go hand in hand. By understanding, honoring, and mindfully harvesting nature's resources, today's sustainable home can take almost any form. With a solution for everyone, even the most simple energy-saving choices can become the most liberating both for one's bank account and peace of mind. Whether opting for life off the grid or simply occupying a smaller structure made from local and recycled materials, the spectrum of techniques available to live in a more environmentally sensitive manner allows us not only to dream big but to dream within budget.

1. The Hybrid Collector
(Photovoltaic thermal hybrid solar collector/PVT)

New developments in solar technology now allow homeowners to collect both heat and electrical energy from the sun within a single system. Placed on the sunny side of the roof, these hybrid panels can produce most if not all of a home's electricity and heating requirements. The combination PVT panels are more efficient in both production and space saving than using photovoltaic and solar thermal panels on their own.

2. The Façade

The façade not only defines the overall appearance of a house but also its environmental performance. When building from scratch, the combination of high-performance insulation, airtight seals, and energy-efficient glazing works together to stabilize the indoor climate year round. If renovating an existing residence, it is important to remember that an efficient façade depends on all aspects of the structure relating to one another. If a high energy rating insulation is installed without replacing the old drafty windows then the two components effectively negate one another. However, if a comprehensive strategy proves unviable due to budget, historic preservation regulations, etc. then the simple act of choosing a more ecological insulation still goes a long way towards buffering the environmental impact generated during construction.

3. The Window

The window often represents the easiest and most economic way to improve a home's energy usage. By simply replacing the old glass with an insulated glazing, the high-performance material reduces heat loss in the winter and solar gain in the summer. For a more complete approach, replacing the windows may also mean updating the framing, and in time, the rest of the façade.

5. The Roof

A well-insulated roof can make all the difference in regulating a home's indoor climate. Accommodating a range of budgets, many different ways to insulate the roof exist including wood fiber, cellulose, and wool insulation. The process of adding the insulation must happen at the point when the entire roof is ready to be replaced.

6. The Expansion

While the main function of an addition is to gain space, these extensions present new opportunities for incorporating green design elements. Ideally oriented towards the south and engaging efficient insulation and airtight construction, the new space can double as a winter garden and temperature buffer between the outdoors and the main house.

7. The Grey Water Tank

Storage tanks collect rainwater and certain types of waste water for reuse around the house. This grey water can be used to flush toilets and irrigate the garden.

8. The Heat Pump

A heat pump taps thermal energy from an underground reservoir and directs it into the house for heating. Reversible heat pumps that provide both heating and cooling are also available.

4. The Floor

From choosing sustainably harvested flooring like cork or bamboo to integrating radiant heating, how one treats this interior finish can dramatically change a home's energy rating. Radiant floors and walls replace the need for inefficient radiators and create a stable and comfortable indoor climate. The only downside to radiant heating or cooling systems is that they require extensive intervention to install, but once in place they quickly live up to their positive reputation.

Illustration "Energiesparhaus", Armin Schieb/Sepia.

Building better!

by Hans Drexler

> "You never change things by fighting the existing reality. To change something, build a new model that makes the existing model obsolete."
>
> Buckminster Fuller

What is Sustainability?

Sustainability essentially describes an approach whereby natural resources are only used in quantities and at a rate compatible with their capacity to regenerate. According to the most basic definition coined by the Brundtland Commission[1] in 1987, sustainability means finding a balance between the needs of the present and of future generations.[2] This definition is based on the underlying concept of human needs. Housing must be considered in this context too, as it fulfills a whole range of basic human needs. Abraham Maslow, a psychologist who developed a theory about human needs, differentiates between "deficiency needs" (essential needs like eating, sleeping, safety) that have to be met to survive, or to live happily (i.e. social needs), and "growth needs" (such as achieving recognition and self-actualization).[3] He explains that at a certain level our deficiency needs are satisfied and no further progress is possible or would be beneficial. The "growth needs," on the other hand, are essentially unlimited. The category of essential needs also includes shelter, which fulfills our need for security by offering protection from the elements and from predators. At the same time, housing directly or indirectly addresses other needs as well. An apartment, for example, is a social space that enables a sense of community and family life. Ultimately, a house or apartment can be associated with esteem and can contribute to self-realization. This psychological and emotional factor is closely tied to the values and self-perception of the individual.

The question of sustainability is inevitably linked to the concept of human needs as it is precisely these needs that give rise to carbon emissions and the exploitation of resources. It would certainly be easier if humans, especially in developed nations, would alter their unsustainable lifestyles and patterns of consumption. Experience shows us, however, that this is unlikely. Our civilization and presumably human nature are not geared toward restraint and modesty. Rather, our economic systems are built on the idea of continual growth and each of us is conditioned to want to improve our lives, which in turn increases our levels of consumption. The challenge we face today is to find a way to meet our needs in a manner that is sustainable and ecologically compatible.

There are three basic strategies with which sustainable development can be achieved: efficiency, consistency, and sufficiency. The most common strategy deployed at present is efficiency, i.e., maximizing the productivity of resources, energy, or work hours that have been invested. The efficiency approach ties in well with the market-oriented logic of economic processes. Closely related is the concept of consistency, which strives to preserve material resources by creating closed-loop life cycles. By recycling products and raw materials, these resources circulate continually within the industrial cycles. Consistency can also refer to the exclusive use of renewable raw materials and energy sources. An alternative approach to a sustainable lifestyle would be to replace quantitative growth with qualitative growth. For example, a smaller but better designed apartment can offer higher quality of life than a larger one with a poor layout and orientation. These approaches can be categorized under the term "sufficiency," which questions what levels of consumption are appropriate or sufficient.

1.1.
What is Sustainable Architecture?

Architecture is arguably mankind's least sustainable activity. It consumes enormous quantities of material and vast areas of land, and it destroys natural habitats. Cities expand to occupy an ever greater portion of the surface area of our planet. The roads, railways, pipelines, and cables that connect these cities cut through every tract of pristine nature. Even the most remote areas of the planet are exploited for their natural resources, contaminated by waste, or altered by climate change. All these impacts are closely related to buildings. The operation and maintenance of buildings account for the greatest part of the consumption of energy, carbon emissions, and production of waste. Since buildings are in use for decades, these impacts are predetermined far in advance.

In light of this fact, it is surprising how little time most architects spend thinking about the impact their buildings have on the environment, the future, or even the people that live or work in them. Unlike craftspeople and engineers, who are pragmatists operating within or acting upon physical reality, architects have to maintain a peculiar distance from the context in which they work, and to the world in general. This distant relationship comes about through the separation of the world as it really exists and the world that architects must create in their minds if they are to transcend reality and facilitate creativity.

The critical distance architects maintain is generally harmless enough. Many architects concern themselves with issues of design that might seem arcane to the general public, solving problems to which most people would be oblivious. Yet as the results of these decisions proliferate, their consequences are having an impact on a far wider scale. The imaginative power of architects, as they create buildings and cities, and thereby alter entire landscapes, indirectly contributes to the transformation of the entire planet. Unfortunately, however, such transformation does not come about through consideration or design. It is no more than a byproduct of a lifestyle to which we have grown accustomed. The last chapter of this introduction will discuss the reasons for this development and will suggest alternatives.

Despite the inherent contradiction, the term "sustainable architecture" seems plausible. This may simply be because we are inured to it from the constant bombardment of books and other media releases that assert the sustainability of particular buildings. Yet most of those claims prove to lack substance, and to bear little scrutiny. The plausibility of the concept may, however, rest on firmer foundations, as this book will seek to show. Since architecture and the built environment present so many challenges for sustainable development, it is a field where there is much room for improvement. Architecture has enormous potential to induce what Bruce Mau called "Massive Change."[4] The projects in this book give encouraging examples of how architecture can be part of the solution rather than part of the problem.

1.2.
The Single-Family House as a Typology

If "sustainable architecture" is a contradiction in terms, the term "sustainable single-family house" seems like a logical impossibility. Of all building typologies, the single-family house is probably the least sustainable. As with many technologies, its impact only becomes apparent when seen on a large scale. On the scale of a city, the low density of suburban estates of single-family houses means comparatively high land consumption per housing unit or person. It also stimulates a great deal of traffic, which in turn needs more roads and other infrastructure to support it. Because population density in most of these areas is so low, a public transit system is not a viable alternative to transportation by car. Long distances to places of work, commerce, or culture discourage alternative modes of transportation like cycling or walking. Therefore, energy consumption for traffic increases significantly with the decreasing density of cities or districts.[5]

As a building typology, the single-family house has some disadvantages that appear either less often or not at all in other typologies. The small overall building volume leads to an unfavorable ratio of surface area to volume, the so-called SA/V ratio. Smaller geometric bodies have a larger surface area in relation to their volume than a body of the same shape but larger dimensions. For example, a cube of 10 m × 6 m × 6 m (the dimensions of a compact single-family house of 120 sq m) has an SA/V ratio of 0.43, but a cube in a hypothetical apartment block, measuring 50 m × 30 m × 30 m, has an SA/V ratio of 0.087. Since the envelope of the building is the most technically sophisticated part of the construction, a smaller building means a more complicated, resource-intensive, and therefore more expensive construction. The building's surface area also affects its energy consumption. Buildings with a more adequate SA/V ratio perform significantly better in almost every climate. Their small size means that single-family houses consume more energy per floor area than larger building typologies.[6]

Single-family houses also tend to be less efficient in organization. On most suitable sites, there are fewer constraints on planning, and therefore less effort is made to make the floor plan efficient and to make the best use of every square meter.

This is not only a problem of design, but also one of image. The single-family house is an emblem of an affluent lifestyle that is almost by definition inefficient. Like a large automobile or other luxury items, it is valued because of its limited availability. It sets its owner apart from those with less buying power. Anyone can afford a small apartment, but few can afford their own house. Therefore a certain generosity of space is an integral part of the concept. Still, the single-family house is more than mere representation, it is a manifestation of aspiration. People dream of a place that belongs to them: a home. A home is a place of security, privacy, peace, and identity.

Despite its fundamental disadvantages, the single-family house is an important typology in the architectural discourse. In architecture, each individual building can be regarded as a small-scale testing ground for sustainable development on a broader scale. The personal level of the relationship between client and architect often yields outstanding results. If we were to develop sustainable solutions for a single building, the same logic could be extended to a small district or even an entire city. There are many encouraging examples of buildings that produce more energy than they need for their operation, or of construction methods that use materials that are recycled and can be recycled many times. The relevance of these achievements must not be underestimated. Only by built example can it be demonstrated that change is possible. In this respect,

Building Better can play an important role. This book gathers many examples and concepts, every one of which can be an inspiration to someone interested in better solutions for the future. The variety of examples shows another characteristic of sustainability: there are many different approaches to sustainable design.

Four Dimensions of Sustainable Development

The Brundtland report already introduces the basic principles behind most aspects of sustainable building. It is based on three pillars of sustainable development: the environment, the economy, and society.[7] This structure has been integrated into many rating systems to evaluate sustainablity in the construction industry, such as the SIA 112 (Switzerland), DGNB-System[8] (Germany) and BREAAM[9] (Great Britain and international). These different aspects can be illustrated more clearly using the four dimensions of sustainable development, which are discussed in the first part of this introduction: the ecological dimension is concerned with the interaction between humans (culture) and the environment (nature), the economic dimension looks at interdependencies within our economic and financial systems, while the social and cultural dimensions encompass the impact on society and the effects of cities and buildings on individuals. Discourse on sustainable building embraces a wide range of other topics that are only indirectly connected to the original question of resources. The four dimensions can provide the basis for a holistic approach to optimizing buildings, and help to ensure that the reduction of resource use is not achieved simply by reducing the quality of the architecture or the performance and comfort of a building.

2.0.
Ecological Dimension

The climate change debate is just one of numerous examples that show why it is important to find sustainable and ecological solutions for architecture. The construction and operation of buildings is crucial to climate change as buildings are responsible for a high proportion of environmental pollution, accounting for 32 percent of total global final energy use and 51 percent of electricity consumption worldwide in 2010.[10] According to the report of the Intergovernmental Panel on Climate Change (IPCC) from 2014, the building sector produced 19 percent of carbon emissions in 2010.[11] Other environmental indicators also demonstrate the significance of the built environment: about 50–60 percent of the world's waste is caused by demolition, refurbishment, and the construction of new buildings. Yet, there is great potential in buildings for improvement and efficiency optimization that can and must be tapped. Over the past thirty years, it has been possible to reduce the primary energy consumption required to operate new buildings by about 80 percent, which has led to the expectation that most buildings in the near future will operate according to the principles of zero-energy or active houses. The EU Commission aims to introduce "nearly zero-energy" buildings as a new standard for all public buildings by 01.01.2019.[12]

2.0.0.
Energy Efficiency: Less Bad is Not Good[13]

Reducing negative consequences, for its own sake or to save the planet, is not sufficient motivation to influence people's behavior. Even if efficiency gains are perceived as a good thing, at least on an abstract level, there is little in the way of tangible benefit or experience. Another problem that arises is the so-called rebound effect.[14] Many achievements in efficiency are canceled out because consumption rises when prices fall, or when goods and services become more readily available or are perceived as having a diminished ecological impact. For example, all efforts at saving fuel through the design of advanced engines or other technologies are rendered meaningless as newer car models constantly increase in size and weight, and even more importantly as the number of cars on the roads continues to rise.

Behavioral changes come about mostly through politics, the economy, or through positive motivation. If goals of sustainability are to prevail among architects, planners, and clients, then achieving those goals must bring improvements that can be experienced on a daily basis. One example of such a concept is the "Sunlighthouse" in Pressbaum near Vienna, Austria, designed by Jury Troy Architects, a project that reverses the argument of the passive house concept. This concept is based on minimizing the overall energy consumption of buildings. For example, windows might be restricted in size depending on their orientation. One consequence of this might be a clearer distinction between interior and exterior spaces, contradicting the prevailing ideas of contemporary housing. In contrast, the idea of the active house is to balance energy gains and losses, or for savings to outweigh consumption. If the outcome is a net gain, there is no need to define specific thresholds or methods by which that outcome is reached, or to specify the characteristics of its components. What is important is the balance between losses and gains. In this concept, then, windows are not seen as energy loss factors but rather as a central architectural element that supplies the interior with natural light and fresh air, creates visual references, and collects solar energy. The increase in spatial quality is as important as the reduction of the negative impacts. The building produces an annual energy surplus. Within 30 years of operation this positive energy balance will also have compensated for the construction of the building and the energy that it entailed. The volumetry of the building is designed in response to its geographical and climatic context. The building is spatially complex and its multifaceted structure successfully overcomes the above-mentioned doctrine of compactness. The combination of material homogeneity and spatial complexity leads to a design in which the energy strategy is manifest in space itself.

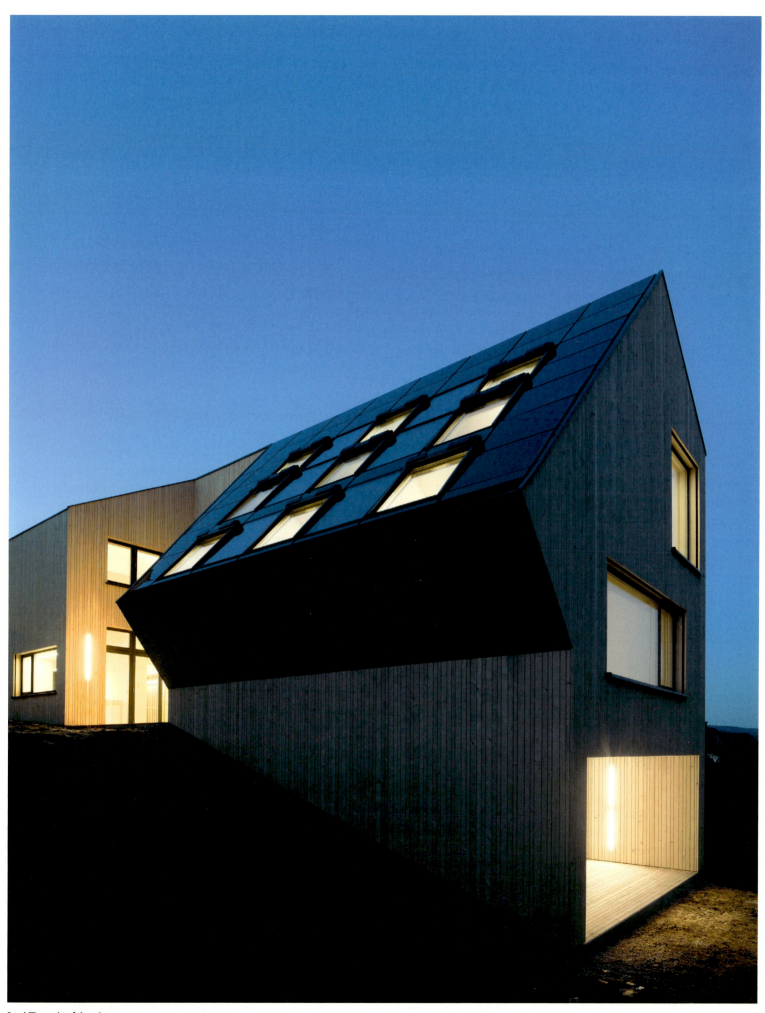

Juri Troy Architects
Sunlighthouse, Austria
→ Page: 40

In the same spirit, the architectural integration of the PV system in the roof is an integral part of the building design.

What is technically possible tends to be much more advanced than of the built reality. Prototypes allow exploration of this territory, enabling the testing of technologies that might in future help to improve many buildings. The network "Effizienzhaus Plus" monitors a range of active houses with the aim of better understanding the performance of these new buildings. An example of a building that produces more energy over the course of a year than it consumes is the BME-Odooproject built for Europe's Solar Decathlon, a carbon neutral house that merges an efficient energy automation system and photovoltaic panels with techniques for passive heating and cooling. Since production and consumption are not synchronized, most active houses use the grid as a buffer, feeding in surpluses during summer and compensating higher consumption in winter. One approach of great interest for future buildings is self-sufficiency. Self-sufficient buildings, i.e., ones that no longer rely on the grid as a buffer, would reduce the need for infrastructure. If we could design most buildings to be self-sufficient rather than to be dependent on external resources, the problem of sustainable energy for buildings would be solved. As of yet, the necessary technology is still expensive and its production resource-intensive.

2.0.1.
Rebuilding Old Stock

With regard to new buildings, impressive efficiency gains can be achieved when all aspects of their design and construction are planned to be sustainable from the outset. The greater and far more important challenge is how to deal with buildings that already exist. The dimensions of this dilemma can be better understood by way of example: new buildings are a more adequate solution in terms of sustainable development as they use less energy, but with new construction at an average rate of one percent per year in Germany, it would take 100 years for the entire building stock to be replaced with more sustainable structures. Older buildings have to be upgraded if sustainable development is to be achieved in the near future. The importance of this is underlined by the fact that modernizing buildings to minimize consumption has, in most cases, less impact on the environment than building from scratch. Many components of an older building can be reused, which eliminates the need to produce new structural components and cuts waste, as the remains of the old building do not have to be disposed of. Also important are old buildings' significance with respect to the cultural identity of towns and communities. The diversity of a city lives from the juxtaposition of its architectural styles and eras. The challenge facing us today is to adapt these buildings to meet modern requierments for comfort, to reduce energy consumption to a tolerable level, and to preserve the identity of the building within the urban landscape. Renovation and refurbishment may of course require compromises when it comes to efficiency, detail planning or usage, but it is in these areas that skilled architects can excel: they should be capable of developing the best solutions no matter the conditions they are given.

In essence, there are four strategies to deal with older building stock: firstly, buildings can be preserved as they are, accepting in the process that energy consumption will be much higher because the levels of comfort expected today, especially with regard to room temperature and hot water, are far greater than the building was originally capable of providing. This strategy makes sense and is imperative in the case of important historic buildings whose cultural value can only be preserved when the original building remains intact. The second strategy aims to integrate refurbishment measures into the building in such a way that the original structure can be optically and technically preserved as much as possible. By applying this approach, historical buildings, for instance, can be fitted with improved technical systems, and external walls can be insulated from the inside, while ensuring that the impact of the intervention and changes to the façade are kept to a minimum.

The third strategy involves the deliberate separation of old and new, but united in an overall composition. An astounding example of this is the project "House Rot-Ellen-Berg" (see page 62) by Architekten de Vylder Vinck Taillieu. A charismatic old building was gutted and rebuilt internally by erecting a smaller new building within the older structure. The façade facing the street and other external walls were kept in their original condition. This house-in-house principle results in a smaller, warm winter house, and a larger, unheated space that is only used when the weather and fluctuating interior temperatures permit. What distinguishes this project from others is the clear articulation of the contemporary elements of the new inner structure. The walls made of aluminum and glass, the modern wood-based materials, and the girders left untreated clearly demarcate the two parts of the building, thereby initiating an exciting dialogue between old and new.

Architecten de Vylder Vinck Taillieu
House Rot-Ellen-Berg, Belgium
→ Page: 62

The "Hunsett Mill" by Acme also pursues this strategy, although in this case, old and new are kept apart in two distinct buildings, sparking a dialogue between the typology of the "pitch-roof house" of the older building and the new annex, which is continued inside.

Acme
Hunsett Mill, Stalham, UK
→ Page: 56

The fourth strategy for dealing with existing buildings is the synthetic reconstruction of buildings that can no longer be supported from a cultural-architectural point of view or because of their poor condition. Such buildings often have to be completely renovated and structurally upgraded, resulting in an entirely new building that offers a homogeneous synthesis of old and new.

2.0.1.0.
Recycling: Design to Disassemble

The high number of different materials required to construct a building translates into a great amount of waste at the end of its useful life. The construction industry in Germany, for example, is responsible for 55 percent of the country's total waste.[15] Current developments in construction have led to fears that the amount of waste will only increase in the future. Firstly, the life expectancy of buildings is continually decreasing and, secondly, a whole range of materials are closely interconnected within the construction, making it impossible to reuse the constituent components. Composites consist of numerous base materials bonded together with insoluble adhesives, creating a huge pile of hazardous waste for the future. Producing this amount of waste is as much of a burden on society and the environment as the production of new materials, which again consumes energy and raw materials.

Sustainable buildings must be constructed differently from the outset. Alternative methods are required to join individual components together so that they can later be disassembled. Structural layers have to be built in such a way that they can be maintained and replaced independently of each other, as the life expectancy and load of each component is different. It is crucial that technical building systems can be easily replaced and upgraded to keep up with technological advances, and in case they need to be adapted to altered conditions (availability of resources and energy supply). "Design for Disassembly" is an approach to designing buildings that cannot only be erected, but also reconstructed, disassembled, and reused with little damage. The design and construction already factor in the eventual disassembly of the building. This approach to building is an important prerequisite for establishing a construction industry that manages building materials and components in closed-loop cycles in accordance with the cradle-to-cradle principle:[16] cradle-to-cradle[17] production eliminates the concept of waste. Products are manufactured from raw materials that can be fully recycled. To ensure that all resources can be reused, it must be possible to separate buildings into their constituent materials and components. Developing concepts to achieve this purpose is one of the greatest challenges facing architects today. This development must occur on two levels: on the first, the structural level, it is essential to develop new systems for joining components, assembly and disassembly procedures, and recycling systems that will make reuse a financially viable option. The second, the material level, focuses on materials and resources that can either be easily and fully recycled or that are biologically degradable. Braungart and McDonough describe two different approaches to recycling: the technosphere (technical cycles) for materials that continually circulate in a closed loop as raw materials for industry, and the biosphere (biological cycles) for biological growth and composting processes.[18]

In individual cases, new buildings' resource consumption can be decreased by using recycled materials. For "Orient House IV and Artist Studio", Orient, NY, a project of Ryall Porter Sheridan Architects, planks salvaged from demolished buildings in the region were used for the façades of both buildings. This recycling method not only mitigates the environmental impact but also gives the building a very individual character through the heterogeneity and patina of its façade.

2.0.1.1.
Renewable Resources

Nature has its own very effective recycling system. Suitable materials can be broken down into their constituent components, composted, and reused as fertilizer for products within biological material cycles. In Europe, wood has been the most popular renewable resource for centuries, and its use is still widespread today. Improved methods in fire protection, advances in automated lumber cutting and processing technologies, and the development of new wood products have opened up a variety of possibilities in the timber industry over the past twenty years. Solid wood constructions have seen a revival since the development of multilayered panels (cross-laminated timber), and glued laminated timber (glulam) has facilitated new building methods. The advantage of this type of construction is

Ryall Porter Sheridan Architects
Orient House IV and Artist Studio, Orient, NY
→ Page: 222

the robustness of the building, the combination of high heat storage capacities with good insulation, and most particularly the haptic and aesthetic qualities of the material's surface. The latter can be experienced inside the "G House," Normandy, France, designed by Lode Architects (see page 206), where the untreated wooden surfaces create the atmosphere of the rooms and give the whole building its distinctive character. Moreover, the construction can be easily built in a comparatively short amount of time thanks to the high degree of prefabricated materials.

Other renewable and locally sourced materials were used in traditional building that became mostly obsolete with the rise of industrial products and modern construction methods. If a greater proportion of renewable materials are to be used in the building sector, it needs to be determined whether and how these natural resources can be deployed in contemporary construction. Architects Tegnestuen Vandkunsten explore the use of a combination of seaweed and wood in their "Modern Seaweed House" (see page 148). In the interior of the building, the seaweed has been covered with a white fabric that gives shape and plasticity to the walls and ceilings.

Tegnestuen Vandkunsten a/s
The Modern Seaweed House, Denmark
→ Page: 148

2.1.
Economic Dimension

The far-reaching consequences of the financial and economic crisis of recent years demonstrate the importance of the economic dimension of sustainable building on a global scale. The crisis was triggered in 2008 by the subprime mortgage meltdown in the United States, the result of banks approving too many mortgages to people who were unable to afford them. Enormous sums, estimated at 9.865 billion US dollars,[19] were invested in real estate for which no buyers or tenants existed. The financing of these buildings was thus not guaranteed on the long term. The economic impact of building can also be immense for the individual. On average, Europeans spend about 28.4 percent of their disposable income on their living accommodation.[20] Added to that are the indirect costs of using other buildings (trade, retail, public buildings) as well as the services they provide, and the infrastructure required to operate buildings and cities, paid for through charges, fees, and taxes. The optimization of these investments, and operation and maintenance costs is an important topic within sustainable development.

Economic logic has permeated our whole society. For this reason, the economic viability of sustainable solutions has an enormous influence on their success and marketability. We will only have a serious chance of increasing demand for these products among consumers and decision makers when we can offer sustainable solutions at competitive prices. It has to be said, however, that with respect to private single-family houses, the economic incentives of sustainable design

Lode Architecture
G House, Normandy, France
→ Page: 206

and life cycle cost analyses, based on both short-term and long-term costs, are not very effective in practice. In most cases, the running costs (operation and maintenance) are not fully taken into account, which means that planning cannot be optimized accurately.

2.1.0.
Affordable Housing

The economic dimension of sustainable development can also be looked at from another angle. The provision of living space is a key objective for society, and more specifically for architecture. An important part of sustainable development is to develop construction techniques and buildings that make it possible for everyone, even those with low incomes, to afford a roof over their heads. The typology of the single-family house may well be associated with luxury homes but numerous simple constructions can be assigned to this category too. Designing a simple and adequate low-cost building that can also deliver a high level of spatial quality and detailing is a challenge that few architectural firms can take on, as there is generally only a small budget available for planning. In this light, humble projects with outstanding architectural qualities are even more remarkable. The small building called "The Nest" by Studio 1984 in Muttersholtz, France is one example of a building that creates a living space with the most simple of means. It consists of a jointed, solid wood frame filled with straw bales to create walls, floors, and ceilings. The bales of straw are protected from the elements by a large, overhanging roof. The building, with an area of 15 square meters, was built for just 14,000 euros.

Studio 1984
The Nest, France
→ Page: 138

"How much is enough?" is the question of all questions that Robert and Edward Skidelsky attempt to answer in their book of the same name.[21] At the heart of their hypothesis is the question as to why people in developed countries actually work so much. As we do not need to struggle for our basic survival, there is only one answer: to afford a better lifestyle. Applying this theory to the subject of housing, the question could be reformulated: would it not make more sense to work less and live in more modestly sized apartments instead of working longer hours in order to afford superfluous living space? In Germany, the amount of living space per capita has risen from an average of 19.2 square meters in 1950 to 45 square meters per person today.[22] We also need to take a critical look at our ideal of the detached family house on the outskirts of a city. An analysis of cost and time benefits is useful here: how many work hours are required to realize the dream of a house in the suburbs? How much time are you prepared to spend commuting from your place of residence in a more affordable location to your place of work or to shops and amenities?

The project "Diogene", by the Renzo Piano Building Workshop, is named after the Greek philosopher Diogenes, who chose to live in a barrel and thought everything else superfluous. It offers interesting answers to these questions. If we were to content ourselves with the 5.76 sq m (2.4 m × 2.4 m) that the prototype offers, this would take the sting out of many current problems. Small though it is, the building offers high-quality spaces, answering more or less all living requirements. It includes a water treatment facility and, above all, produces its own energy.

2.2.
Cultural Dimension: "Sustaining Identity"[23]

The built environment fundamentally shapes the way we experience the world, making architecture one of the most important forms of cultural expression. The city is an expression of society's understanding of itself, and it determines communal life and social processes. There is more at work here than the mere superimposition of centuries of differing notions of architecture, technology, culture, and society: the city is also the result of a collective creative process involving the participation of thousands of people. This cultural discourse is directed and filtered to a far lesser extent in a city than, for instance, in a museum. Books, museums, films, and music are all consumed in a selective and more or less conscious way. Like no other cultural product, the city offers an everyday experience. It is a living space that does more than just collage individual buildings and intellectual concepts: it fundamentally shapes, indeed facilitates, the totality of our communal life and of society on all levels. Every building can be seen as a building-block in this collective cultural effort.

Unlike the city, and unlike public buildings, houses are at the service of individual identification as they play a part in founding the identity of its inhabitants, for example, that of a family. Such a house can be of profound significance, either positive or negative. However, the built enviroment acquires cultural significance only when it transcends individual experience, for culture emerges through discourse. This discourse is the process by which new ideas are integrated into culture.

The projects collected in this book, and indeed the book itself, are an example of this cultural discourse. The book addresses questions that concern everyone, such as "how should we live?" and seeks out and discusses possible answers to these questions.

2.2.0.
Learning from the Past: Autochthonous (Vernacular) Building Forms

Sustainable building is not a new idea. On the contrary: many traditional buildings were built sustainably, purely from necessity. Only since the Industrial Revolution has the availability of materials and energy been artificially amplified to an extent that created the false impression that resources were infinite. Before the Industrial Revolution, and still today in societies with preindustrial economies, the availability of building materials and energy, such as that used to heat buildings, was and is extremely limited. This limitation creates the necessity to treat available resources with frugality and care. According to the simplest definition of sustainability, derived from a forestry handbook[24] of 1713, if the quantity of resources (wood) taken from the natural system (the forest) within a certain time span does not exceed the quantity of wood that grows in the same period, such a management system can be called sustainable. Still, it should not be forgotten that management and building in preindustrial societies was not always sustainable. Indeed, the need for rules to be introduced in support of a sustainable economy by Hans Carl von Carlowitz arose from the fact that economic growth and the intensifying use of resources had already led to a dangerous depletion of woodland in the early modern period, and this needed to be stopped. Jared Diamond, in *Collapse—How Societies Choose to Fail or Succeed*,[25] explains how various traditional societies, facing the challenge of economic sustainability, have either failed or developed further. Two of the examples he analyzes are of particular interest to the construction sector. Easter Island's[26] indigenous civilization collapsed due to the deforestation of the island. Indeed, all palm trees were cut down in order to build the wooden ramps required to erect the famous statues and their platforms. A positive example, on the other hand, comes from Japan during the Tokugawa Shogunate (1603–1868), when the impending deforestation of the archipelago, as wood was taken for construction and for firewood, was averted by the imposition of strict limits on consumption and on the exploitation of the forests.[27] Most societies, however, developed a more or less sustainable way of life before the Industrial Revolution. Only as new sources of fuel and energy were developed, in particular fossil fuels (first lignite and coal, later oil and gas), did it become possible to abolish the dependence on time and locality in the generation and consumption of energy. In other words, it was now possible for consumption to exceed what could be grown or produced in the local area or at the given time.

Encoded within traditional or autochthonous building forms is time-honored knowledge of local resources and artisanal methods. The building tradition thus becomes an important agent of culture that is formative not only for the individual, but also for society as a whole. Sustainable construction must engage with the continuation of such traditions. Because buildings today come about by quite different processes, it cannot work with the same techniques and technologies as traditional building forms. Nonetheless, it is important that the building culture should continue to develop.

Many of these construction methods are also the result of a long process of optimization, adapting to the local climate and available building materials. The exhibition and catalogue *Learning from Vernacular*[28] offers a good overview, using models and analyses to present the results of a project headed by Professor Frey Pierre at the EPFL Lausanne. What these examples have in common is that they employ passive building strategies, thus offering an alternative to the prevailing high-tech strategies of contemporary architecture. Ingenuity in the design of the overall building volume, usage zoning, and the development of building construction can make it possible for the building to be run with low energy consumption. Typical building forms have developed in relation to the local climate. In colder regions, roof designs react to snow and wind. Compact structures are the rule, with small windows that leak less heat to the cold exterior. In dry and hot climates, extremes of temperature occur between day and night, so that buildings must have a high storage mass that cushions the daily fluctuation. Very dense development structures are also found here, e.g. in old centers of Arabian cities, because these limit solar irradiation. Other strategies found here include vertical zoning and usage that migrates in response to the building's changing temperature throughout the course of the day. One example is the Hakka houses that are a traditional building form of Fujian Province in China. These consist

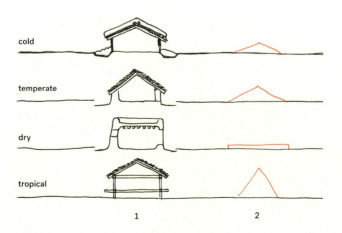

Manfred Hegger et al., "Energie Atlas: Nachhaltige Architektur (Konstruktionsatlanten)," 64. Drawing DGJ.

Kekeng Toulou Cluster: Hakka Round Houses in Fujian, China.

Section of a Hakka Round House in Fujian, China.
Both images: Anna Nikodem "Vertical Village" (M.A. Münster School of Architecture, 2013). Drawing DGJ.

of a massive outer shell of masonry defining a communal internal space, in which an open wooden construction forms a residential unit for a household. On the one hand, the building form has a social motivation, forming a defensive structure against attack. On the other hand, the form provides ideal protection against solar radiation and a high storage mass that guarantees a pleasant living environment.

In tropical climates, buildings are raised above ground level because of the heavy seasonal rains. The culture reacts to the year-round high temperatures by designing buildings in as open a form as possible so that breezes can pass through the structure. In spite of the high temperatures, air movement makes the tropical conditions bearable because a person's body temperature is reduced by sweating (adiabatic cooling). This traditional building technique was employed in the "Blooming Bamboo Home" in Vietnam (see page 142). The walls here consist of open bamboo lattices through which the breeze can blow. As is often traditional in tropical construction, the buildings are raised on stilts so that wind can also blow beneath the structure. Here too, elevation provides protection from standing water during heavy rains, and from vermin.

2.2.1. Local Building Materials

Another characteristic of traditional architecture is the use of local building materials. Local resources with a low degree of processing have a much smaller negative impact on the environment. For example, the clay needed for clay houses was traditionally extracted from the ground immediately adjacent to the building site. Because clay, unlike bricks, is not fired, its manufacture uses a minimum of energy. Another advantage of this building technique is that clay is soluble in water, so that after its use in a building, it reabsorbs into the landscape. Other building techniques are based on wood from sustainable local forestry. All over the world, there are outstanding examples of historical buildings constructed in this way.

A building tradition that is based on local materials can also foster identity, hence functioning as an agent of cultural sustainability. Where entire cities are built in a stone that is available locally, a strong overall identity of appearance comes to characterize the city in spite of a great wealth of individual architectural styles. Brick buildings are traditionally widely used in many regions, because in many places bricks can be made locally from clay or mud. Since the color of brick depends on the chemical composition of the local clay, traditional brick buildings in a particular area generally have a typical coloration, which can range from light yellow across a wide spectrum of reds to dark brown. An example of a contemporary house that takes up this kind of local building tradition in its choice of materials and its artisanal processes is the "House for All Seasons" in Shijia Village, China (see page 112). What is particularly interesting here is that the spatial organization also follows traditions of historical building typologies. Internally, the building forms several residential courtyards, like the traditional *siheyuan*, through which the living spaces are opened up, and these form the functional heart of the building.

H & P Architects
Blooming Bamboo Home, Vietnam
→ Page: 142

H & P Architects
Blooming Bamboo Home, Vietnam
→ Page: 142

Rural Urban Framework
A House for All Seasons, Shijia Village, China
→ Page: 112

2.2.2.
Another Modern Architecture

The Industrial Revolution and the resources it made available facilitated unprecedented wealth and improvements in millions of people's living conditions. Yet resistance to its consequences began to emerge soon after it began. Above all, many people found urban living conditions to be intolerable. In architecture, the most important movement proposing an alternative to industrial modernity was the Arts and Crafts movement in Britain and America. In continental Europe, similar ideas were pursued in Art Nouveau and Jugendstil. Essentially, the proposal was to reconcile industrial civilization with the artisanal tradition, and technology with nature. Advocates of Arts and Crafts recognized that industrialization and urbanization had caused people to become alienated from their natural way of life. They responded with efforts in all spheres aimed at making this new society more human, and reconnecting it with nature. Ebenezer Howard's "Garden City" was an idealized urban environment in this spirit. It offered a synthesis of town and countryside, enabling people to live a largely self-sufficient lifestyle within the individual clusters. Frank Lloyd Wright countered the technocratic, centralized city of the modernists with his own proposal of 1932, "Broadacre City." This was based on the originally American idea of a decentralized, suburban city, in which each citizen would be allocated an equal parcel of land—one acre, or 4,000 m², so that one could supply themselves and their family by working it. Because of the necessarily low density, this urban utopia led to enormous traffic problems, which Wright hoped to solve with the notion of private helicopters. Imagining the building as embedded in its natural context is typical of Frank Lloyd Wright's understanding of architecture. Wright designed a number of residential homes, of which the most famous, "Fallingwater" (1935–1937), is conceived as part of the landscape. But Wright's earlier "prairie style" displays the same approach in a different way. Because the flat terrain of the Mid-West offers few points of reference to integrate building volumes, the surrounding prairie itself becomes the design model for the interior of the building. The landscape is integrated within the house, creating a new type of space that subverts and abolishes the distinction between indoors and outdoors in buildings of the early modern period, especially those by Mies van der Rohe.

But Wright's buildings display a new dimension of architecture in more than just overall design. Improving ease and comfort is now the central concern. In the prairie house designs, a large, central hearth always forms the center, or heart of the building. The roof, room structure, and façade are designed to guarantee those inside a supply of fresh air, as Reyner Banham showed in his comprehensive study *Architecture of the Well-tempered Environment*.[29]

2.2.3.
The Cultural Identity of the City and of Suburbia

The detached house is inextricably linked to the idea of the verdant suburb. The appeal of the suburbs lies in their liminal location: proximity to the urban center provides an economic basis as jobs are available. It also offers shopping opportunities, cultural attractions, and educational facilities, such as schools and universities. This urban quality is connected to the idea of living close to nature.[30] Low building density and green space indeed lend a rural quality to the suburb. Families in particular look to the outskirts of the city to provide a healthy living environment that is safe and in contact with nature. The idea of living close to nature romanticizes the countryside. In reality, suburbanization leads to the destruction of such natural and rural spaces. Besides the land needed for actual housing, much more land is also requisitioned to construct the necessary infrastructure: roads, sidewalks, and public buildings.[31]

An alternative model to the expansion of the peripheries of conurbations is the recolonization of disused spaces in cities. Making use of the smallest residual spaces with sophisticated architecture is a particularly difficult challenge to planners, and one that Pitman Tozer Architects have taken on (see page 52). Their "Gap House" makes use of a narrow gap just three meters across in a typical district of terraced houses in London. The building uses the somewhat wider rear portion of the land to bring luminosity into more rooms through a lightwell and skylights, creating exciting spatial references.

2.3.
Social Dimension

The modernist movements aimed to improve living conditions and to ease social grievances. Sustainable architecture today must continue this important discourse. The current discussion on the reorganization and renovation of cities is often inadequate. This

Pitman Tozer Architects
Gap House, London, UK
→ Page: 52

One of the typological problems of the single-family house is that it tends to be poorly adaptable to the future challenges of architecture. In all societies, the average age of the population rises in accordance with the country's level of industrialization. To meet the challenges that result from this, but also to make buildings usable by anyone, it would be necessary for newly constructed buildings to be entirely accessible. This requirement is reasonable not only in regard to the equal rights of people whose mobility is limited, but also in regard to the long-term usability of buildings. If single-family houses are ultimately to be used as homes by the elderly, it is shortsighted to plan them in ways that prevent old people from using them.

A Methodological Discourse

"It is fundamentally the confusion between effectiveness and efficiency that stands between doing the right things and doing things right. There is surely nothing quite so useless as doing with great efficiency what should not be done at all."

Peter Ferdinand Drucker

inadequacy stems from the fact that the discussion is separated from the social dimension, a dimension concerned with creating affordable housing, achieving a representative mix of social groups within the city, and asserting a clear agenda to avoid gentrification. Urban gentrification often appears as an unavoidable consequence of the modernization of buildings and urban districts, and leads to a displacement of citizens from downtown areas and attractive neighborhoods. As a result, increasing segregation takes place along subtle social boundaries between wealthy neighborhoods and neighborhoods where the more financially and socially disadvantaged demographics live, as they simply cannot afford rising rents. A socially mixed urban realm is still the core of a democratic society and state. As Thomas Sieverts has pointed out, a democratically and socially evolved consciousness can only develop based on the real day-to-day experience of society as a whole.[32]

We might examine the detached, single-family house and ask ourselves how suitable this type actually is in offering a context of life that reflects the way people really live. The family is seen as the nucleus of society, and the single-family detached house is seen as the preferred venue in which family life runs its course. Considering today's altered models of living and dynamic changes within families, most family houses are in fact only used for this purpose over a relatively short period of time in their intended way, until the children move out, for example. It is then reasonable to ask, from a sociological standpoint, whether this residential form has any value as a model for the future.

The definition of sustainability in the Brundtland report has been criticized for putting human needs first. This focus is above all a product of the global perspective of the UN. It aimed at a just distribution of resources worldwide, among rich and poor, and among present and future generations. However, looking at developed countries today, it is obvious that the main problem is the level of consumption, i.e., the so-called needs themselves. This issue is implicit in several aspects of the discussion of single-family houses. Specialist discourse on sustainable building is mostly only concerned with discussing methods for solving a given building assignment more efficiently. Yet efficiency on its own is not a solution to the mismatch between rising demand and dwindling resources. The questions of what or why something should be built aren't asked as often. In the case of single-family houses in particular, sufficiency and effectiveness (in contrast to efficiency) are important questions. Savings in building and operating costs per square meter of residential space are canceled out by the rebound effect described above. In terms of residential property, this means in practice that people demand more space per person. The desire for more residential space seems to know no natural bounds. Seen as a whole, then, it is sensible not just to think about sustainable solutions in the building of single-family houses, but also to ask the fundamental question of why single-family houses play such an important part in our culture. This question cannot be answered within the bounds of the discipline, but must be addressed in terms of the relationship between the individual and the world, and the idea of architecture that emerges from that relationship.

2.4.
A World Within the World

More than other building typologies, the single-family house is an icon of Western culture. The dream of the single-family house distils something fundamental in Western consciousness. It is a manifestation of individualism. The idea that the individual is at the center of culture and society can be traced back to the Enlightenment in general and to René Descartes in particular. In his philosophy, the mental capacities of the individual were the central instance of the production of knowledge. He applied his newly-developed analytical method to mathematics (geometry and algebra), but it became even more influential as a philosophy of science and scholarship. The analytical method is based on the assumption of an independent outside observer (the subject) of a system or the world in general (the object). This observer is enabled, by virtue of his or her mental capacities alone, to understand and, in consequence, act upon the system or object. The Cartesian method puts the individual at the center.

This observational method has other consequences quite apart from the central role it accords to the individual. Reality is no longer regarded as a continuum of effect. The core of the analytical method consists in the dissection of reality into subsystems that are small enough that meaningful descriptions can be given within them.[34] This isolation is assumed to be necessary in order to distinguish causes and effects within the profusion and complexity of reality, and to predict how a system or object will behave. But this conceptual isolation spawns a real one, for the solutions that are developed refer only to the subsystem artificially isolated. This assumption negates the state of the "fundamental interconnectedness of all things."[35] Reality cannot really be subdivided into part-systems.[36] Moreover, this isolation is not always only spatial, but can also be temporal. The subsystem is considered over the short term, in the here and now, and its future state is not an object of consideration.

From a holistic perspective, this isolation appears problematic. The local solution of a problem often has unintended consequences elsewhere. A short-term measure can produce consequences that are harmful in the long term. Many of the problems discussed above derive from local and short-term strategies, the global and long-term consequences of which are catastrophic. A few decades of dependence on fossil fuels consumes resources that took millions of years to form. Climate change is one of the many unintended consequences here. The methodical problem is that humanity as a whole, as well as individual societies, have outgrown the strategies that long ensured survival. These methods date from a time when it seemed reasonable to define an isolated segment of reality, because sufficient resources existed within and around that segment so that it seemed possible to regard the subsystem as valid, while the consequences of doing so seemed manageable, because the world seemed inexhaustibly large in comparison to what was being consumed.[37] Yet as long ago as 1972, a report to the Club of Rome warned of an exhaustion of resources and the vulnerability of the environment.[38] Since then, many resources have duly been exhausted and many ecosystems have gone beyond their capacity for regeneration.

During the Enlightenment, nature was seen as an orderless chaos, to which the enlightened man brought structure and order by his actions.[39] This notion has given rise to the fundamental distinction between culture (architecture) and nature. Architecture is not thought of as part of nature and its processes, but as an external, indeed contrary, system. Consequently, when architecture is understood in this way, its inherent task is assumed to be to replace nature with what is assumed to be the superior anthropogenic system. This dichotomy of nature and culture thus also redefines the role of architecture. These issues of epistemology and philosophy of science are in a variety of respects important and highly relevant to sustainable architecture, which:

→ has an impact on the understanding of nature and culture.
→ has a formative role in individuals and their desire for a private sphere.
→ has a formative role in the self-image of the architect and the discipline.
→ determines the method by which architecture is conceived and produced.
→ shapes the understanding of form and space in modern architecture.

2.5.
Individualism and Private Spaces:
From the Villa to the Single-Family House

It would be stretching credibility to assert that a philosophical concept or analytic method has led to the fragmentation of society. More plausibly, it could be argued that Descartes' theory extrapolated the trajectory of Western society at the time. What caused society to fragment was the liberation of the individual from external bonds. The revolutions and political changes that ensued can be regarded as a shift of power from the central entities of monarchy, state, and church, to the individual. Democratizing tendencies are a logical consequence of that shift. But the fragmentation is also relevant on a sociological level. Church congregations, guilds, and extended families were waning both in size and importance. One indicator for this development is that the average number of persons per household in Western societies dropped from 5.0 in 1893 to 2.5 in 2000.[40] The single-family house is the built expression of the concept of individualism. It is a world within the world, a microcosm for a small group or an individual, creating the illusion of a space that is fully controlled and self-sufficient.[41]

Privacy and private space slowly evolved with individualism during the age of Enlightenment. Before that time, privacy was not a relevant concept for society or architecture. For the Romans of antiquity, privacy was the state of deprivation from taking part in public affairs, the *res publica*, that sphere of political, cultural, and social life that was the privileged preserve of the free man.[42] Privacy was therefore not held in high regard. For most of history, few would have a house of their own, and even those who did would share those premises with servants, extended family, and others. Bill Bryson explains how the concept of privacy in England developed during the sixteenth century.[43] Before this time, houses were mostly "halls," i.e. large common spaces for all activities of life (and livestock) where no distinction was made between public and private areas. To create such newly conceived private spaces, houses had to be differentiated internally, being subdivided into an increasing variety of spaces for different uses and inhabitants. In the urban context, houses began to move apart from each other, occupying the open landscape made available by the demolition of the fortifications that confined the growth of most cities until the nineteenth century. This tendency would later lead to the formation of suburbs as houses spread out in greater numbers.

From the dawn of the Enlightenment, theorists of architecture turned their attention to the villa, the precursor of the single-family house. Andrea Palladio, whom Pevsner calls the first professional architect,[44] and who may be regarded as the prototype of the author-architect, specialized in villas, which constitute the greater part of his output. The villa now became the symbol of a new genre of architecture. Palladio's villas are no longer bound to the urban context, but are located amid the landscape, freed from all constraints. The landscape here becomes a frame that is also designed, but without exerting a design influence on the building. Instead Palladio, in his *Quattro libri* of 1642, compiles a plethora of rules for building methods, materials, dimensions, and proportions that are modeled to some extent on Vitrivius' *The Ten Books on Architecture*. However, the rules he proposed would prove less significant in the subsequent reception of Palladianism than the very idea that such methods and rules were possible for architecture. Palladio and his Neoclassicist followers established a relationship with antiquity and its strictly ordered building forms. In particular, architecture was associated with scientific method by introducing intrinsic rules.

The transposition of the architectural discourse from public and sacred buildings to private houses reflects the valorization of the individual over society or abstract overall concepts such as kingdom, church, or state. The citizen as enlightened individual moved to the center of the culture. Accordingly, portraiture depicting rich and influential citizens now became an important genre in painting. Wealthy and progressive citizens as patrons acted as drivers of culture with their commissions for paintings, sculptures, villas, and palaces. The Renaissance villa is the architectural icon of the Enlightenment in three respects. Firstly, it is a work of art created by an author-genius. Secondly, as a typology, it frees the building from the urban structural context and its constraints. Thirdly, it is a private building project that represents the citizen as individual.

Here a distinction must be introduced between the mostly suburban single-family house and the villa or country house. The villa was not a Renaissance invention, but was an aspect of the Roman heritage rediscovered and propagated by Palladio and his Neoclassicist successors. The Roman villa was a residence in the countryside. Most villas were centers of agricultural production and at the same time the temporary or permanent residence of the landowner and his family. Most pre-modern country houses or cottages were related to agriculture. Only after World War II did the rural single-family house as a wholly residential building become a widespread phenomenon within the reach of the middle classes. It is no coincidence that its success parallels that of the culture of the automobile, for cities with their expanding suburbs would create large distances that could only be covered on a daily basis by auto. Automotive traffic made suburbia possible and accelerated its development. Just like the automobile, the single-family house had become a middle-class consumer product due to the introduction of industrial production pioneered by Henry Ford, which made houses and cars more affordable. The development of private houses was mostly due to a general increase in wealth. The same pattern can still be seen in most countries: as prosperity increases, a greater portion of the population tends to live in single-family houses.

2.6.
Architecture with a Capital 'A'

The single-family house also became an important genre for classical modernism. Many of the most important buildings of the twentieth century are single-family houses, such as Le Corbusier's Villa Savoye, Mies van der Rohe's Farnsworth House, and the Case Study Houses. The importance of these milestones lies in their exemplary function. Single-family houses are a kind of Petri dish, a microcosm in which new ideas can be implemented in a more radical way than in larger, more complex projects. This radicalism is also related to the smaller number of people involved in the design process. Descartes, in *Discours de la méthode [pour bien conduire sa raison, et chercher la vérité dans les sciences]* explicitly refers to the role of the architect and the superiority of an individual accomplishment over a collective one.[45] This manifests itself in the method by which architecture is produced: the creative act is the heart of the production. This creation from the pure reason and creativity of the author is central to the authorial "Architecture with a capital A," contrasted with "architecture with a small a," which Bernard Rudofsky calls "anonymous architecture."[46] Anonymity is characteristic of a different understanding of self. In Architecture with a capital A, the author is at the forefront as an individual and the originator of the design.

Traditional, anonymous architecture has no authors. It is the result of a collective effort that not only grows from the knowledge and skills of many people, but is also based on local, traditional knowledge. To a certain extent, it emerges from society and context. Accordingly, complex and multifaceted relationships to nature, landscape, climate, and society are encoded within it. Architects (capital A) do not see themselves as agents within an existing reality, but as creative geniuses using their intellectual power alone to invent a new reality that is better than the existing order of things. The white sheet, or the sketch roll, embodies this distanced relation to reality. Reality is either negated altogether, or else it is reduced to a working basis, to which, as the work process continues, a constant accretion of new sheets of sketching paper creates an increasing distance, burying and suppressing it.

The understanding of space in modern architecture is also informed by Descartes. The ideal here is the three-dimensional Cartesian grid. Within this neutral, uniform, infinite geometric space, all points and directions are of equal value and may be used and connected as desired. As a construct (the uniform column grid designed to free space from direction and limitation), a design principle (regular façade grid), and a structure of urban planning, the grid is the most important determinant of modernist planning. Yet this understanding of space is profoundly alien to the nature of things. Real space, or the "lived space"[47] about which Franz Xaver Baier writes, always contains direction. It is distorted by gravity. It has a before, a behind, an above, and a below. Nor is space infinite—nor, indeed, is it geometric, but rather topological, i.e., affected by things and their relationship to one another. This infuses reality with an incalculable abundance of directions and movements that the neutral Cartesian space seeks to negate. Le Corbusier's "Plan Voisin"[48] for Paris is an extreme example of the negation of the lived space. It envisaged demolishing an area of around 240 ha[49] in the historic heart of Paris to the north of the Île de la Cité, from Place de la République to the rue du Louvre, and from the Gare de l'Est to rue de Rivoli, and building in its place a modernist residential city and a separate commercial city.[50] The plans negate and replace the context of the organic city rather than attempting to acknowledge and develop it. The distance modern architecture adopted from its context is also apparent in *Vers une architecture*.[51] Le Corbusier's references for his new architecture are selected buildings with no landscape context, and machines that symbolize mankind's independence from nature and context: the ocean liner, the airplane, and the automobile. His only references to architectural history are to abstract geometric rules and proportions, through which he suggests that the principles and methods he proposes were already valid in the past, but were never formulated with his degree of clarity. The formal language of this architecture is thus also informed by the same simplification. In *Vers une architecture*,[52] Le Corbusier traces architecture back to the geometric space, the Platonic body, and the human observer and creative genius, who is capable of recognizing the internal geometric contexts and expressing them in design. By its negation of context, modernist architecture also becomes universally applicable. Methods and solutions can be employed without regard to context, culture, or climate. Philip Johnson commented on this tendency that the modernists displayed in the title of his 1932 MOMA exhibition, *The International Style*. Architecture in modernism became a global movement. At the same time, however, Johnson's use of the word "style" carries a hint of irony, suggesting that this is no patented solution of global problems, but rather an intention in design in which aesthetic predilections are just as important as they ever were.

The example of the Modulor reveals a fundamental conflict within modernism. The Modulor makes the human individual the measure of all things. Not only is this measuring system based on the human body, it also betrays a claim to human hegemony, as man seeks to bring the world into an order that seems reasonable to him. Yet at the same time, this standardization has the effect of suppressing individuality and difference. Le Corbusier's idea of the dwelling as a residential machine shows this attitude. If the house is a machine to live in, housing becomes a technical problem to be dealt with efficiently and decisively. As a consequence of this attitude, the people inside the house become a standardized product. The Modulor is an attempt to enforce this: it specifies an exact height (183 cm) for the human body, then uses this to derive the dimensions of the "machines to live in." Here again, the analytical method is applied. The human body is isolated from the context and simplified to a degree that allows for general rules to be identified. Clearly, anyone not measuring 183 cm in height would have to adapt to the reality imposed.

It must be said that Le Corbusier had the greatest affection for the newly arrived machines that surrounded him in the increasingly modern world. In *Vers une architecture*, he devotes almost a third of the text to exploring how these machines might become the reference for new modern architecture. By classifying the building as a machine, however, he makes architecture more a technical discipline than a cultural practice. Ever since, architects have been striving to build machines that are poetic and beautiful even though they are machines, rather than to abolish the contradiction by acknowledging that buildings are not machines and nor are people standardized entities of raw material to be processed. There are many examples of post-war mass residential architecture, in both the east and the west, which redefined scale and generated monotony. This then became the point at which postmodernist criticism began. Modernism canceled thousands of years of traditional building culture and invented architecture anew. This reinvention harbored an emancipation of the creative genius from traditional sources, an emancipation that continues to be influential as it exerts a powerful stimulus on the discipline.

2.7.
New Planning Methods: A Holistic Approach

Although sustainable building is arguably the most important and most pressing discourse in the discipline of architecture, the achievements necessary to make the majority of buildings and cities sustainable are modest on closer inspection. On the level of the individual building, savings in energy and resource consumption can be significant, and might be as high as 90 percent. However, potential improvements do not translate into an overall reduction of resource consumption. The focus on buildings' operational energy and carbon emissions has detracted from a holistic discourse on sustainable architecture. Problems of sustainability and ecology tend to be so complex and abstract that it is difficult for people to relate their personal or professional decisions to them. Doing the right thing has no consequence that could be experienced in everyday life. Challenges are still met with ignorance at best and resistance at worst. Energy efficiency, benchmarks, life cycle costs, and certification systems seem to tangle into a knot that hinders architects in their creativity. Rather than being seen as an inspiration or as a design challenge, they are experienced as a limitation that restricts freedom in the creative process. This perception is closely related to the lack of comprehensive strategies, methods, and tools to integrate the issues of sustainable design into the planning process. What is still missing are strategies that address sustainability as a design issue.

The first part of this introduction discussed specific themes and aspects of sustainable building. Even specialist discourse in recent years has above all been concerned with describing sustainability in construction, developing long lists of criteria and systems of certification and evaluation. This discourse makes a valuable contribution as it demonstrates all of the aspects comprised within sustainable building. However, with respect to the sustainability of buildings, we find ourselves in a double-edged situation. We know with some precision what a sustainable building is, but we lack methods to control a design or plan a process that respects these criteria. Not without justification, then, most architects regard these criteria and systems as technical problems and not as part of the discipline itself. This discourse of technicality has created the false impression that there are technical components that will make a conventional building sustainable. But sustainability is not an extra feature that can be added to a conventional building, like a photovoltaic module or a heating pump. Rather, sustainability is an attitude, an integral part of the design, the construction, and the architecture. Above all, then, it needs methods and strategies to be developed that enable us to ask the right questions and answer them through the design process.

There is another widespread misunderstanding that prevents the discipline's necessary development. Many architects believe that good architecture (whatever that is) is inherently sustainable. The thought process is superficially plausible: buildings that are of good quality and well suited to their use will remain in use for longer. Indeed, if the word "sustainability" were synonymous with "durability," this argument would be conclusive. However, sustainability is much more complex.

Throughout history, architecture has consistently appropriated new themes as it has developed methods of design and construction that address these themes in the planning process; such themes are now understood as part of the core role of the architect. Examples include stability and statics. Naturally, stability against collapse was always an important challenge in all buildings, but most buildings made in the artisanal tradition were built with large redundancies in their structure. Static calculations have only been used as a computational planning method since the nineteenth century. The possibilities afforded by these calculations have since given rise to new constructions and building typologies. The audacious engineering structures of the nineteenth century, such as Joseph Paxton's Crystal Palace (1851) or the Eiffel Tower (1887–1889) were possible because stability could be calculated during the planning process, and because materials were of a reliably uniform quality. As well as the need for new planning methods, the example highlights another important aspect. The development of the load-bearing system is now part of the architect's job. The engineer now has an undisputed place in the planning team and process. The integration of new planning content, then, demands new experts, but also new expertise for the architect. A somewhat new architectural language has developed through the implementation of new planning methods, with the use of new building materials like steel, glass, and reinforced concrete.

The discipline must implement sustainability in a professional way within the planning process. There already exists a spectrum of professional consultants involved in these processes, working in the interests of issues of energy efficiency and sustainability, and preparing and executing certifications. It is becoming increasingly clear that the subject cannot be readily treated separately from the actual processes of design. Comprehensive engagement with all aspects of sustainable building thus often begins at such a late stage in the planning process that adaptations can only be made at great financial cost and with considerable delays. Integrating sustainability in planning processes requires new planning methods. The task of the future will be to develop better methods and tools to achieve this. In a preliminary proposal, Dominique Gauzin-Müller suggests a new conceptual framework for sustainable building based on the themes of the architectural plan, and offers starting points for the plan:[53]

→ Human use—social and cultural dimension, spatial program, requirements
→ Location, territory—urban planning, landscape, land consumption
→ Material, technology—building structure, energy and material consumption, resources
→ Energy and comfort—energy consumption, comfort

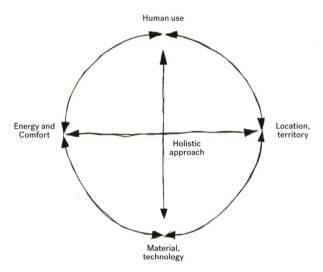

However, architects will also need wider training and a shift in orientation. In the nineteenth century, the introduction of engineering methods led to a debate on the fundamental direction of the discipline. The artist-architects, arguing for training at fine art academies, opposed the engineer-architects trained at the new technical colleges. To some extent, these two directions continue to exert their influence today. The dichotomy, however, also expresses a fundamental ambivalence in the discipline, which is neither purely technical nor purely artistic, but must pay due attention to both equally. The holistic approach to sustainable architecture must abolish this dichotomy; it must therefore also constitute a broadening of the concept of creativity to include not only facility in design but also analytical and scientific processes. The notion that creativity is only necessary in artistic or design processes is antiquated. Design is not the antithesis of scientific work, nor must it set itself free from supposed scientific fetters. Design and science share common origins.[54]

2.8.
Responsibility of Architecture

The role of the client must also be discussed here. To a certain extent, the architect is only a service provider, following the client's instructions. Key decisions such as choosing the type of residential form and the location are generally made by the client, creating a framework within which the architect then works. Client and architect thus share joint responsibility for the sustainability of the architecture, and should steer the processes in a sustainable direction through their dialogue. An important factor here is that the architect must demonstrate different planning variants through consultation, analysis, and the presentation of advantages and disadvantages.

The client's decisions on these matters are not made in a vacuum, but are integrated within a social, economic, and political context. Political specifications determine the availability of land and its potential use. Many potential developers would prefer to build in inner cities if suitable land with planning permission was available. The conditions to facilitate or favor sustainable solutions must also be created on a political level. The construction of single-family houses, for instance, is abetted when cities continually make new land available for construction on the edges of conurbations in order to attract new citizens with plenty of buying power. In democracies at least, this political will is supported by a social consensus that, up to a point, reflects the wishes of the majority of the electorate.

It is high time for architects, clients, and society in general to face their responsibilities to the future. Architecture as a discipline owes society answers to the urgent questions of our time. Architects must embrace the themes of sustainability as an opportunity to develop planning themes, and this book contains many inspiring examples. When conceived as an integral element, sustainability is not the enemy of design. On the contrary, it stimulates concepts, designs, and constructions whose aesthetic value lies in the fact that they make sense, and engage in a dialogue with their context.

If people are to be inspired to change, they need positive examples of how this change can improve their lives. Sustainable buildings must not only be more ecological, they must also be more useful, more comfortable, and more beautiful.

Hans Drexler, Dipl. Arch. ETH M. Arch, studied architecture at TU Darmstadt, ETH Zurich, Bartlett London, and at Städelschule in Frankfurt. He was a research fellow under Professor Hegger at TU Darmstadt. His scientific research focuses on the integration of sustainability within architectural processes in design and planning. Hans Drexler is an associated partner at Büro Drexler Guinand Jauslin Architekten. His "Minimum Impact House" has received many accolades. Since 2009, he is a professor at msa | münster school of architecture.

1. United Nations World Commission, "Chapter 2—Towards Sustainable Development" in *Our Common Future: Report of the World Commission on Environment and Development*, (Brundtland Report), http://www.un-documents.net/our-common-future.pdf. (accessed 05/2014)
2. United Nations World Commission, *Our Common Future: Report of the World Commission on Environment and Development*, (Brundtland Report), http://www.un-documents.net /our-common-future.pdf. "Sustainable development is development that meets the needs of the present without compromising the ability of future generations to meet their own needs. It contains within it two key concepts: The concept of 'needs,' in particular the essential needs of the world's poor, to which overriding priority should be given; and the idea of limitations imposed by the state of technology and social organization on the environment's ability to meet present and future needs." (accessed 05/2014)

3. Abraham Maslow, "A Theory of Human Motivation" in *Psychological Review* Vol. 50 #4 (1943), 370–396.

4. Bruce Mau, *Massive Change, A Manifesto for the Future Global Design Culture* (London, 2004).

5. Peter W. G. Newman et al., "Gasoline consumption and cities: a comparison of US cities with a global survey", in *Journal of the American Planning Association* (1989).

6. A typological study compared buildings of different sizes but the same physical construction in respect of their total energy consumption for heating, cooling, and lighting. The results showed that a single-family house uses approx. 45% more energy than a building with eight residential units. Cf.: Roman Brunner et al., *Das Klima Als Entwurfsfaktor: Architektur und Energie*, second revised edition (Lucerne, 2013).

7. United Nations World Commission, "Section I. THE GLOBAL CHALLENGE, 2. The Interlocking Crises" in *Our Common Future: Report of the World Commission on Environment and Development*, (Brundtland Report), http://en.wikisource.org/wiki/Brundtland_Report. "2. The Interlocking Crises. 11. Until recently, the planet was a large world in which human activities and their effects were neatly compartmentalized within nations, within sectors (energy, agriculture, trade), and within broad areas of concern (environment, economics, social)." (accessed 04/2014)

8. Deutsche Gesellschaft für Nachhaltiges Bauen e.V. (Stuttgart, 2008), http://www.dgnb-system.de/de/system/dgnb-nachhaltigkeitskonzept/?pk_campaign=kachelsystemvorstellung. (accessed 04/2014)

9. BRE Global Ltd internal, London, http://www.breeam.org/. (accessed 04/2014)

10. Intergovernmental Panel on Climate Change (IPCC) Working Group III, Potsdam Institute for Climate Impact Research (PIK) Climate Change 2014: Mitigation of Climate Change IPCC Working Group III Contribution to AR5, http://mitigation2014.org/report/final-draft/. "In 2010, the building sector accounted for approximately 117 exajoules (EJ) or 32 percent of global final energy consumption and 30 percent of energy-related CO2 emissions; and 51 percent of global electricity consumption." (IEA, 2013). (accessed 04/2014)

11. Intergovernmental Panel on Climate Change (IPCC) Working Group III, Potsdam Institute for Climate Impact Research (PIK) Climate Change 2014: Mitigation of Climate Change IPCC Working Group III Contribution to AR5, http://mitigation2014.org/report/final-draft/. "19 percent of all global 2010 GHG emissions." (accessed 04/2014)

12. European Parliament and Council Directive 1010/31 EU, May 19th 2010, on the total energy efficiency of buildings (new version). The revised version of the EU Directive published on June 18th 2010 in the Journal of the European Union (Issue L 153/13). "Nearly zero-energy buildings. (1) Member states affirm that (a) all new buildings will be nearly zero-energy buildings by December 31st 2020, and that (b) new buildings used by authorities as owners will be nearly zero-energy buildings from December 31st 2018." Quoted from: Melita Tuschinski, ed., http://www.enev-online.de/epbd/2010/index.htm. (accessed 05/2014)

13. Michael Braungart and William McDonough, *Cradle to Cradle* (San Francisco, 2002), 45.

14. Tilman A. Santarius, *Der Rebound-Effekt* (Wuppertal, 2012), 12.

15. Statistisches Bundesamt, Abfallaufkommen (einschließlich gefährlicher Abfälle), 05/2013, http://www.umweltbundesamt.de/daten/abfall-kreislaufwirtschaft/abfalllaufkommen. (accessed 04/2014)

16. Michael Braungart, and William McDonough, Cradle to Cradle (San Francisco, 2002).

17. Ibid., 104.

18. Ibid., 93.

19. Wendy Edelberg et al., Final Report of the National Commission on the Ca*uses of the Financial and Economic Crisis in the United States*, submitted by the Financial Crisis Inquiry Commission (Washington, 2011).

20. Antonio Puente, "Statistik kurz gefasst. Bevölkerung und soziale Bedingungen. Der europäische Verbraucher in der erweiterten Union" (Brussels, 2005), http://www.eds-destatis.de/de/downloads/sif/nk_05_02.pdf. (accessed 04/2005)

21. Robert Skidelsky and Edward Skidelsky, *How Much is Enough? Money and the Good Life* (New York, 2012).

22. Bundesinstitut für Bevölkerungsforschung, press release #9/2013, 2013, Wiesbaden, http://www.bib-demografie.de/SharedDocs/Publikationen/DE/Download/Grafik_des_Monats/2013_07_pro_kopf_wohnflaeche.pdf?blob=publicationFile&v=3. (accessed 04/2014)

23. Kirsten Schemel, *Sutaining Identity*, lecture MSA 2013. The title references a lecture of the same title given at the Münster School of Architecture by Prof. Kirsten Schemel, December 2013.

24. Hans Carl von Carlowitz, *Sylvicultura oeconomica* (Leipzig, 1713), 105.

25. Jared Diamond, *Collapse—How Societies Choose to Fail or Succeed* (New York, 2005).

26. Ibid., 89 ff.

27. Ibid., 298 ff.

28. Pierre Frey and Patrick Bouchain, *Learning from Vernacular: Pour une nouvelle architecture vernaculaire* (Lausanne, 2008).

29. Reyner Bahnham, *Architecture of the Well-tempered Environment*, second ed. (New York, 1984), 116, first published (New York, 1969).

30. Thomas Sieverts, *Zwischenstadt—zwischen Ort und Welt, Raum und Zeit, Stadt und Land* (Basel, 1997), 1. "Es ist, anders ausgedrückt, die Sehnsucht nach der Verbindung von Hirtenromantik und Stadtkomfort." ("It is, in other words, a longing for the reconciliation of bucolic romanticism and urban comfort.")

31. Hans Drexler et al., Fachgebiet EE der TU Darmstadt, *Minimum Impact House—Prototyp für nachhaltiges Bauen* (Wuppertal, 2008). Analysis of a typical new residential area in the north of Frankfurt showed that an average area of 333.7 m^2 was requisitioned per residential unit, and a further 69.6 m^2 built over.

32. Thomas Sieverts, *Zwischenstadt — zwischen Ort und Welt, Raum und Zeit, Stadt und Land* (Basel, 1997), 154.

33. Peter Ferdinand Drucker, "Managing for Business Effectiveness" in *Harvard Business Review* May–June 1963 (Boston, 1963), 53–60.

34. René Descartes, *Discourse on the Method of Rightly Conducting One's Reason and of Seeking Truth in the Sciences*, (London, 2013) first published Paris, 1637: "The second (precepts), to divide each of the difficulties under examination into as many parts as possible, and as might be necessary for its adequate solution.
The third, to conduct my thoughts in such order that, by commencing with objects the simplest and easiest to know, I might ascend by little and little, and, as it were, step by step, to the knowledge of the more complex; assigning in thought a certain order even to those objects which in their own nature do not stand in a relation of antecedence and sequence."

35. Douglas Adams, *Dirk Gently's Holistic Detective Agency* (London, 1987).

36. Peter Eisenhardt et al., *Du steigst nie zweimal in denselben Fluß* (Hamburg, 1998), 21: "Bezugnehmend auf die notwendigen Bedingungen wissenschaftlicher Denkweise und ihre Folgen für die Wirklichkeitsauffassung der Wissenschaftler, nämlich ihre Unterwerfung unter die Illusionen der Abstraktion, stellen wir Postulate auf, wie man die Wirklichkeit möglichst abstraktionsfrei auffassen könnte. Wir sagen: 1. Die Wirklichkeit ist prozessual und keineswegs statisch, sie wird und ist wesentlich in der Zeit. 2. Die Wirklichkeit ist diskret und heterogen, keineswegs kontinuierlich und homogen-identisch. 3. Die Wirklichkeit ist lokal und keineswegs global überschaubar, sie ist jeweils nur örtlich—an den Orten möglicher Beobachtung- strukturiert. 4. Die Wirklichkeit ist Wechselwirkung, nicht an sich seiend, sie ist

überhaupt nur, insofern sie auf einen Beobachter (der zum Beispiel auch ein Meßinstrument sein kann) eine Wirkung ausübt und von diesem Beobachter eine Wirkung erleidet. Dieser wechselseitige Prozeß, in dem lokal diskrete Größen ausgetauscht werden, konstituiert erst die Wirklichkeit." ("With reference to the necessary conditions for scientific thought and their consequences for the scientist's perception of reality, i.e., the subjugation of perception to the illusions of abstraction, we suggest how reality might be perceived with as little abstraction as possible. We propose: 1: reality is processual and far from static, but develops and exists in time. 2: reality is discrete and heterogeneous, rather than continuous and homogeneous/identical. 3: reality is local and cannot be surveyed on a global scale, being always structured locally, at the venues of possible observation. 4: reality is interaction, not a thing existing in itself—it only exists at all where it exerts an influence on an observer (the definition of 'observer' here would include a measuring instrument) and is influenced by that observer. Indeed, this reciprocal process in which local, discrete values are exchanged, is what constitutes reality.").

37. cf. Douglas Adams and Mark Carwardine, *Last chance to see* (London, 1990).

38. Donella H. Meadows et al., *The Limits to Growth. A Report to The Club of Rome* (New York, 1972).

39. Charles-Edouard Jeanneret, (Le Corbusier), *Towards an Architecture* (New York, 1986), 227, first published in French *Vers une architecture* (Paris, 1923): "Plan. The Plan is the generator. Without a plan, you have lack of order, and wilfulness. The Plan holds in itself the essence of sensation. The great problems of tomorrow, dictated by collec-tive necessities, put the question of 'plan' in a new form. Modern life demands, and is waiting for, a new kind of plan, both for the house and for the city."

40. Mason Bradbury et al., "Longterm dynamics of household size and their environmental implications" in Population and Environment A Journal of Interdisciplinary Studies, (New York, 2014), quoted from http://csis.msu.edu/sites/csis.msu.edu/files/Longterm%20housing.pdf. (accessed 04/2014)

41. The notion of individualism, libertarianism and privacy as discussed here is closely related to Western societies. Other cultures lead to other social models. In China, to single out one of many possible other concepts that could be named here, the public and the private sphere are less clearly distinct. As Dieter Hassenpflug explains, the Chinese city does not know our concept of the public space. In European cities, the public space is generated by the communication of mainly private buildings with the public realm. The façade defines a spatial boundary of the public and the private spaces, and acts as a display that communicates from the individual (citizen) to the public (society). China's society is based on communities on the small scale, and the state. The public space can therefore not be constituted by spatial distinction or communication. Exterior spaces in Chinese cities (Hassenpflug calls them open spaces) are of a commercial or representative nature. Commercial spaces use the image of the public space for commercial purposes, generally as market places of different kinds or for commercial recreational activities. The power of the state is represented in open urban spaces as well, the most famous example being Tiananmen Square in Beijing. Those spaces are in scale and design very different from the public spaces in European cities, which underlines their different purpose. Of course public gatherings, especially political ones, are not allowed in these spaces, which explains their representative rather than public character. The effect of the absent public character Hassenpflug describes as "intimization," the use of urban spaces for private purposes: Chinese people like to use urban spaces to dry their laundry, to dance, to dine, or to gather in smaller or bigger groups. Interior spaces, meanwhile, are often closed to the urban spaces. The Hutong, one of the most important traditional housing typologies, is an enclosed courtyard house. In modern China this tradition translates into large-scale compounds that are also enclosed housing complexes where sometimes thousands of people live together. Housing in China is generally based on the idea of a community occupying an enclosed communal space, very different from the private spaces in Western houses.

42. Hannah Arendt, *The Human Condition* (Chicago, 1958), 38. "In ancient feeling..."

43. Bill Bryson, "Chapter Three—The Hall" in *At Home: A short history of private life* (London, 2010).

44. Nikolaus Pevsner et al., *Lexikon der Weltarchitektur*, third ed. (Munich, 1990), 476.

45. René Descartes, *Discourse on the Method of Rightly Conducting One's Reason and of Seeking Truth in the Sciences* (London, 2013) first published (Paris, 1637): "Of these one of the very first that occurred to me was, that there is seldom so much perfection in works composed of many separate parts, upon which different hands had been employed, as in those completed by a single master. Thus it is observable that the buildings which a single architect has planned and executed, are generally more elegant and commodious than those which several have attempted to improve, by making old walls serve for purposes for which they were not originally built."

46. Bernard Rudofsky, *Architecture Without Architects: A Short Introduction to Non-Pedigreed Architecture* (New York, 1964).

47. Franz Xaver Baier, *Der Raum. Prolegomena zu einer Architektur des gelebten Raumes* (Cologne, 2000).

48. The 1925 Plan Voisin was named for its sponsor, the French aircraft manufacturer Société Anonyme des Aéroplanes G. Voisin.

49. Cf.: Fondation Le Corbusier (Paris, 2014), http://www.fondationlecorbusier.fr/corbuweb/morpheus.aspx?sysId=13&IrisObjectId=6159&sysLanguage=fr-fr&itemPos=151&itemSort=fr-fr_sort_string1%20&itemCount=216&sysParentName=&sysParentId=65. (accessed 04/2014) Centre Pompidou, Le plan Voisin 1 - L'hypothèse de Le Corbusier, http://www.airsdeparis.centrepompidou.fr/viewtopic.php?t=109. (accessed 04/2014) Massachusetts Institute of Technology, Tunney Lee et al., "Density Atlas", http://densityatlas.org/casestudies/profile.php?id=99, "47'972 m^2". (accessed 04/2014)

50. Andreas Krasser, *Le Corbusier—Städtebautheorien*, http://www.andreas.krasser.com/downloads_sonstiges/LeCorbusier.pdf. (accessed 04/2014)

51. Charles-Edouard Jeanneret (Le Corbusier), *Towards an Architecture* (New York, 1986), 277, first published in French *Vers une architecture* (Paris, 1923).

52. Ibid., 153 ff.

53. Dominique Gauzin-Müller, "Nachhaltig Bauen: Lowtech oder Hightech?" in Hans Drexler and Adeline Seidel, *Building the Future: Maßstäbe des nachhaltigen Bauens* (Berlin, 2012), 25.

54. Otl Aicher, *Die Welt als Entwurf: Schriften zum Design* (Berlin, 1991) "Die Tugend der Wissenschaft überträgt sich auf das Entwerfen. Die Tugend der Wissenschaft ist Neugier, nicht das Wissen. Wir entwerfen, weil wir suchen, nicht weil wir wissen." ("The virtue of science is transposed to design. The virtue of science is curiosity, not knowledge. We design not because we know, but because we quest.")

Vo Trong Nghia Architects
Stacking Green
→ Page: 246

Projects

Ábaton Arquitectura

Sustainable features

- → Natural ventilation
- → Photovoltaic power
- → Hydro power
- → Southern exposure
- → Overhangs for shading
- → Insulating shutters
- → Off-grid
- → Local and recycled materials
- → Solar panels
- → Adiabatic cooling

Off Grid Home

Cáceres, Spain

This off-grid home serves as a sustainable retreat that generates its own power and water supply. The gracious farmhouse combines a rustic sensibility with passive house principles including natural ventilation, the use of local materials, and a layout optimized for solar gain.

Set on a sweeping five-hectare estate, this project transforms an abandoned stable into an elegant family home. The two-level house, located at the foothills of the Gredos Mountains in western central Spain, turns its locational challenges and access to standard amenities into an opportunity for sustainable innovation. Both contextually and environmentally sensitive, the charmingly rustic dwelling enjoys a rich life off the grid.

High on a hill and far from city water or the electrical grid, the home instead relies on photovoltaic solar power during the summer and hydro power in the winter for its year round energy needs. The building's original orientation also benefits from southern exposure, allowing the sun to still serve as the main source of heat during the winter. Solar panels soak up the plentiful Spanish sun throughout the year, affording the residents the rare luxury to live off the grid and on their own terms. At the same time, a generous eave prevents too much sun from entering the home during the summer and balances out the level of sun exposure during the course of each season. Large wooden shutters slide over the exterior like a second skin. Sweeping open during the day, these shutters cover the large windows at night. This shifting façade element not only lends the interior and exterior a variety of aesthetic atmospheres but also conserves the home's daily solar gain for nighttime heating.

T he residence's considerable distance from city water balances out due to its optimal placement below two fresh streams and the integration of water turbines. This reliable source of pure water readily meets the occupant's drinking and bathing needs. A swimming pool running along the side of the house also doubles as a holding tank for use in irrigation.

Opting for an approach focusing on conservation, the interior of the residence carefully relates to the outdoor environment. Here, nature blends into almost every room in the house. In this gracious and modern interior, bathrooms offer views of the internal patio and its stone water fountain while bedrooms with generous picture windows overlook the pristine countryside. Rising out of the forest clearing, the house basks in the regal ambiance of the surrounding oak, chestnut, alder, and willow trees.

Executed on a modest budget, the entire house was completed for under $415,000. Given the stable's crumbling state, a mix of cement and local stone was applied to the updated façade. Inside, light metal pillars replaced the supporting walls. The haylofts in the upper area are converted into bedrooms and the expansive central lounge behaves as an active, multi-purpose social space. Seamlessly merging new and old elements, the house introduces numerous sustainable materials. These environmentally conscientious choices include recycled stone, weather-beaten oak wood, concrete, limestone floors, and recyclable steel.

A few of the preserved qualities from the original stable consist of the u-shaped, load-bearing rough stone walls, the permeable south façade, the slope of the roof, and the set back on the upper floor. The updated layout's most notable differences appear in the spatial split between the ground floor and upper level as well as the introduction of an open courtyard. This elegant courtyard, lined with rugged stones, directs natural light indoors and helps with the building's thermal control through the central placement of a sleek water element. Minimalist in design, the low lying fountain sends a cool breeze wafting into the open living room. The five-bedroom, three-bathroom house also incorporates a charming one-bedroom, one-bathroom cottage for guests.

An understated outdoor water element produces natural adiabatic cooling for the interior. By cooling the surrounding air, the water feature maintains a fresh indoor climate.

The estate lies on the intersection of two valleys with moderate sloping platforms facing south. Protected by the surrounding mountains, this southern hillside overlooks the Tiétar valley and is the first natural barrier the clouds encounter when coming inland from the Atlantic Ocean. This atmospheric barrier results in an unusual amount of rainfall for an otherwise dry region. These exceptional conditions contribute to a natural microclimate that mitigates the harshness of the weather found at this altitude—approximately 1,100 meters above sea level. The shape of the valley combined with its slope and orientation work together to produce a constant southern breeze, which reduces the extreme temperatures typical during the summer months. Such temperate results dramatically ease the home's dependency on energy.

Carefully referencing the original structure on the site, the new home keeps the same southern orientation and material choices. This peaceful coexistence between materials, historic periods, and the natural environment reinvents the image of sustainable and contemporary housing. The thoughtful reinterpretation of the original structure and its commitment to ecology crafts a distinctive blend of architecture that honors the past while anticipating developing needs. Preserving and building on the characteristics of the site's historical legacy, the residence leaps off the grid and into the future.

Large wooden shutters afford the residents the flexibility to adjust the amount of desired sun exposure into the house according to the season and time of day.

Sustainable features:
- Natural ventilation
- Photovoltaic power
- Hydro power
- Southern exposure
- Overhangs for shading
- Insulating shutters
- Off-grid
- Local and recycled materials
- Solar panels
- Adiabatic cooling

Sustainable materials:
- Oak wood
- Recycled local stone
- Concrete
- Limestone floors
- Steel

City/country:
Cáceres, Spain

Year:
2010

Plot size:
5 hectares

Building size:
257 m²

Number of rooms/residents:
6 bedrooms/N/A

Overall budget:
$415,000

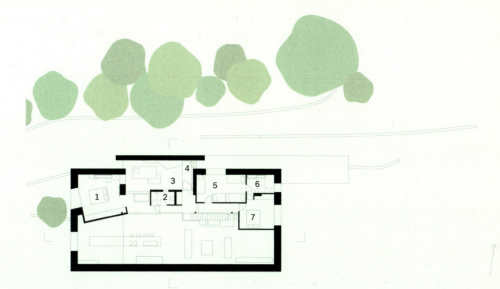

First floor plan

First floor plan
1. Bedroom/bathroom
2. Bathroom
3. Inner courtyard with fountain
4. Entrance
5. Children's bedroom
6. Children's bathroom
7. Bedroom

Ground floor plan
1. Bedroom/bathroom
2. Living/kitchen
3. Bedroom/bathroom
4. Utility room

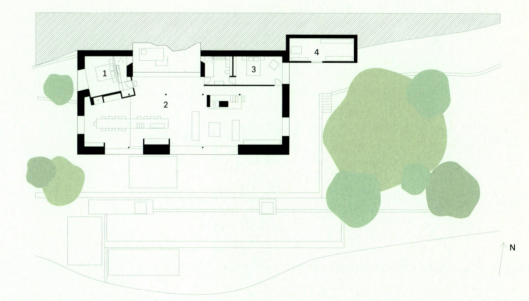

Ground floor plan

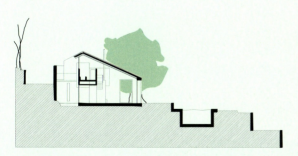

Transverse section

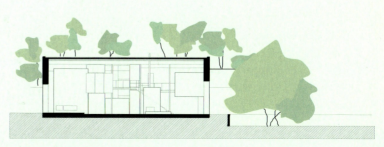

Longitudinal section

Bercy Chen Studio

Sustainable features

- Green roof solutions
- Hydronic ceiling and floor loops for thermal comfort
- Adiabatic cooling
- Diamond electrode water purification system
- Smart pool as thermal mass
- Vacuum pump glazing
- Rainwater collection system
- Geothermal heat pump
- Latent energy storage

Edgeland House
Austin, Texas, USA

Formally and ecologically experimental, this captivating and efficient home—built on a former brownfield site—pairs an insulating roof of local wildflowers with low-emissivity glazing and adiabatic cooling. Geothermal heating and numerous passive cooling measures ensure a comfortable indoor/outdoor climate year round.

Located on a rehabilitated brownfield site, this bold residence functions as a modern re-interpretation of one of the oldest housing typologies in North America—the Native American pit house. This traditional, typically sunken dwelling takes advantage of the earth's mass to maintain thermal comfort throughout the year. Edgeland House's relationship to the landscape proves similar to these timeless dwellings both in terms of approach as well as building performance. Such similarities involve the appearance of an insulative green roof and a seven-foot excavation that channels the earth's mass for cooling during the summer while still keeping in heat throughout the winter. This one-of-a-kind setting presents a rare opportunity to challenge the status quo of ecology, sustainability, and architecture alike.

This project sets new standards for sustainability while providing rich aesthetic qualities through its small footprint and integrated mechanical features. Innovative and high-performance mechanical systems combine integrated hydronic HVAC heating and a green roof to maximize energy efficiency. The innovative implementation of such sustainable technology enhances rather than contradicts the dwelling's architectural agenda.

More than the sum of its individual parts, the sustainable features present in the Edgeland House work together to form a holistically integrated mechanical system. This cutting-edge approach increases building performance while simultaneously reducing the project's carbon footprint. The two-bedroom house, with 2.5 bathrooms nestles under a lush green roof with a sophisticated rainwater collection system of gutters and pipes built in. Featuring local plant life and native grasses, the slanted roof planes provide thermal insulation that helps maintain cooler temperatures in the summer and warmer temperatures in the winter to reduce energy costs year round. Hydronic floor and ceiling loops are used in lieu of a forced air system. This efficient heating and cooling alternative establishes thermal comfort in the interior by passing temperature controlled water through embedded copper tubing.

A geothermal heat pump adds to the home's broad climatic strategy. Here, the earth is used as a heat source in the winter and a heat sink in the summer to minimize the operational costs for heating and cooling. Vertical ground loops also transport water through the earth's mass to stabilize the overall temperature and reduce excess loads on the heat pump.

The house also engages a number of sustainable materials. These ecologically minded elements range from the most apparent green roof to the more demure vacuum pump glazing that lightly partitions the interior spaces from the exterior walkways and pool area. Reducing glass emissivity by 12–25%, the glazing introduces a vacuum-sealed air cavity between the panes. Structural detailing made from recycled steel minimizes the amount of waste typically associated with construction sites while phase change materials provide latent energy storage. This storage reduces the mismatch of supply and demand in a mechanical system—an important solution for the conservation of energy.

Both visually and functionally, the residence behaves as a site-specific art installation and an extension of the landscape. The program, divided into two separate pavilions for

Centrally located, a triangular pool provides adiabatic cooling for the house while a cantilevered green roof above keeps the home well insulated.

living and sleeping, requires direct contact with the outside elements to pass from one to the other. This open relationship to the outdoors and the natural climate encourages a fluid connection between inside and out.

Unifying the two distinct sides of the house, an iconic triangular pool juts out into the landscape. This smart pool doubles as an extra thermal mass for the residence and links to the main hydronic system. The bespoke pool serves as an added cooling element during the sweltering Texan summers. When the glass partitions slide open, a fresh breeze from the pool wafts through both interior volumes.

A collaboration with Lady Bird Johnson Wildflower Center reintroduces over 40 native species of plants and wildflowers to the home's green roof and across its generous plot. This carefully chosen vegetation helps protect the local ecosystem while further blurring the house into the surrounding nature. The dramatic architectural result of these ecological efforts strikes a balance between the industrial and natural aspects of the site.

The now pristine plot, set on a one-acre bluff, formerly housed an oil pipeline. After careful excavation and soil testing for contamination, the project now serves as the symbolic bridge between the manmade zone on one side of the land and the natural river on the other. From brownfield to verdant residential oasis, this project unveils the contemporary face of sustainability. Healing the land and ameliorating the scars of the site's industrial past, the daring residence raises awareness about nature, its finite resources, and the diminishing landscape.

Longitudinal section

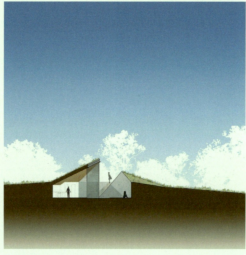

Transverse section

Sustainable features:	City/country:
→ Green roof solutions	Austin, Texas, USA
→ Hydronic ceiling and floor loops for thermal comfort	Year: 2012
→ Diamond electrode water purification system	Plot size: 4,050 m²
→ Smart pool as thermal mass	Building size: 130 m²
→ Vacuum pump glazing	Number of rooms/ residents:
→ Rainwater collection system	2 bedrooms/ 2 residents
→ Geothermal heat pump	Overall budget: N/A
→ Latent energy storage	

Sustainable materials:

→ Green roof
→ Vacuum pump glazing
→ Recycled steel

Floor plan

1. Entrance
2. WC
3. Kitchen
4. Livingroom
5. Smart pool
6. Patio
7. Bedroom
8. Bathroom
9. Bedroom
10. Bathroom
11. Mechanical room
12. Guest trailer

Floor plan

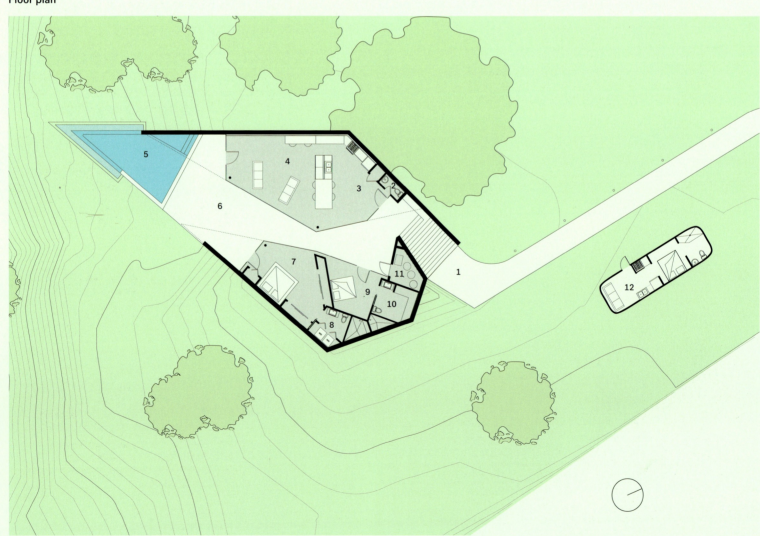

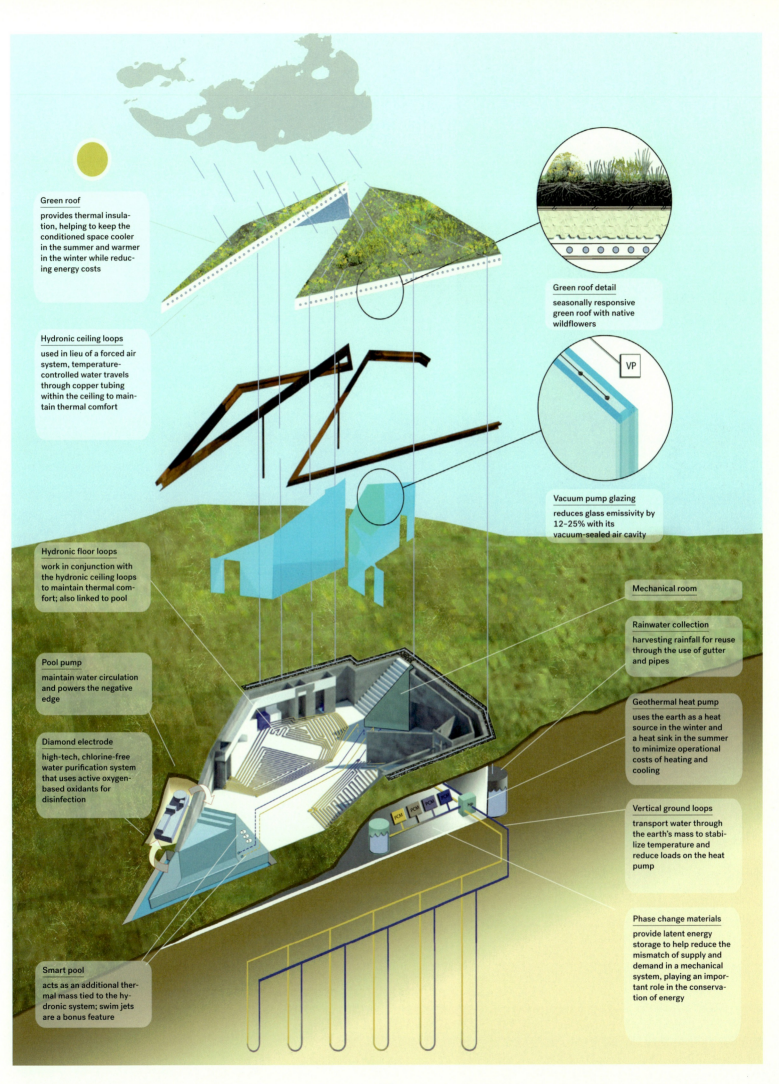

Juri Troy Architects

Sustainable features

- → Carbon neutral house
- → High-performance heat pump
- → Photovoltaic roof panels
- → Thermal solar panels for hot water
- → Heat recovery system
- → Passive house strategies
- → Solar gain
- → Natural ventilation
- → Local materials
- → High-performance insulation
- → Rainwater collection system

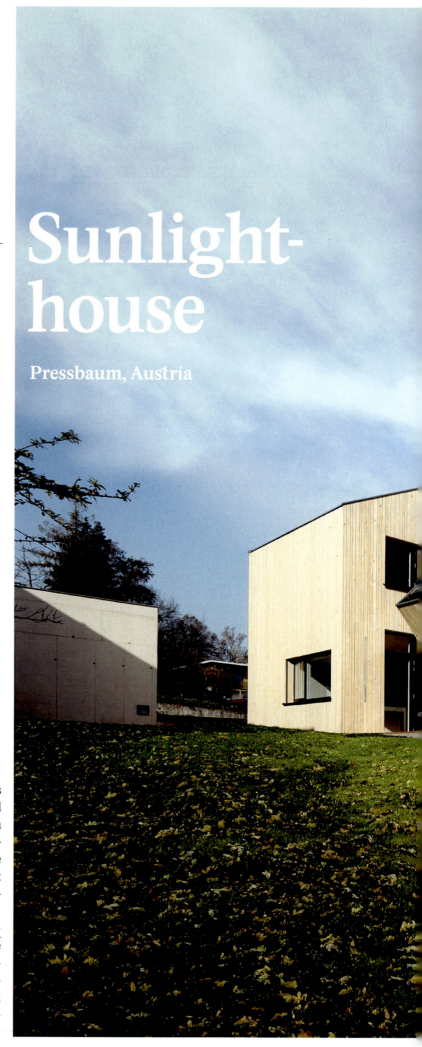

Sunlighthouse

Pressbaum, Austria

A carbon neutral model home stands as a prototype for future sustainable housing. Channeling the power of the sun, the highly efficient house generates all of its own energy through photovoltaic panels, and passive heating and cooling strategies.

This single-family home outside of Vienna stands as the first CO_2 neutral residence in Austria. Launched by the Velux company as part of their pan-European experiment, the project began as a competition between nine Austrian architecture firms to develop a prototype for the model home of 2020. The eye-catching winning project integrates the most advanced approach of progressive and sustainable building and living.

Exploring themes of innovation and transferability, the sustainable model home taps the full potential of the plot. The house capitalizes on the impressive views of the site and sunlight exposure while maximizing privacy between the existing residences. Achieving the rare combination of energy efficiency and ambitious architecture, the house will erase its ecological footprint within the next thirty years.

Optimized to maximize sun exposure, an angled roof filled with photovoltaic panels meets the home's energy needs while granting the building a distinctive appearance.

Sunlighthouse produces more energy than the transport, building, and daily consumption of the project combined. An energy concept for the building—developed in collaboration with the Danube University of Krems—includes an array of efficient technology. The building equipment comprises a high-performing heat pump, 48 m² monocrystalline photovoltaic roof panels, 9 m² thermal solar panels for hot water, and a controlled air system with heat recovery. Other energy-saving techniques extend to the building's exterior, with optimized heat insulation and the use of efficient windows that fulfill passive house requirements.

True to its name, the Sunlighthouse's total window area equals 42% of its floor area. These windows expand the interior's access to daylight, lowering overall energy consumption and dependence on artificial light. The average daylight reaching each room registers five times higher than that of a typical dwelling. Strategically positioned roof and façade windows provide stunning views and maximize passive solar energy. Enabling optimal natural ventilation during summer months, these high-performance windows minimize thermal losses during the winter time. Functioning as a small power station, the visionary design paves the way for a new guard of environmentally conscious and sustainable residential architecture.

All materials used underwent strict evaluations based on their ecological qualities. The Austrian Institute for Construction Biology and Ecology (IBO) also benchmarked the CO_2 valuation for all assembled materials. Challengingly positioned on a hill, the residence required concrete foundations. Instead of using ordinary Portland cement, which suffers from a poor CO_2 rating, the design instead utilizes blast-furnace-slag to mix the concrete. This technique, a spin-off product from steel production, boasts an extremely low CO_2 output. Also tackling the area of insulation, the project sourced efficient and ecological choices including sheep wool and recycled cellulose.

The six-room home's bright, sloping planes are clad in spruce wood planking. Locally grown and processed, the sustainably sourced wood features prominently in the overall design. Treated with white pigmented natural oil to prevent darkening, the elegant cladding unifies the interior and exterior in a continuous luminous wrapper. This delicate surface treatment further accentuates the ample views of the lush wilderness present throughout the house. A grid of skylights interspersed with iridescent, navy solar cells creates an iconic slanted feature wall that stands out from the rest of the demure yet modern exterior.

In spite of the home's challenging plot, the final result far exceeds expectations. The slender and long piece of land declines toward a beautiful but heavily shaded woods with high trees in the southeast. A dense hedge in the northeast and a high wall in the southwest further shield the site from light. Additionally, two closely situated neighboring houses on either side impact the amount of privacy available. Digging into one of the site's main slopes, the design overcomes these situational constraints of light and privacy while simultaneously capturing views of the lake nearby. Such an appealing outcome and design concept becomes a valuable tool for others to learn from, as affordable plots in a mountainous country like Austria rarely offer ideal conditions.

After opening to international visitors for a year, the project continues to provoke an ongoing dialogue on themes of sustainability and contextual sensitivity. The home, now sold to a private owner, carries on a comprehensive monitoring of its energy usage. These real-time energy values allow for a continuing comparison between the simulated and actual results. This constant feedback and energy data will influence and help streamline the next generation of sustainable housing prototypes. In the meantime, the contextual, aesthetic, and environmental impact of Sunlighthouse grows with time. From the ethical standards upheld with the construction crew to the uncompromising commitment to environmental quality and resource conservation, this project reinvents the typology of sustainability, cultivating a symbiotic relationship between energy efficiency and aesthetic sensibility.

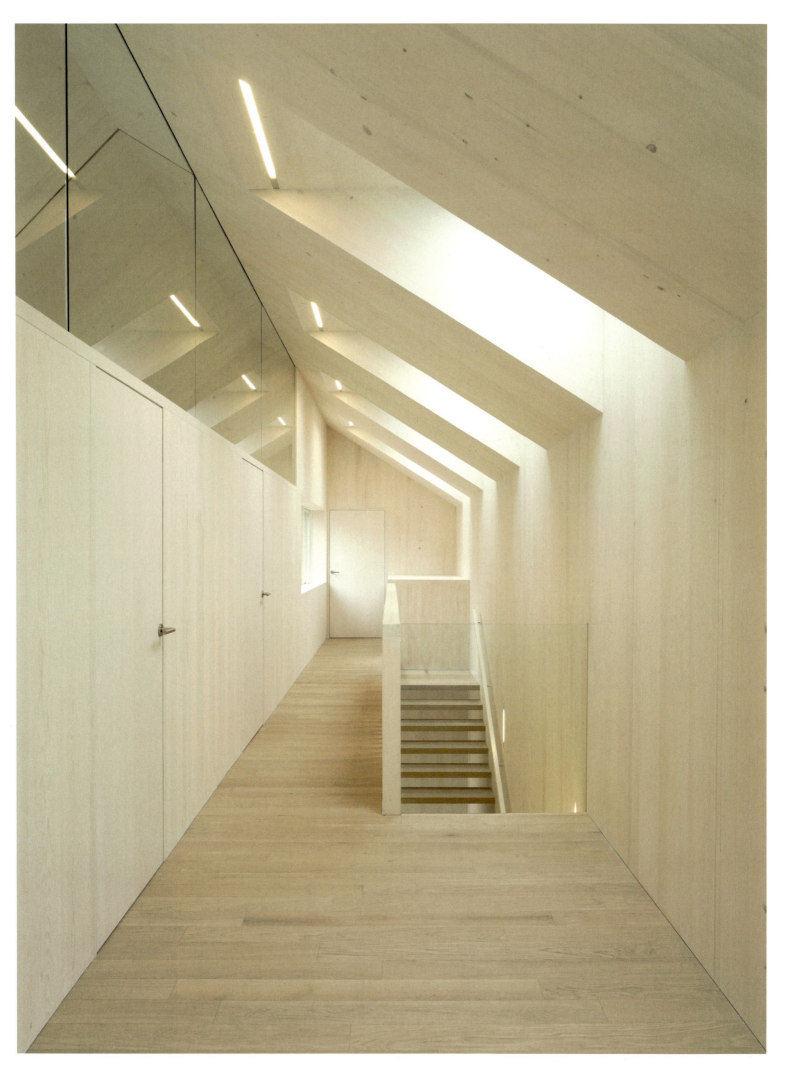

Sustainable features:
- → Carbon neutral house
- → High-performance heat pump
- → Photovoltaic roof panels
- → Thermal solar panels for hot water
- → Heat recovery system
- → Passive house strategies
- → Solar gain
- → Natural ventilation
- → Local materials
- → High-performance insulation
- → Rainwater collection system

Sustainable materials:
- → Sheep's wool and recycled cellulose insulation
- → Slagstar eco concrete
- → Local timber
- → Untreated wooden façade
- → Flax impact sound insulation
- → Recycled tiles

City/country:
Pressbaum, Austria

Year:
2010

Plot size:
1,292 m²

Building size:
131 m²

Number of rooms/residents:
3 bedrooms/ N/A

Overall budget:
N/A

Site plan

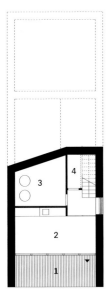
Ground floor plan

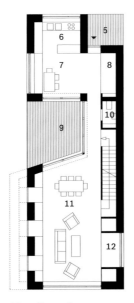
First floor plan

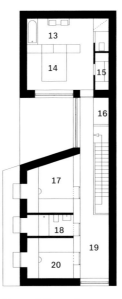
Second floor plan

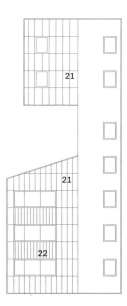
Roof plan

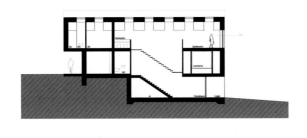

Ground floor plan
1. Loggia
2. Leisure room
3. Engineering room
4. Storage room

First floor plan
5. Entrance
6. Kitchen
7. Dining room
8. Wardrobe
9. Terrace
10. Toilet
11. Living room
12. Reading alcove

Second floor plan
13. Bathroom
14. Master bedroom
15. Wardrobe closet
16. Working area
17. Children's room (bedroom)
18. Children's bathroom
19. Playing area
20. Children's room (bedroom)

Roof plan
21. Photovoltaics
22. Solar panels

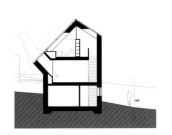
Elevations

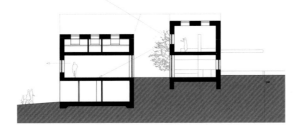

Sections

BLAF Architecten

Passive House with Textile Skin

Asse, Belgium

Sustainable features

- → Zero emission, carbon neutral house
- → Passive house standards
- → Solid construction materials for heat accumulation
- → High-performance insulation
- → Airtight construction
- → Southern oriented glass façades for solar gain
- → Mobile sunscreens
- → Geothermal heat exchanger
- → Renewable energy systems
- → Natural ventilation

With a skin made from EPDM rubber, this interactive and airtight house enjoys a zero emission carbon rating. Sunscreens composed of fiberglass fabric keep the southern oriented and glazed upper story adaptive to the shifting path of the sun.

Belgium is one of the most dense, yet endlessly dispersed areas in Europe. This existing model for spatial development, often based on private ownership of land, no longer proves justifiable. Rather than criticize this unsustainable situation, the ambition of this inspiring residence instead explores an alternative and positive update to the local residential typology. The goal for this zero emission project provokes a behavioral shift in architectural discourse that extends across spatial, social, and ecological levels.

The residence repurposes a leftover lot from a 1960s housing development. Close to schools, work, and public transport, the sustainable house also promotes a sustainable lifestyle. This unconventional design returns the formally private front yard back to the community. By designing the front yard of the residence as a semi-public playground and by using the front façade as a larger-than-life drawing board, the house becomes a more social and hospitable element in the neighborhood. The unexpected introduction of the semi-public space rejects the allotment's rigid concepts of privacy and territory.

Passive house principles, combined with the topography and orientation of the site, develop an efficient skin design that embodies the family's values for transparency, flexibility, and interaction. The ground-floor façade facing the basketball court features a sustainable EPDM rubber surface that forms a giant canvas for chalkboard artists and neighborhood children. An upper story, clad in a UV-resistant, glass-fiber fabric, presents a façade composed entirely of sunshades. These dark sunscreens become automated at window areas and otherwise stay fixed on wooden frames. Responding to both the daily climatic needs of the house and the personal needs of the occupants, these mobile textile shades assist with both privacy and solar filtering. The built-in flexibility of this shading system significantly changes the appearance of the house at different times of day,

Solid construction materials, including concrete and brick, aid in the accumulation and storage of heat. The bright interior engages a light color palette, directly contrasting with the slate black exterior. Living areas and the children's rooms are situated on the upper floor to enjoy an added heat gain of 2°C from the extensive glazing. Below, the parents' bedroom and bathroom nestle into the slope of the site. This ground level also holds a home office and a storage room.

The residence applies a wide assortment of sustainable features. Designed for a couple and their three children, the house was completed on a budget of approximately $401,000. Cellulose and wood fiberboard make up the home's efficient insulation. These high-performance materials keep the walls, floor, and roof well insulated throughout the year. The airtight, carbon neutral dwelling utilizes generous glass façades along its south side to capture maximum solar gain. Built according to passive house standards, the home's yearly energy consumption for heating stays limited to an impressive 15 kWh per square meter. A geothermal heat exchanger further supports these efficient energy ratings.

A set back on the upper level creates space for an outdoor terrace. With floor-to-ceiling glazing on all three sides, the terrace keeps the family connected to the outdoors even on this elevated level. Promoting cross ventilation between the two sides of the house, the generous glazing framing this courtyard space also provides a visual link between the living and

The home's upper level, clad in floor-to-ceiling gazing, embeds operable sunscreens into the façade to control the amount of desired sun exposure.

children's area. A glazed central stairwell brings light into the lower part of the house. Golden curtains line this glazing to regulate the amount of privacy and climate control desired between floor levels. Circular skylights punched out of the roof add further illumination to the social family spaces over the year.

The ability to easily transform the exterior of the house combined with an inviting basketball court marked by vibrant neon lines encourages an active outdoor lifestyle. As the family and local community begin to engage with the chalkboard house, what begins as a stark, black, monolithic residence evolves into a whimsical social canvas for creativity and interaction. The home's malleable exterior finishing allows it to remain responsive to the changing sentiments, aesthetics, and dreams developing between the family and their neighborhood.

This chalkboard house offers a refreshing reminder of the aesthetic and social possibilities that can be harnessed through sustainable design. Carbon neutral and environmentally conscientious, the lighthearted design seamlessly bridges technical specifications with a childlike sense for the imaginal. Strengthening both the neighborhood and the family unit, the interactive residence casts off the stuffy preconceptions associated with sustainable design. Instead, this playful project demonstrates that ecologically-minded architecture can capture both a high energy rating and one's imagination.

Sustainable features:

→ Zero-emission, carbon neutral house
→ Passive house standards
→ Solid construction materials for heat accumulation
→ High-performance insulation
→ Airtight construction
→ Southern oriented glass façades for solar gain
→ Mobile sunscreens
→ Geothermal heat exchanger
→ Renewable energy systems
→ Natural ventilation

Sustainable materials:

→ Cellulose and wood fiberboard insulation
→ EPDM rubber cladding
→ Glass fiber fabric

City/country:
Asse, Belgium

Year:
2009

Plot size:
680 m²

Building size:
184.1 m²

Number of rooms/residents:
4 bedrooms/5 residents

Overall budget:
$401,000

Site plan

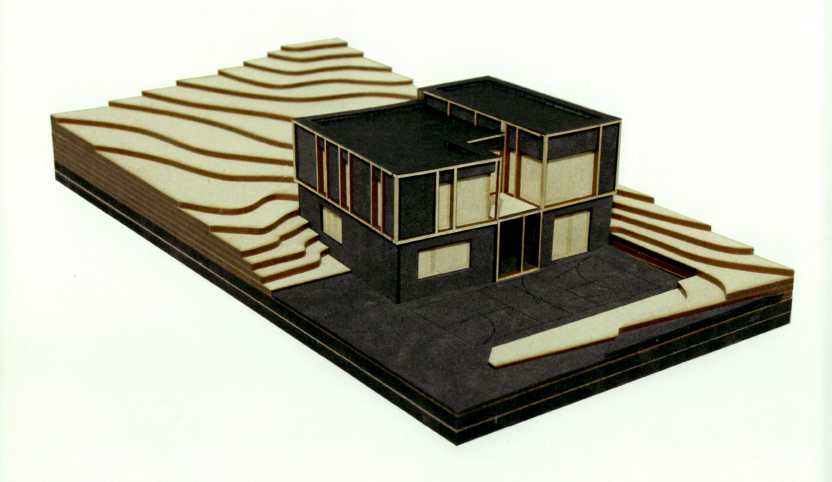

Ground floor plan

1. Children's area
2. Children's bathroom
3. Children's bedroom
4. Living room
5. Dining room
6. Kitchen
7. Terrace

First floor plan

8. Master bedroom
9. Technical room
10. Storage room
11. Master bathroom
12. Entrance
13. Office
14. Spare bedroom

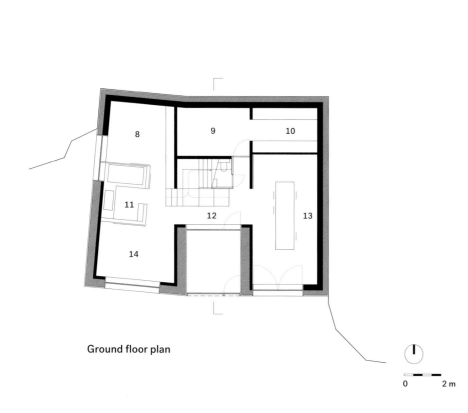

Ground floor plan

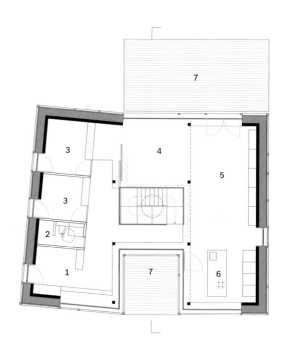

First floor plan

0   2 m

North elevation

South elevation

East elevation

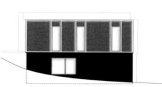

West elevation

Transverse section

Longitudinal section

Pitman Tozer Architects

Sustainable features

- 30% less energy usage than typical house
- Code of Sustainable Homes: exemplary rating
- High-performance insulation
- Solar gain
- Ground coupled heat pump
- Radiant heating
- Rainwater harvesting system
- Natural and sustainably sourced materials
- Energy-efficient glazing
- Natural ventilation
- Passive house strategies

Gap House

London, UK

A tiny, high-performance infill residence consumes 30% less energy than a typical new home. Built according to the Code for Sustainable Homes, the house's numerous passive features encompass efficient insulation and glazing, natural ventilation and solar exposure, radiant heating, rainwater collection, and locally sourced materials.

Rising out of a narrow 2.3-meter-wide infill plot, this compact and efficient townhouse shakes up its conservative West London context. The slender, terraced residence proves that sustainable architecture remains an achievable option even on the tightest of urban sites. Without compromising efficiency, the ecological house incorporates a number of green strategies including passive solar gain, high levels of insulation, and a ground coupled heat pump and rainwater harvesting system. This holistic approach to sustainability further minimizes the home's already small carbon footprint.

The low-carbon building maximizes light and space within the constraints of a tight and awkward site. Originally a side alley and rear garden for the adjoining property, this infill space now remarkably accommodates a spacious feeling four-bedroom family home. The two-faced residence presents a closed and introverted appearance toward the street. Successfully hiding the larger residence just behind, the public view of the home appears almost uninhabitable in its narrowness. From the back, the multi-level house spills out onto a generously sized courtyard. This ultra-private outdoor space connects to an open plan living, dining, and kitchen area via floor-to-ceiling foldable doors. These doors allow this lower level to open up completely to the courtyard, generating natural ventilation and a flexible boundary between inside and out. Crimson accents found in the kitchen and patio walls add a striking visual continuity that flawlessly blends home and garden.

The smart design results in a working home that uses approximately 30% of the energy of a typical house built to meet current building regulations. This considerable energy saving reduces heating bills by up to $1,340 annually. Receiving an exemplary grade 4 rating under the Code for Sustainable Homes, this micro residence produces macro energy saving results. These impressive energy ratings are achieved through a combination of passive strategies and high-performance materials.

High levels of insulation in the walls and roof combined with passive solar gain optimize the home's heating requirements. Sustainable lamb's wool insulation is used for all the internal walls and floor. Three bore holes measuring 50 meters deep in the rear courtyard coupled with a heat pump installed in the plant room manage all the heating and hot water needs for the house. This effective system also supports the radiant floor heating throughout the building. A rainwater harvesting system, designed specifically to suit the constrained nature of the site, cuts down on excess water consumption. The collected rainwater is reused to flush the toilets.

Foldable glass partitions connect the ground floor living and dining room to a private courtyard, naturally illuminating and ventilating the space.

The townhouse relies heavily on natural materials. Connecting the multiple residential levels, a sustainably sourced composite larch board forms the main stair structure. This central twisting timber stair, delicately pulled away from the walls, brings daylight deep into the living spaces on each floor. In addition to channeling light into the seemingly dark property, the geometrically complex, self-supporting stair acts as a four-storey stack for passive ventilation in the summer.

With an almost invisible street façade, the unassuming wedge can easily go unnoticed between its two prominent neighbors. The main entry to this townhouse, marked by three levels of modern windows with wooden shutters, keeps within the demure formal language of the street. These windows and the extensive glazing found on the back side of the house engage high-performance, low-energy windows. These windows are then set into timber frames made from sustainable spruce wood.

The complex interior organization achieves a solution where each habitable room enjoys ample daylight and a spacious atmosphere, even within the narrowest part of the house. The smaller bedrooms stack together at the front of the residence facing the street while the rear organization takes on an unexpected cascading configuration. Wet rooms and storage areas occupy the parts of the plan without access to natural light. A hidden courtyard at the rear of the site forms a private oasis for the family. This courtyard floods the ground floor reception space with daylight and cools the interior with welcome fresh breezes throughout the summer months.

Designed and built for the partner of the architecture practice and his family, the townhouse functions as an interactive case study for the firm. The challenges of the design and the limitations of the site afford the partners the unique opportunity to put new strategies for carbon reduction and energy production into practice. These sustainable results and their associated systems can be continually monitored, adapted, and updated based on the evolving energy goals over the course of the home's lifespan. With $50,200 of the $860,000 budget set aside for sustainable materials, the project demonstrates that green design need not come with a hefty price tag or ideal site conditions. Charmingly understated, this emissions cutting townhouse enables its architects to literally practice what they preach.

Sustainable features:
- 30% less energy usage than typical house
- Code of Sustainable Homes: exemplary rating
- High-performance insulation
- Solar gain
- Ground coupled heat pump
- Radiant heating
- Rainwater harvesting system
- Natural and sustainably sourced materials
- Energy-efficient glazing
- Natural ventilation
- Passive house strategies

Sustainable materials:
- Lamb's wool insulation
- Sustainably sourced spruce wood and composite larch board
- Low-energy windows

City/country:
London, UK

Year:
2007

Plot size:
N/A

Building size:
185 m²

Number of rooms/residents:
4 bedrooms/N/A

Overall budget:
$860,000

Ground floor plan
1. Courtyard
2. Living room
3. Dining room
4. Kitchen
5. Utility room
6. Heat pump
7. Hall

First floor plan
1. Study
2. Bedroom 1
3. Bathroom
4. Hall
5. Bedroom 2

Second floor plan
1. Conservatory
2. WC
3. Hall
4. Bedroom 3

Third floor plan
1. Bathroom
2. Hall
3. Bedroom 4

Third floor plan

Second floor plan

First floor plan

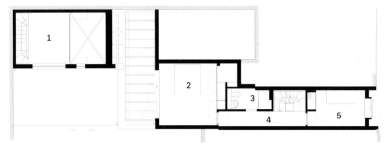

Ground floor plan

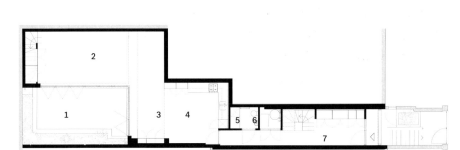

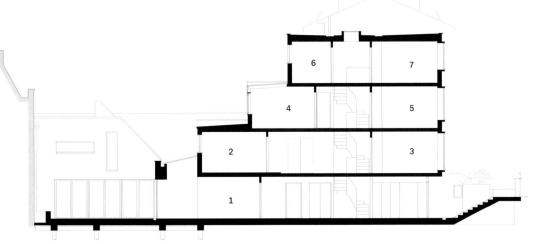

Longitudinal section

Longitudinal section
1. Kitchen
2. Bedroom 1
3. Bedroom 2
4. Conservatory
5. Bedroom 3
6. Bathroom
7. Bedroom 4

Acme

Sustainable features

- → Ground source heat pumps
- → Passive solar heating
- → Independent water well supply
- → Minimally invasive foundations
- → Prefabricated structural system
- → Airtight insulation
- → Thermal mass
- → Sustainable and locally sourced materials

Hunsett Mill

Stalham, UK

The prefabricated wooden addition works with locally sourced materials, high-performance glazing, and a passive solar heating system. Aided by minimally invasive foundations and a charred cedar shell, the extension minimizes its environmental impact.

A remote former water pumping mill and single family home take up residence in the historic Norfolk Broads National Park. The house accommodated the Keeper of the Mill until 1900, when the advent of electricity rendered wind-powered pumps obsolete. Since the end of its working life, the house has been used as a private residence. Standing adjacent to the historic mill, the home and its new addition represent an important piece of the local heritage.

Conceived as a shadow of the existing house, the new addition purposefully retreats behind the mill. The addition of a dark, angled volume that mirrors the silhouette of the existing brick building obscures the visual transition between old and new. Massing and proportions for the extension remain subordinate to the original building, while the charred timber cladding settles the radical structure into its context.

Interspersed with squares of energy-efficient glazing, the extension incorporates charred cedar board cladding for natural weatherproofing.

According to the client's request, the previous three-bedroom space turns into a five-bedroom dwelling. The extension overcomes limitations of size and height restrictions by creating an open ground floor layout. On this open level, three small, double-height areas give the impression of spaciousness. Adding to this open feeling, large windows look out toward the mill and scenic marshes. Centered around a fireplace, this ground floor shifts in level to form distinct kitchen, dining, and living rooms. The second level contains all five bedrooms. Two bathrooms on this floor intersperse with the voids of the double-height spaces below.

All internal walls and ceilings consist of an exposed timber structure. The walls release a subtle scent and appear to glow in the afternoon light. Doors built into these timber walls match in thickness and finish to ensure a continuity of material, texture, and appearance throughout the house. Integrated fittings, wardrobes, and the fireplace also nestle into the timber walls, further optimizing the limited space. The majority of the floors are finished with limed, dark baked oak planks to complement the golden hue of the larch timber walls.

With a desire to make the new intervention as ecologically responsible as possible, the design focuses on the minimization of carbon footprint and energy expenditure during construction. Simple, natural, and sustainable materials are used throughout the residence. Engineering out any superfluous elements, the structure exclusively features solid cross-laminated timber walls, slabs, and roofs. This primary structural element functions as an effective insulating member and thermal mass to regulate the internal temperature and limit the need for excess heating. Ground source heat pumps, passive solar heating, and an independent water supply ensure almost complete self-sufficiency.

FSC-certified, the timber appearing in this project comes from sustainable forests where more trees are planted than felled. The strict guidelines applied to the harvesting of the wood also extend to the welfare of those producing the material. Additionally, the enforcement of reasonable transport distances for the wood ensures that all materials stay local. This verifiable material life-cycle approach assures that the house maintains a carbon negative footprint.

The laminated timber core of the building operates as an inherently low-waste system. By designing and fabricating components off-site using digital techniques and CNC milling, the amount of on-site construction time and material waste were significantly reduced. This sustainable system also respects the health and safety of the laborers working during the build.

A lightweight, factory-produced structural solution reduces the foundations to small, diameter driven piles. The use of concrete also restricts the ground bearing slab that sits in the floodplain. In this way, the house minimally impacts the earth it rests upon. Similarly, no byproducts were released into the ground or river, safeguarding the ecological balance of the delicate landscape.

This rustic yet contemporary building boasts high standards of insulation, airtightness, solar efficient glazing, and thermal mass. A centuries' old technique of timber preservation, known as superficial charring, weatherproofs the addition in a low-maintenance rainscreen cladding. These cedar boards enjoy a superior longevity and their charred surface finish requires little maintenance and no chemical treatments. Contrasting with the brick construction of the mill cottage, the blackened cladding introduces a clear distinction between the original building and the extension. The rough texture of the charred boards also contrasts with the crisp details of the mirrored frameless windows of the extension.

Surrounded by tranquil wetlands full of rare and endangered wildlife, the landscaping strategy for the 4500 m² garden selects local species that blend with the surrounding ecosystem. These contextually sensitive plantings also help frame the architecture and enhance its timeless atmosphere. Advocating for a life in harmony with both nature and history, this modern take on the classical farmhouse sets the stage for a new era of vernacular ecology.

Sustainable features:
- → Ground source heat pumps
- → Passive solar heating
- → Independent water well supply
- → Minimally invasive foundations
- → Prefabricated structural system
- → Airtight insulation
- → Thermal mass
- → Sustainable and locally sourced materials

Sustainable materials:
- → FSC-certified cross laminated insulating timber
- → High-performance glazing
- → Charred cedar boards

City/country:

Stalham, UK

Year:

2010

Plot size:

4500 m²

Building size:

213 m²

Number of rooms/residents:

5 bedrooms/N/A

Overall budget:

N/A

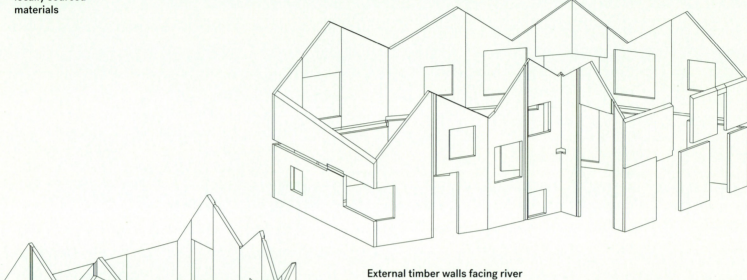

External timber walls facing river

Timber walls at junction to existing house

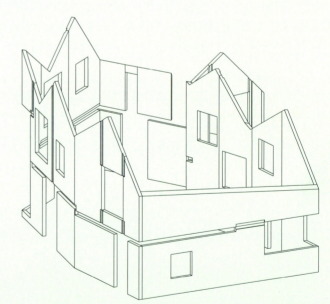

External timber walls facing garden

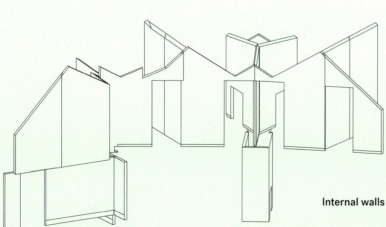

Internal walls

Assembly drawings for the "timber structure"

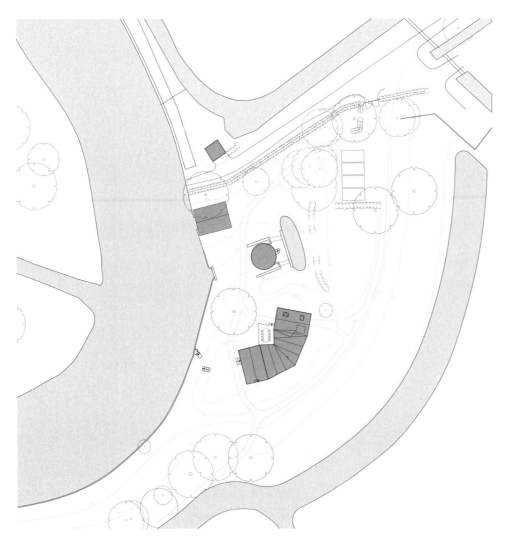

Site plan

Section

61

Architecten de Vylder Vinck Taillieu

Sustainable features

- Recycled materials
- Structural and historical preservation
- Natural ventilation
- High-performance insulation
- Compact floor plan
- Reduced thermal bridges
- Vapor barriers
- Prefabricated structural system

House Rot-Ellen-Berg

Oudenaarde, Belgium

Creatively retrofitted, a dilapidated inn enjoys a second life as a flexible residence. An act of historic preservation, the layered home consists of repurposed and recycled materials as well as high-performance insulation and a prefabricated structural system that reduces thermal bridges.

At the foot of the Koppenberg, a famous hill in the Flemish Ardennes, a charming but run-down old inn enjoys its second life as a refurbished family house. The delicate project, set in a typical Flemish village of brick houses, functions as a balancing act between preservation and modernization. Respecting and redefining existing resources, a new house appears inside the quaint original shell.

A house of glass with an industrial aesthetic takes up residence within the extant brick structure. Creating a smaller winter home inside a bigger summer house, the glazed interior façade protects a compact and efficient residence within. This reduction in floor plan results in a more modestly sized dwelling that requires less energy to heat. Additionally, this ample internal glazing forms a tight seal in the winter, allowing the interior to behave as a type of residential greenhouse.

By layering old and new structures, the residence produces a stable and well-insulated interior climate. These in-between spaces keep the inside ventilated during the summer while acting as a buffer from the cold air outside during the winter. For optimized heating performance, a stone stove stands in the center of the space. This central positioning of the stove, with its back to the former fireplace, also establishes a dialogue between the original structure and its contemporary update. The tiled wood stove, a slow and steady heating instrument, uses the local wood available on the 1490 m² property.

The south façade of the brick building remains in its original state while the north face undergoes a considerable overhaul. This exterior transformation supports the interior winter house as it leans against one wall of the old structure. Featuring a high-performance flax wool insulation, the prominent structural wall receives its own unique exterior surface treatment. Here, the roof's new grey cement tiles wrap down and over the side wall. These shingles generate a distinctive pattern reminiscent of the home's original brickwork. Wood fiberboard insulation and vapor barriers avoid the thermal bridge often present in the connection point where the roof construction joins the walls of the house. Forming a unified transition between wall and roof, past and present, the considered material choice alludes to the updated interior hidden just inside.

This sleek, geometric tiling also contrasts with the untouched and slightly dilapidated front façade. Marked by an inviting red door, the old-fashioned entry sequence warrants a second look thanks to the addition of an unexpected trompe-l'œil oriel window extending out over the pitched roof above. Referencing the antique shape of the original entry windows from the front, the window's two sides reveal a mirrored finish. This unconventional use of mirror obscures the perception of the added volume of the window, instead replacing it with reflections of the sky. A subtle use of mirror also appears along the roof gutter line to camouflage a newly added, exposed concrete beam.

Designed as a continuous space, the ground floor heating unit steadily transfers heat over the multiple levels of the interior. The three-bedroom house for a family of four flexibly demarcates more private areas with level changes and the introduction of kelly green curtains that can open and shut as needed. Doubling as a method of both climate control and space saving, layers of the house can be added and subtracted to shrink or enlarge the interior over time.

Previously used for storage, an attic area underneath the pitched roof becomes an integral part of the new residence. Illuminated by two dormer windows and the glass curtain wall separating the renovated interior from the rustic exterior, this cozy space transitions into an open loft. Accessed via a removable stair, the intimate mezzanine under the rafters still remains connected to the open layout below.

Creating a type of greenhouse effect, floor-to-ceiling glazing separates the old structure from the new interior and illuminates the upper mezzanine area.

Executed on a budget of approximately $97,000 for the interior, exposed wood and metal structural framing give the house a work-in-progress feeling. Inspired by the classic Meccano construction set, the dressed down interior celebrates a structural honesty with yellow girders, silver columns, plentiful glass, and black rubber stripping. The house cuts down on assembly time and construction costs by engaging a hybrid of prefabricated structural systems. With one system for constructing cement formwork and the other derived from techniques for building hothouses, the diverse assembly process adapts to the highly specific context.

Challenging conventions of sustainability, the home rejects a purely technical approach to the topic. Instead, the residence stands as a reminder of the importance of preservation, living within one's means according to the season, and sourcing local and replenishable materials. Saving a piece of regional history, the project identifies numerous opportunities for improvement and experimentation. The house of today finds its place in the house of yesterday.

Sustainable features:
- → Recycled materials
- → Structural and historical preservation
- → Natural ventilation
- → High-performance insulation
- → Compact floor plan
- → Reduced thermal bridges
- → Vapor barriers
- → Prefabricated structural system

Sustainable materials:
- → Flax wool insulation
- → Wood fiberboard insulation
- → Insulated interior glazing

City/country:
Oudenaarde, Belgium

Year:
2011

Plot size:
1,490 m²

Building size:
86 m²

Number of rooms/residents:
3 bedrooms/ 4 residents

Overall budget (only interior):
$97,000

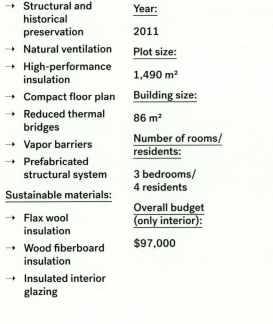
Site plan

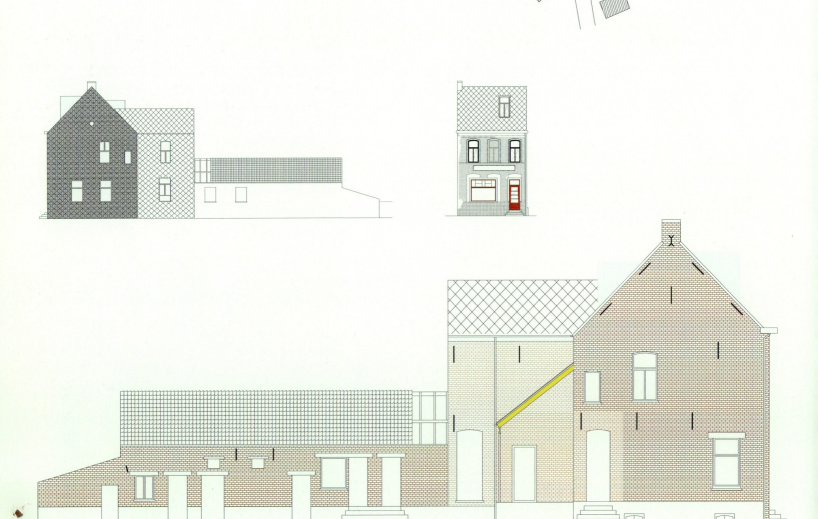
Elevations

Second floor plan

1. Bedroom
2. Office
3. Double-height space

First floor plan

1. Living room
2. Bedroom
3. Bathroom
4. Double-height space

Ground floor plan

1. Garden
2. Terrace
3. Entrance
4. Living room
5. Kitchen

Sections

1. Entrance
2. Living room
3. Kitchen
4. Bedroom
5. Bathroom
6. Office
7. Double-height space

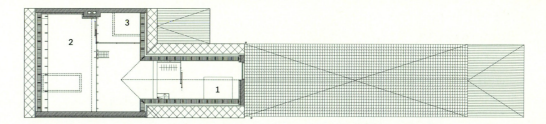

Second floor plan

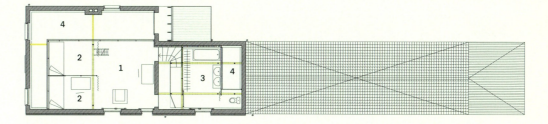

First floor plan

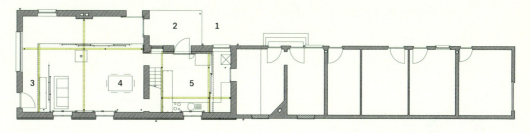

Ground floor plan

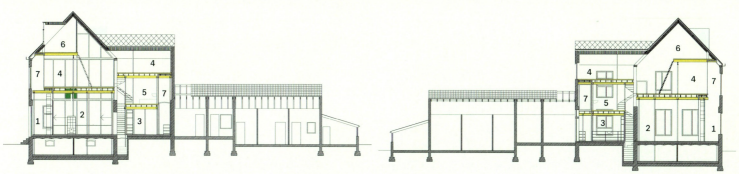

Sections

Aray Architecture

Sustainable features

- → Solar hot water
- → Rainwater collection system
- → Green roof solutions
- → Natural ventilation
- → Locally sourced and recyclable materials
- → Passive insulation
- → Double walls
- → Passive heating and cooling

Shirasu House

Kagoshima, Japan

Composed of locally manufactured bricks made from volcanic soil found in the region, this residence enjoys the material's multiple sustainable benefits. In addition to providing natural ventilation, fire protection, and insulation, the double brick walls also support a green roof and solar panels for supplying hot water.

A sustainable house with volcanic soil brickwork, known as "Shirasu", commands a prominent corner of a residential neighborhood in southwest Japan. Instead of depending on standard sources of energy to combat the region's high temperature and humidity levels, the residence reintroduces ecology into the built environment. Named after the Japanese word for soil, the inward oriented house engages the native and natural material in an unexpected way. The ancient material, dating back 25,000 years, affords an economical and sustainable tool for achieving passive heating and cooling. The design of the cave-like brick house, responds to the client's wish for an environmentally friendly house in a hot and humid region.

Standing as the home's most sustainable and energy efficient material, the locally produced, fireproof soil bricks incorporate a number of climatic features including humidity conditioning and thermal storage. The exterior walls of the double-layered brickwork are molded from a mixture of cement and Shirasu particles. This reinforced mixture strengthens the exterior supporting walls while crafting a steady thermal and insulated interior environment. Reducing the thermal load to the interior, the inner walls become the main finish materials for the rooms while adjusting for indoor humidity. The spaces between the bricks act as an aerated zone to prevent condensation. Combined with raw ore from the volcanic soil, these inner walls improve the adsorption of moisture. During the summer, these two layers of volcanic bricks work together to maintain a cool interior. Over the winter months, these same materials produce a warm climate reminiscent of the hotter times of year.

For improved ventilation, the ground floor layout consists of a single open space with no partitions. A triangular atrium visually connects the two floors and spreads daylight into the lower level. This atrium also enhances the home's efficient natural ventilation. A centrally placed skylight exhausts warm air and brings fresh air down into the main spaces. The family dining room and kitchen appear in the center of the lower level. Standing off to one side, the double-height living room aligns itself under the atrium. Glass sliding doors extend this open living space onto an outdoor deck and garden, promoting interaction between the house and the city. A rainwater collection and recycling system provides water for this outdoor garden. Further minimizing the home's reliance on external resources, solar panels generate the hot water supply for the house.

The two-story house accommodates a family of six. An understated, inset door serves as the main entry to the residence. Built into the inner brick wall, this entrance leads to the communal family space and a slender timber and steel staircase that connects the two floors of the house. In addition to hosting the shared children's room, the home's upper level also integrates a study room, library space, and luminous sunroom. This sunroom opens onto an enclosed rooftop terrace. Perforations in the brick enclosure offer protected vantage points for observing the happenings in the neighborhood from the comfort of the small outdoor space. A green roof above completes the building's natural insulation strategy. Deflecting weight onto the bricks below, the green roof improves the home's energy efficiency while positively impacting the quality of the urban environment.

Corresponding to the shape of the site's corner lot, the home's floor plan takes on a dynamic position toward the street. With no nearby house to block the sunlight, the dwelling enjoys southwestern solar exposure. This advantageous site allows the house to receive plentiful sunlight throughout the day. Land and sea breezes from the northwest circulate the air across the house. Certain bricks are purposefully removed to form a wall of ventilation from inside to out. The gaps in the façade buffer the harsh rays of the sun while filtering in light and framing glimpses of the surrounding neighborhood. Negotiating between the clients' wishes for an approachable but protective shell, the house introduces tilted exterior walls. These angled surfaces compress the building as they reach the second-storey, reducing the home's monolithic appearance and resembling a scaled-down residential pyramid. The unusual geometry also facilitates an airflow stack effect, as the hot air draws up and out of the building.

With an exposed interior and exterior structure made entirely from repurposed local materials, the introverted brick house demonstrates the beauty that can come from treating readily available elements in new ways. The sustainable and inward-looking house develops a far-reaching environmental agenda, from recycling to solar energy. A showcase for a rare, plentifully available, and naturally efficient material, the residence doubles as a learning tool for the community. Subtly sophisticated, the structure underlines the merits of linking architectural practice with ecological solutions.

Thick double walls of volcanic soil bricks insulate the house. Gaps between these bricks generate natural currents and frame views of the neighborhood.

Sustainable features:
→ Solar hot water
→ Rainwater collection system
→ Green roof solutions
→ Natural ventilation
→ Locally sourced and recyclable materials
→ Passive insulation
→ Double walls
→ Passive heating and cooling

Sustainable materials:
→ Volcanic rock bricks
→ Green roof

City/country:
Kagoshima, Japan

Year:
2013

Plot size:
228.9 m²

Building size:
88 m²

Number of rooms/residents:
2 bedrooms/4 residents

Overall budget:
$366,000

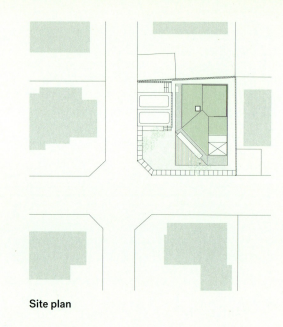

Site plan

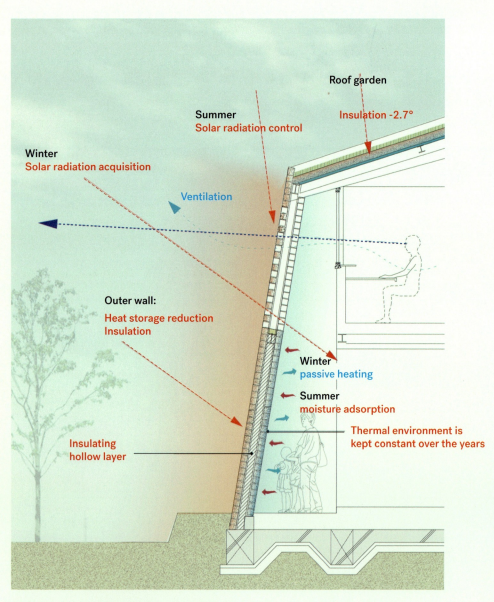

The space between bricks form an insulating layer to reduce the thermal load from the outside.

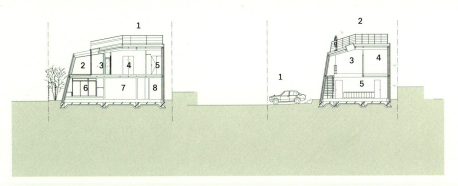

Longitudinal section	Transverse section
1. Roof garden	1. Parking
2. Terrace	2. Roof garden
3. Sunroom	3. Study room
4. Children's room	4. Children's room
5. WC	5. Dining room
6. Bedroom	
7. Dining/kitchen	
8. Bathroom	

Longitudinal section

Transverse section

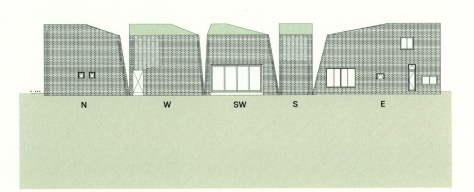

Elevations

Ground floor plan

1. Entrance
2. Dining/kitchen
3. Living room
4. Bedroom
5. Deck
6. Parking

First floor plan

1. Library
2. Study room
3. Atrium
4. WC
5. Children's room
6. Sunroom
7. Terrace

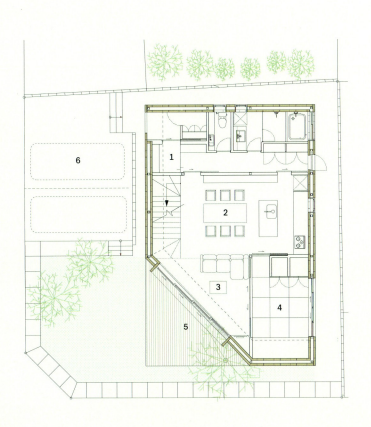

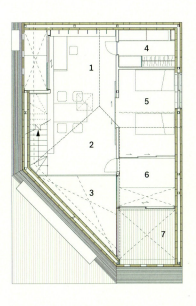

Ground floor plan

First floor plan

75

Barton Myers Associates

Sustainable features

- → Southern orientation
- → Native vegetation and low water-use plantings
- → Recycled materials
- → Thermal mass
- → Natural ventilation
- → Clerestory vents
- → Radiant coil hydronic heating system
- → Photovoltaic array
- → Solar hot water system
- → Fire resistant structure and landscaping

Montecito Residence

Montecito, CA, USA

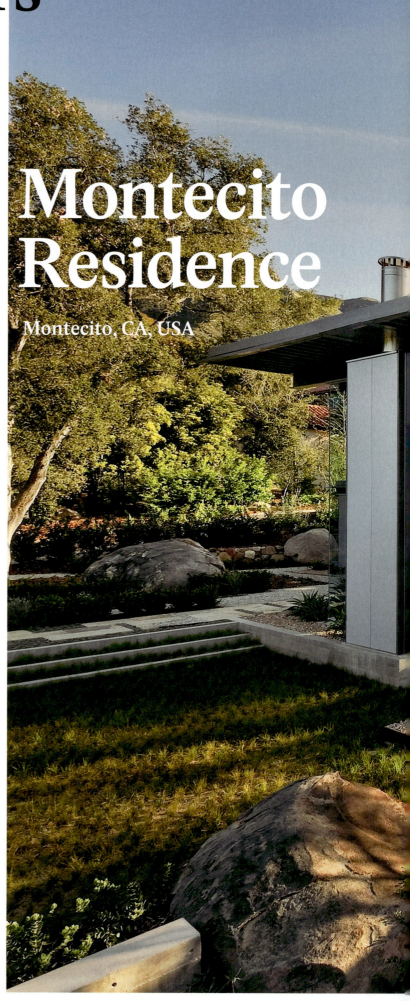

A triumph of steel house design, this recyclable and fire resistant structure delicately negotiates with nature. Framed by native vegetation that requires little water, the naturally ventilated residence embeds solar hot water and radiant heating systems.

Just south of Santa Barbara, this captivating residence is the latest work from the pioneer of steel house design, Barton Myers. Built for a couple and their extended family that visits often, the home nestles into the secluded hills of Montecito on a sweeping 4360 m² plot. Mixing the best of Californian modernism with green design, the project negotiates an environmentally sensitive site. This pristine habitat includes dense vegetation and large boulders and sits adjacent to a seasonal creek.

The recyclable steel construction includes roll-down doors that allow the interior to enjoy natural ventilation and seamlessly connect with the outdoor patio when open.

The three-bedroom residence consists of a large main house, a 50 m² detached garage, and an extant guest house. A generous sun deck structure runs along the length of the 16-m lap pool. Wrapped around a tranquil courtyard and a massive boulder, the floor plan of the main residence separates into two wings: one public and one private. The public wing holds the living and kitchen areas while the private wing accommodates the bedrooms, bathrooms, and a library. Inspired by Japanese garden design, the unique topography of the site largely influences the interior layout. Treating natural obstacles as opportunities to add character to the house, the iconic steel residence navigates around the prominent boulders and protected oaks sprinkled over the land.

By using steel construction and standardized off-the-shelf industrial components, the resulting dwelling supports an integrated relationship between indoor and outdoor living. Framing an intimate courtyard, the buildings encourage the rugged site to embrace the house. The residence, designed in the tradition of other Barton Myers steel houses, features an exposed structural frame, overhead roll-up doors that connect to outdoor spaces, concrete floors, exposed steel decks, and the addition of infill insulated metal panels for the enclosure. This project represents the architect's fourth iteration in an ongoing exploration of how green design and industrial materials can relate to and enhance the natural landscape of Southern California. The intention behind the design strategy creatively envisions a flexible prototype for sustainable housing.

The project's sustainability features, site layout, glazing strategy, and fire mitigation techniques act as the integral components informing the overall design. Each of the main buildings orients to capture prevailing winds, southern light, and partial ocean views. North-facing clerestory windows offer views of the nearby mountains while letting in the morning light. Environmentally sensitive native landscaping comprises Mediterranean vegetation and plantings with low water requirements. All driveways and walking surfaces, composed of permeable paving, promote water infiltration across the grounds.

Introducing a high quantity of recycled content, the main house is composed of a steel structure and steel insulated infill panels. The floors, made up of sealed concrete slab on grade, utilize recycled fly ash. These floors are positioned to provide thermal mass and heat carrying capacity to mitigate the diurnal swing of the Southern California climate. Large, operable overhead doors and sliding pocket doors enable the owners to completely open up the home to the garden. This spatial flexibility erases the physical barriers between the interior and exterior, merging them into a single continuous space.

A concrete floor slab in the main living wing extends to the outdoor areas, seamlessly linking the interior and exterior when the operable sectional doors slide open. Taking into account the partial ocean views and adjacent neighboring buildings, the home organizes around internal site features. This more introverted layout allows each family member access to nature, garden, and natural light. Despite its relatively modest size when compared to the neighborhood's standards, the layout's strong relationship to the surrounding nature makes the home feel much larger that its actual floor plan.

The home does not utilize mechanical cooling, relying instead on coastal breezes and airflow through clerestory vents. These natural ventilation and cooling techniques keep the interior at a comfortable temperature over the warmer months of the year. For added heating, the building includes a radiant coil hydronic system in the slab. White elastomeric sheeting with a high albedo for solar reflection cover the roof. The garage also hosts a photovoltaic array while a solar hot water system for domestic hot water and pool heating perches over the bedroom wing.

In a region of canyons particularly vulnerable to seasonal wild fires, the house and landscaping are designed for fire mitigation. The steel construction, with no wooden secondary or wall members, proves inherently fire resistant. The building also incorporates fire sprinklers and strategic landscaping around the perimeter. Barton Meyers's own residence and studio in Toro Canyon, an area of extreme fire hazard, serves as the original prototype for this home. Lessons from this earlier structure include steel fire shutters over all glazing. These steel shutters and operable façade systems grant the home a unique ability to adapt to environmental changes and challenges without sacrificing its timeless splendor.

Sustainable features:
- Southern orientation
- Native vegetation and low water-use plantings
- Recycled materials
- Thermal mass
- Natural ventilation
- Clerestory vents
- Radiant coil hydronic heating system
- Photovoltaic array
- Solar hot water system
- Fire resistant structure and landscaping

Sustainable materials:
- Permeable paving for water infiltration
- Recycled steel structure and insulated infill panels
- Recycled fly ash
- High albedo roofing

City/country:
Montecito, CA, USA

Year:
2009

Plot size:
4,360 m²

Building size:
300 m²

Number of rooms/residents:
4 bedrooms/ 2 residents

Overall budget:
N/A

Floor plan
1. Fire pit
2. Terrace
3. Living room
4. Dining room
5. Kitchen
6. Reading room
7. Storage
8. Bar
9. Pantry
10. Mechanical room
11. Library
12. Guest bedroom
13. Master bathroom
14. Closet
15. Master bedroom
16. Garage
17. Garden room
18. Guest house (existing)

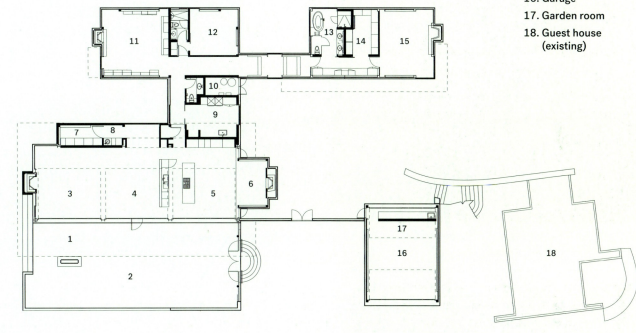

Floor plan

North elevation

East elevation

South elevation

West elevation

Carl Turner Architects

Slip House
London, UK

Sustainable features

- → Solar-assisted ground source heat pump
- → Photovoltaic panels
- → Wildflower roof
- → Rainwater harvesting
- → Reduced water consumption
- → Mechanical ventilation with heat recovery
- → Airtight building envelope
- → High-performance insulation

One of England's most energy-efficient homes occupies a compact infill plot in a residential neighborhood of London. Outfitted with photovoltaic panels, a ground source heat pump, and a rainwater harvesting system, the slender and flexible house also integrates high-performance insulation to complete its airtight construction.

Occupying a narrow infill plot on a street lined with typical London townhouses, this unique home constitutes a new prototype for adaptable terraced housing in the city. Three simple 'slipped' orthogonal boxes break up the bulk of the building and give it its striking sculptural quality. Cantilevering toward the street, the staggered envelope becomes a local landmark of green design. Airtight detailing and high-performance insulation work together to make this mint green home one of the most efficient houses built in the United Kingdom.

Designed to meet the Code for Sustainable Homes Level 5, the eye-catching residence incorporates a spectrum of green features. Working with a budget of approximately $837,000, the shell, internal fit-out, finishes, and sustainable technologies were all sourced with economy in mind. Energy piles utilizing a solar-assisted ground source heat pump create a thermal storage site beneath the building while photovoltaic panels support the home's energy requirements. A roof planted with wildflowers combined with rainwater harvesting and proactive conservation techniques substantially reduce the family's daily water consumption. For climate control, a mechanical ventilation system with heat recovery works together with high-performance, triple-glazed windows to craft a well-insulated interior that stays comfortable year round.

The house presents a live–work layout for the modern family. With the workshop below and the living space above, the spatial organization allows for a great deal of flexibility. The current arrangement features a ground floor studio with a moveable study area. The upper floors contain an open and tastefully appointed kitchen, living, and dining area as well as two bedrooms for the two inhabitants. Depending on the developing needs of the owners, the house can be used as a single home, a studio workspace and apartment, or two individual apartment units. Extra bedrooms can also be quickly added to the open floor plan as needed. This built-in flexibility enables the owners to sublet or downsize if faced with times of financial hardship. Storage built into the walls on the first and second floors optimizes the narrow footprint, granting a surprisingly spacious experience. Such a fluid and adaptable housing model can enliven local communities and produce mixed-use and collaborative residential environments.

Composed of three shifting volumes, the home's spatial arrangement improves light and views. These boxy levels use the full width of the site, maximizing the interior footprint. By bringing the overall volume out to the edges of the property, future buildings can simply adjoin to the flank walls. The shifting planes are clad in milky, translucent glass Linit panels that solve privacy issues, both for the residents and their neighbors. This unusual cladding extends past the top floor to form a secluded rooftop terrace. On the ground level, the lower volume

The airtight building envelope, clad in translucent panels, leads up to a rooftop garden filled with wildflowers and irrigated by the home's rainwater collection system.

retreats inward to introduce a private courtyard in its place. An entry gate, matching the height of its two brick neighbors, engages the same translucent paneling to maintain privacy for the courtyard and visual unity for the exterior. Above, the staggered levels generate outdoor space for intimate balconies. Promoting natural ventilation, these balconies also inspire an active relationship to the outdoors and the surrounding neighborhood.

Perimeter load-bearing timber wall panels, reinforced with a cantilevered steel frame, free up the internal areas from supporting columns. The resulting open plan layout ensures that any added walls or dividers are simple to erect and require minimal construction effort. Concrete flooring appears across the house and sits flush against all walls and fittings. Skylights, generous floor-to-ceiling glazing, and glass sliding doors keep the home illuminated throughout the day. Proving both financially and environmentally sustainable, these modest modifications keep the house responsive to the changing lives and living situations of its occupants.

The prototype brownfield development offers a dense, flexible, and urban living scenario for the ecologically minded. Acting as a vehicle for in-house research on sustainable design, the residence seamlessly integrates the often conflicting aesthetic requirements of architecture and alternative low-energy systems. The energy-efficient model home will undergo future iterations through new developments and as affordable housing. Restructuring the urban townhouse, this project provides a residential prototype flexible enough to account for shifts in economy, the family unit, and ecology. The home's ability to readily accommodate evolving living arrangements does so without sacrificing a deep commitment to sustainability and a green lifestyle. From its soft green color palette to its forward-thinking approach to adaptation, this updated English townhouse sparks a discussion on nature and how best to manage its finite resources right in the heart of the city.

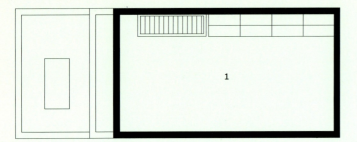

Roof terrace

Roof terrace

1. with photovoltaic panels

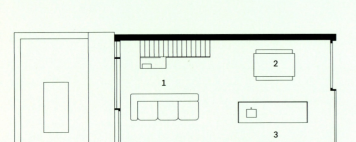

Second floor plan

Second floor plan

1. Living room
2. Dining room
3. Kitchen

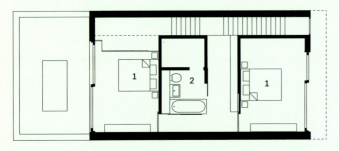

First floor plan

First floor plan

1. Bedrooms
2. Bathroom

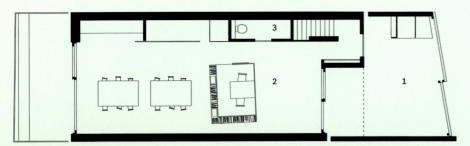

Ground floor plan

Ground floor plan

1. Studio space
2. Living area
3. WC

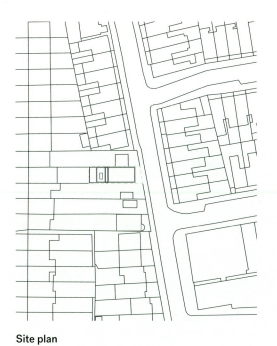

Site plan

Sustainable features:	City/country:
→ Solar-assisted ground source heat pump	London, UK
→ Photovoltaic panels	Year: 2012
→ Wildflower roof	Plot size: 80 m²
→ Rainwater harvesting	Building size: 192 m²
→ Reduced water consumption	Number of rooms/residents:
→ Mechanical ventilation with heat recovery	2 bedrooms/ 2 residents
→ Airtight building envelope	Overall budget:
→ High-performance insulation	$837,000

Sustainable materials:

- → Triple-glazed windows
- → Timber wall panels
- → Steel framing

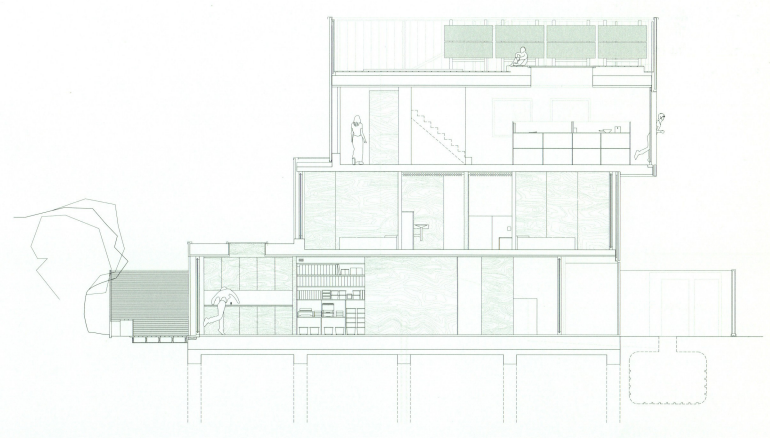

Longitudinal section

Desai Chia Architecture PC

LM Guest House

Dutchess County, NY, USA

Sustainable features

- → Geothermal heating and cooling
- → Radiant floors
- → Natural ventilation
- → Motorized solar shades
- → Photovoltaic panels
- → Rainwater collection
- → Energy-efficient glazing
- → Sustainable landscaping
- → Prefabricated façade
- → Locally sourced materials

A state-of-the-art glass house mixes the best of modern design with a holistic approach to energy-efficient and prefabricated architecture. From geothermal heating and cooling to photovoltaic panels and locally sourced materials, the home advocates for environmental sensitivity and living within one's means.

This elegant glass house takes up residence on a rock outcropping that overlooks a trout pond and serene, open farmland. Designed as a contemplative retreat for weekend visitors, the residence allows one to experience the sweeping 148-hectare grounds with vast, panoramic views. Reminiscent of the great glass houses of the modernist period, this graceful holiday home introduces the added values of energy efficiency and green design.

Deceptively simple in appearance, the house in fact integrates a range of green design strategies and technologically sophisticated systems for energy management. Such sustainable features include geothermal heating and cooling, radiant floors, natural ventilation, motorized solar shades, photovoltaic panels, and rainwater collection for natural irrigation. Windows and sliding glass doors are placed in strategic locations to take advantage of prevailing winds for natural ventilation and cooling. To further aid in climate control, the home's generous glazing utilizes a filtering, laminated UVB interlayer that minimizes solar gain. Ensuring maximum energy performance even when the house stays empty, the electronically controlled shades and heating/cooling system can be conveniently monitored and controlled remotely from the client's iPhone.

A continuous, high-performance glass façade wraps around the main living areas and bedroom. Minimizing heat loss and excessive solar gain, this floor-to-ceiling glazing provides an open flow of space around the perimeter of the house and an unobstructed connection to the surrounding natural landscape. Open views to nature create a stunning backdrop for these minimalist living and sleeping areas. With an open kitchen and living area on one side of the house and the more hidden bedroom wing on the other, the layout acts as a gradation between public and private spaces. A master bedroom and two smaller sleeping nooks with built-in bunk beds provide accommodation for six guests.

Locally sourced wood covers the floors, cabinetry, and wall partitions, granting the home a comfortable and timeless ambiance. The two sleeping nooks, bathroom, and storage rooms are housed within a slatted wood core in the middle of the layout. This custom wooden wall system surrounding the core allows natural light to penetrate through to the interior spaces of the home by day. At night, light emanates from this wood core, casting a warm, inviting glow into the more public living areas. The slatted system also promotes natural ventilation across the entire house, including the sleeping nooks and storage closets.

Sustainable landscape design strategies closely tie into the overall design of the house. A tight palette of native vegetation highlights vistas and other natural features on the property while also managing storm water run-off. Local bluestone slabs and shale excavated from the site form outdoor seating areas and pathways to encourage regular interaction with nature. The terrace, made from this same bluestone slab, sits between the house and a nearby grove of pine trees and provides an intimate outdoor space for entertaining and dining. Bluestone steps from the terrace lead to a more secluded barbecue area and an outdoor shower in the woods.

Nested behind a wall of high-performance glazing, sliding wood panels allow for further customization of the interior climate to mitigate overexposure to solar gain.

Engaging an efficient building solution, the structural design for the residence relies on four steel columns embedded in the wood core. From here, the roof cantilevers out from these four columns to align flush with the exterior glazing. This graceful construction solution minimizes the amount of materials needed to achieve the expansive, open living areas at both ends of the house. The modern façade comprises a thermally robust system of high-performance, triple-paned glass panels that vary in width from ten to twenty feet. Prefabricated off-site and shipped to the location in a single container, the entire façade assembly was erected by crane in just two days. This expedited construction process limited the home's impact on the site.

Built on open farmland in upstate New York, the local climate spans the full range of temperatures and freeze/thaw conditions. This exposure to seasonal climate shifts calls for robust and durable material choices throughout the house. The home also enjoys a solid and stable foundation provided by its location on top of a natural rock outcropping. This rock serves as an ideal base for embedding the residence's geothermal wells and producing the most efficient thermal exchange for the system.

The orthogonal lines of the environmentally sensitive house contrast with the raw nature of the pastoral site. Even so, this bold juxtaposition between the manmade and natural worlds promotes a meaningful relationship between the two. Reflecting off the surface of the trout pond just down the hill, the residence functions as an enticing, glowing beacon on the land. Combining residential splendor with ecological practices, this project proves that a glass house can indeed be an efficient house.

Sustainable features:

→ Geothermal heating and cooling
→ Radiant floors
→ Natural ventilation
→ Motorized solar shades
→ Photovoltaic panels
→ Rainwater collection
→ Energy-efficient glazing
→ Sustainable landscaping
→ Prefabricated façade

Sustainable materials:

→ Locally sourced wood
→ Locally sourced bluestone and shale from the site
→ Native vegetation
→ Triple-glazed windows

City/country:

Dutchess County, NY, USA

Year:

2012

Plot size:

148 hectares

Building size:

186 m²

Number of rooms/residents:

3 bedrooms/ 6 residents

Overall budget:

N/A

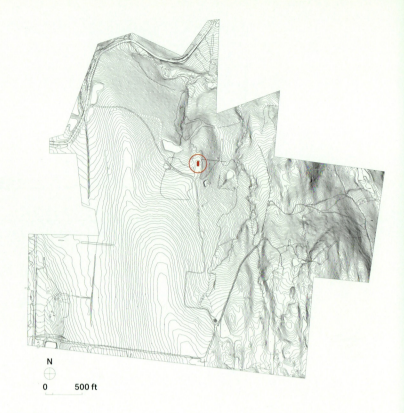

Site plan

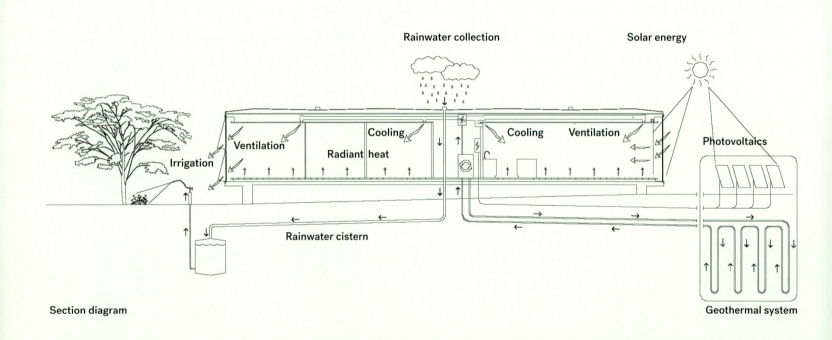

Section diagram

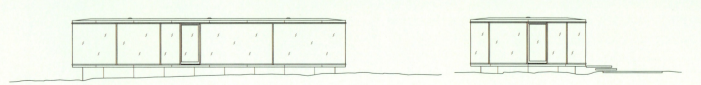

Elevations

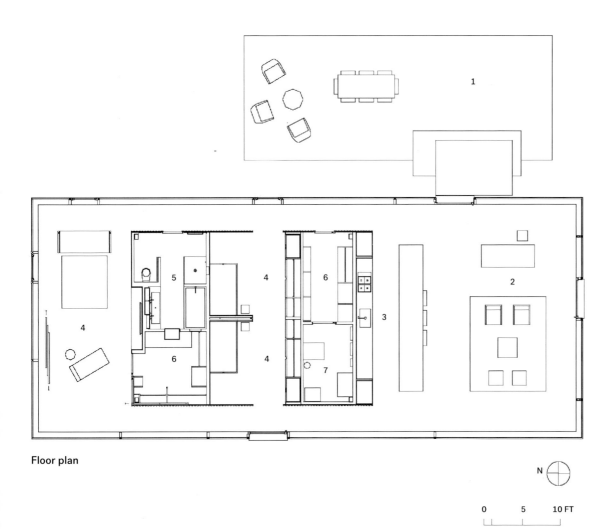

Floor plan

Floor plan
1. Terrace
2. Living area
3. Kitchen
4. Sleeping area
5. Bathroom
6. Storage
7. Mechanical

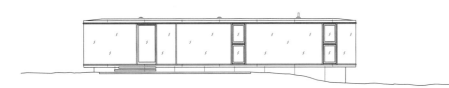

Elevations

FRPO Rodriguez & Oriol

Sustainable features

→ Carbon neutral house
→ Prefabricated structure
→ Two-week assembly
→ Minimally invasive foundation
→ Insulating materials
→ Energy-efficient glazing
→ Green roof solutions
→ Thermal mass

MO House

Madrid, Spain

Prefabricated in just two weeks, this customized house introduces a branching floor plan that navigates around the site's old growth trees. In addition to the use of energy efficient materials and the channeling of cross breezes, an insulating green roof further stabilizes the interior climate.

In the outskirts of Madrid, a single-family wooden house applies a light touch upon its forest setting. Although the programmatic requirements prove relatively conventional, the delicate 1500 m² site requires the house to adopt a complex geometric solution. The powerful presence of the trees and the wish to have a house integrated in the woods influences the disaggregated floor plan.

A number of simple rectangular pieces hold the residence's different programs. These arrayed yet interconnected rectangular boxes fluidly inspire visual and physical connections between the separate spaces. Determining a series of useful and expected solutions, the shifting topological relationships between the rooms also promote a new way of engaging with both house and nature. Corridors lead toward the master bedroom and children's rooms on one side of the house and the kitchen, dining, and living rooms at the other end. These two corridors merge into the main entrance situated at the center of the floor plan. Accessed via a spiral staircase, a single taller box houses a bright study space nestled under the trees.

Adopting a branching and angled floor plan, the distinct boxes maintain a feeling of independence while always remaining in sight of one another. Generous cutouts in the white volumes bring in sunlight and frame picture perfect views of the impressive forest grounds. Fully operable windows on all faces and large sliding doors keep the house naturally ventilated during the warmer months of the year. These plentiful apertures and patios soften the boundaries between interior and exterior, extending the floor plan and the family's activities into the great outdoors.

The MO House belongs to a family of sustainable projects developed by FRPO over the past decade. These projects explore the possibilities of generating architectural complexity out of a combination of simple elements. Throughout the development of these projects, the specifications of each client generates a systematized approach to all design decisions in order to maximize simplicity and utility. The elegant results, represented in this house in particular, combine a number of extremely elementary volumes into a rich spatial experience. By following a few basic rules and engaging elements with adequate proportions, an endless range of appealing residential solutions appear.

A feat of energy efficiency, the unusual layout overcomes considerable sustainable challenges present on the site. The high variety of angles in the joints between spaces makes the house vulnerable to heat loss and challenges its overall energetic performance. Built adjacent to many old-growth pine trees, the foundation system also faced the difficult obstacle of how to protect against invasive roots without doing excess harm to the land.

Tackling the home's heat loss issues, a lighter structural system enables a far more accurate assembly. This accuracy produces airtight corners for thermal optimization and insulation. Built from cross-laminated wood panels, this solid structural material maintains a high insulating performance rating. Retaining precision at all angles, the numerically cut panels form a protective, continuous, lightweight, and extremely thin structure. The CNC manufactured wood panels weigh less than a third of a conventional structural system. This dramatic weight saving solves the home's foundation issues. Instead of an overly aggressive approach, the foundation consists of galvanized steel micro-piles only two meters long. By working with prefabricated elements, the house enjoys an easy assembly and fast construction time. This streamlined construction process limits the carbon footprint and physical impact of the house on the land.

Large apertures appear on all sides of the bifurcating floor plan, inspiring cross ventilation and the flexibility found in indoor/outdoor living.

The home's sustainable strategy centers around a carbon neutral concept. Structure, slabs, and walls, all made of the cross-laminated wood panels, are prefabricated and delivered on site ready for assembly. Combined with the respectful foundation system, the entire basic structure of the house was built in just two weeks. This rapid construction timeline minimizes waste generated by the on-site crew.

Insulation plays a key role in the project's energy strategy. In addition to the insulating wood, prefabricated, high-performance windows limit excess energy spent on heating and cooling. A green roof also acts as a thermal buffer to naturally stabilize the interior climate throughout the year. Slightly elevated over the soil, the micro-piling foundations provide an extra insulation chamber under the floor slab.

Combining prefabricated elements with custom accoutrements, this ecologically sensitive residence harmoniously blends in with its serene forest surroundings. The interrelated network of courtyards, interior spaces, and gardens keep the home in tune with the nuances of the natural world. Built in just a matter of weeks but hopefully lasting for many generations, the uplifting dwelling finds its personality through the sum of its prefabricated parts.

Sustainable features:	Sustainable materials:	City/country:	Plot size:
→ Carbon neutral house	→ Cross-laminated wood panels	Madrid, Spain	1,500 m²
→ Prefabricated structure	→ Green roof	Year:	Building size:
→ Two-week assembly	→ High-performance glazing	2012	295 m²
→ Minimally invasive foundation			Number of rooms/residents:
→ Insulating materials			4 rooms/ N/A
→ Energy-efficient glazing			Overall budget:
→ Green roof solutions			N/A
→ Thermal mass			

Exploded axonometric diagram

Elevation

Site plan

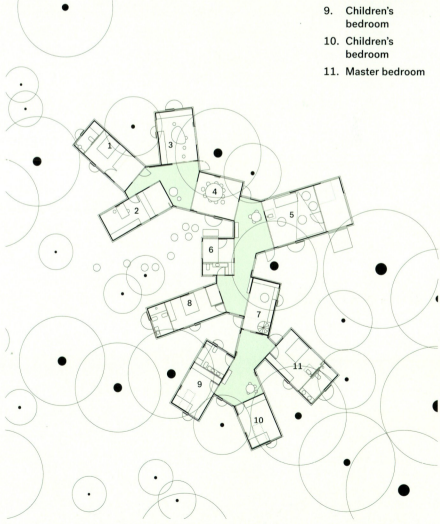

Floor plan

Service area
1. Extra room
2. Utility room
3. Kitchen
4. Dining room

Gathering area
5. Living room
6. Hall
7. Studio

Sleeping area
8. Guest bedroom
9. Children's bedroom
10. Children's bedroom
11. Master bedroom

Volume diagram

Floor plan

John Wardle Architects

Sustainable features

- Indigenous tree plantings
- Double glazing
- Ventilation louvers
- Rainwater collection
- On-site waste water treatment
- Solar hot water
- Locally sourced and recycled materials
- Handmade bricks
- Cross ventilation
- High-performance insulation

The Shearers Quarters

Bruny Island, Australia

With ecology as its driving factor, this charming residence on a remote sheep farm combines a network of passive and active techniques to minimize the structure's impact on the land. The contemporary quarters, made from exclusively recycled and locally sourced materials, includes solar hot water, on-site waste water treatment, and a multi-purpose rainwater collection system.

Part of an historic farming property on the southeastern coast of Tasmania, this alluring residence offers shelter to the local shearers, rural contractors, staff of John Wardle Architects, and guests visiting for annual tree planting weekends and retreats. Positioned on the site of an old sheep shearer's shed destroyed by fire in the 1980s, the new residential structure sits alongside a traditional timber-clad cottage on a bluff overlooking the sea. The striking yet understated building remains sensitive to the delicate ecology of the remote site.

Integrated environmental sustainability stands at the core of the building design. The residence employs operable ventilation louvers and double glazing for effective climate control. For water and energy conservation, the home integrates a rainwater collection system, on-site waste water treatment, and solar hot water. All rainwater collected here is used for drinking, toilets, and showers. Waste water treated on site irrigates a small native plant population. In addition to the solar hot water heater, a wood heater responds to the shifting needs of the year-round occupants.

The house features an extensive assortment of recycled materials. These recycled elements include timber flooring, wood from repurposed apple crates, and reclaimed handmade chimney bricks. Galvanized, corrugated iron cladding wraps the exterior while the warm interior is lined entirely with timber. Taking on a complex, angled geometry, the locally sourced, salvaged, and economical timber lining offsets its fairly labor-intensive installation process. Sourced as individual trees from old rural windbreaks, wood from the native pine tree, Pinus Macrocarpa, makes up the primary internal lining of choice. The two bedrooms and one shared room with bunkbeds are covered with recycled apple box crates. These crates were collected from the many old orchards of the Huon Valley, where the timber has remained stacked but unused since the late 1960s. Introducing a stepped, rhythmic quality into the minimalist sleeping areas, these apple crate surfaces become tactile feature walls that spark the imagination. Rounding off the interior's sustainable wood choices, the flooring comprises of recycled yellow stringybark. The chimney on the residence's eastern elevation completes the home's sustainable offerings. Constructed from original and soft handmade clay bricks, the detached brick chimney forms a dialogue with three similarly composed original fireplaces of the adjoining 1840s dwelling.

Optimized for passive comfort year round, the building occupies a small footprint. The floor plan transforms along its length to shift its profile from a slender lean-to roof at the west to a broad gable at the east. This exploration of the two primary forms found in agricultural structures enables the plan to align exactly with both the slope of the land to the south and the line of the original residence along its north face. Nestling low along the gully, the building's compact footprint shelters the residence against prevailing winds. Openable vents and louvers allow for controlled cross ventilation during the summer. During the winter months, double glazing and high-performing insulation on floors, walls, and ceilings reduce heat loss.

Supported by a small bathroom and laundry room, the three-bedroom dwelling incorporates an open plan living, kitchen, and dining zone. These tranquil areas frame views of the bay on one side and the meadow on the other. An inset veranda on the northern elevation shifts the alignment of the floor plan to make space for a broad living area at its eastern end. With openings on every side, this interior sequence benefits from natural ventilation and unobstructed access to indoor/outdoor living. The generously sized living space opens up to the panoramic ocean views with high-performance, floor-to-ceiling glazing. Reaching their tallest point inside the living room, the angled ceilings grant this elegant enclosure a feeling of infinite spaciousness. Set next to the meadow, the shaded veranda keeps the house cool while exposing the residents to the comings and goings of the ground's expanding sheep population.

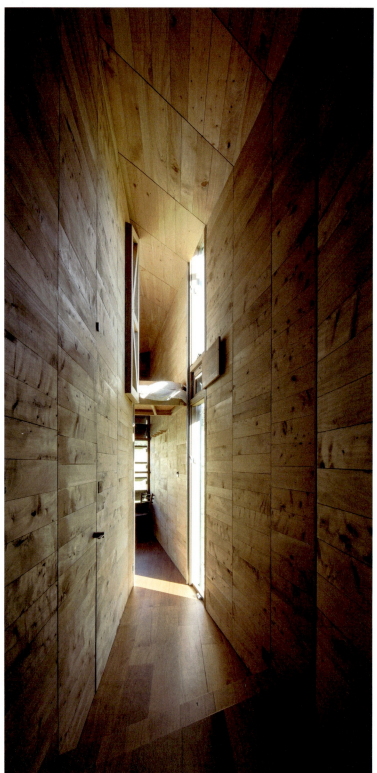

Recycled apple box crates form the walls of the sleeping quarters. This simple, repurposed material gives the spaces a tactile and timeless quality.

With an architect as the client, what began as a simple treatment of a rudimentary shed form now manifests as a far more engaging exploration of detail, material, and ecological building systems. Extensive environmental initiatives undertaken on the property include significant indigenous tree plantings. With over 6,000 new trees planted, more than a quarter of the active sheep farm's 440 hectares of land are now reserved for conservation purposes. A collaborative effort between the region's local artisans and the architects, this experimental and ecological project engages the best aspects of the regional country vernacular. The Shearers Quarters behaves as both a modern green companion and counterpoint to the existing historic cottage.

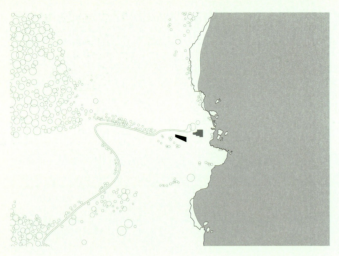

Site plan

Sustainable features:	Sustainable materials:	City/country:
→ Indigenous tree plantings	→ Double glazing	Bruny Island, Tasmania, Australia
→ Energy-efficient glazing	→ Handmade bricks	**Year:** 2012
→ Ventilation louvers	→ Recycled apple box crate	**Plot size:** 440 hectares
→ Rainwater collection	→ Pinus macrocarpa wood	**Building size:** 136 m²
→ On-site waste water treatment	→ Corrugated galvanized iron	**Number of rooms/ residents:**
→ Solar hot water	→ Yellow stringybark flooring	3 bedrooms/ variable residents
→ Recycled materials		**Overall budget:**
→ Cross ventilation		N/A
→ High-performance insulation		

North elevation

South elevation

East elevation

West elevation

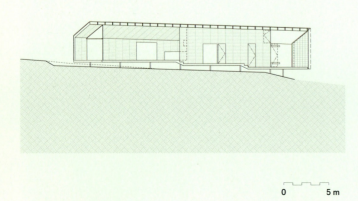

Longitudinal section

Transverse section

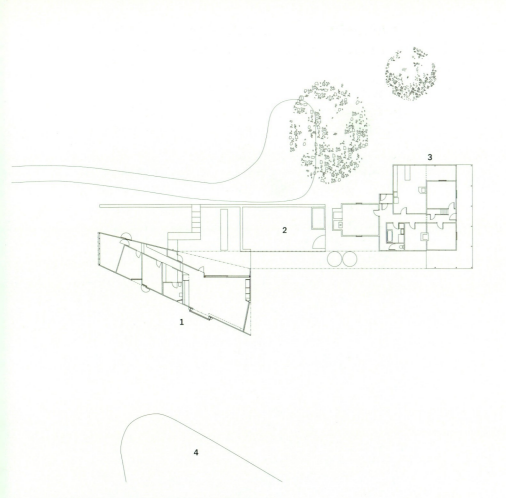

Composite floor plan of new and old structures

Composite floor plan

1. Shearer's quarters
2. Kitchen garden
3. Existing historic cottage
4. Dam
5. Cliff edge

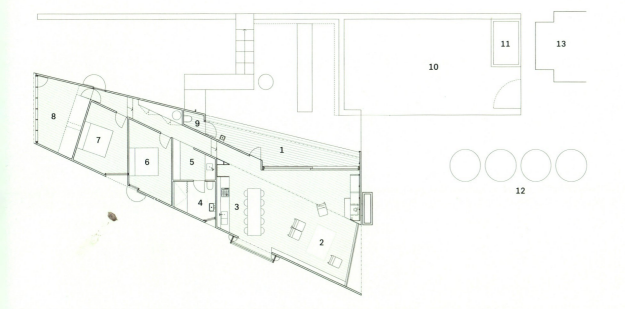

Ground floor plan

Ground floor plan

1. Entrance
2. Living room
3. Dining room
4. Bathroom
5. Laundry/scullery
6. Bedroom
7. Bedroom
8. Bunk room
9. WC
10. Kitchen garden
11. Chook shed
12. Water tanks
13. Original house

Institute for Advanced Architecture of Catalonia

Endesa Pavilion

Barcelona, Spain

Sustainable features

- → Digital fabrication
- → Self-sufficient solar prototype
- → Modular structure
- → High-performance insulation
- → Solar orientation
- → Natural ventilation
- → Photovoltaic cells
- → Southern exposure
- → Overhangs

An experimental pavilion sets new standards for residential energy performance. Remaining efficient in both the summer and winter, the modular, prefabricated structure responds to the path of the sun with thoughtfully placed photovoltaic cells, overhangs, and angled windows.

A futuristic pavilion stands as a self-sufficient solar prototype for sustainable housing. Installed at Barcelona's Olympic Port, the project was built for the International BCN Smart City Congress. Over a one-year period, the striking pavilion was used as a control room for monitoring and testing several projects related to intelligent power management.

The project's philosophy reinterprets architect Louis Sullivan's classic quote "form follows function" into "form follows energy". This formally daring prototype derives from a scalable and contextually adaptable construction system. Composed of modular components, the iconic façade acts as a comprehensive sustainable system that maximizes photovoltaic gain while providing solar protection, insulation, natural ventilation, lighting, and storage. The single component smartly integrates all levels of intelligence that the building needs. By simply adapting the basic geometries, this construction element provides an accessible solution for ecologically-minded design.

Solar calculation software, derived from parametric design algorithms, optimizes the structure's energy values. Each exterior module fans out from the wooden shelter at an aesthetically dramatic and highly calculated angle and length. Appearing in a state of constant motion, these modules are topped with photovoltaic cells that track the arc of the sun across the site. All points respond with mathematical accuracy to the different stresses of its orientation and position.

From within, these modules work together to stage a luminous and flexible interior. As each module responds to its own distinct calculation on the exterior, their internal faces develop a diverse range of uses. These interactive wooden units oscillate from windows to skylights in the more transparent areas and from built-in storage spaces to sleeping lofts in the more opaque parts. By crafting an occupiable façade, the interior enjoys an increased living area within the same building footprint. The multiple apertures at various angles promote a rich relationship with the outdoors and the nuances of the surrounding site.

Panels of oriented strand board (OSB) make up the interior's floor and ceiling planes. This simple material adds to the brightness of the space, as it helps reflect daylight into the shelter's multiple corners. White curtains on long rails track through the interior. These curtains allow further personalization and the demarcation of different spaces and climates as desired.

The final geometry responds to the energy of the place. Set on a bright plot, the memorable façade visibly reacts to the path of the sun. On the north side of the building, the façade becomes closed and protective while opening up to welcome in afternoon sunlight along its permeable southern face. Glass sliding doors on this southern side open onto a gracious outdoor deck with ample shading. High overhangs generate greater energy collection for the vertical windows while simultaneously protecting against the harsh summer sun. Many of the

Operable windows of various sizes and angles circulate the air while capturing the shifting rays of the sun throughout the year.

Topped with photovoltaic cells, staggered modules in a range of sizes track the path of the sun to maximize energy production.

angled surfaces introduce low-lying slanted windows to catch the precious solar rays during the winter months. The operable windows also produce a fresh current for natural ventilation and climate control throughout the year. This environmentally responsive building system adapts to the full spectrum of contexts and orientations, resulting in a wide range of aesthetic and energy efficient outcomes.

Developments in current digital fabrication techniques and energy management bring technology closer to the user through a more open and participatory platform. Readily understandable and accessible, the pavilion encourages a lifestyle empowered by sustainable technology. Here, digital fabrication techniques speed up construction times. Each piece is individually coded, creating an assembly process akin to solving a life-size 3D puzzle.

Out of a $690,000 budget, approximately $124,000 are allotted to sustainable features. Beginning in the construction phase and extending into the day-to-day relationship with the house, all materials, energy usage, and climatic behavior remain purposefully transparent to the inhabitants. This transparency provokes an environmental awareness that extends into all aspects of residential life. According to the designers, solar houses should be built with solar materials. In this instance, the wood—grown with solar power—represents the key structural material for the self-sufficient photovoltaic pavilion.

Self-sufficiency proves a universal challenge for buildings both large and small. Acknowledging that structures of every size face similar obstacles for achieving energy independence, the project proposes an efficient building system capable of adapting in scale, form, and context. The modular system can easily scale up from a single family house to an office tower. Never compromising its efficiency, the scalable method applies the same architectural logic to all usage scenarios. Innovative in both formal and ecological terms, this unique shelter raises the bar for sustainable design.

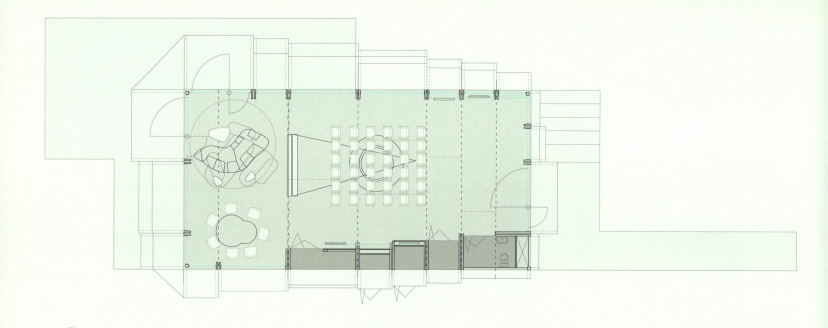

Floor plan

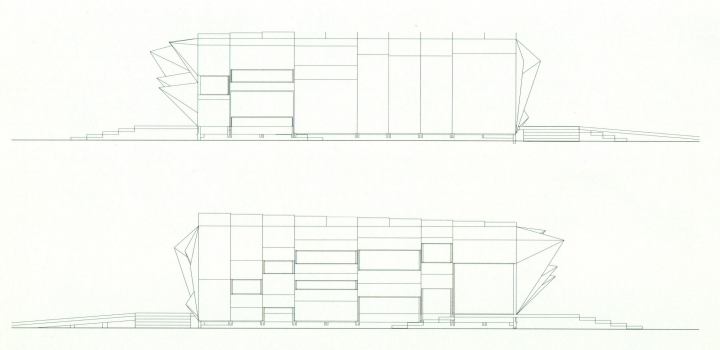

Elevations

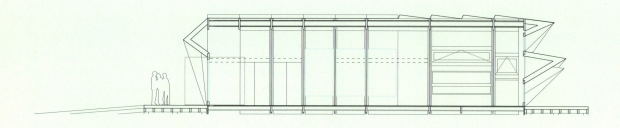

Longitudinal section

Sustainable features:
- → Digital fabrication
- → Self-sufficient solar prototype
- → Modular structure
- → High-performance insulation
- → Solar orientation
- → Natural ventilation
- → Photovoltaic cells
- → Southern exposure
- → Overhangs

Sustainable materials:
- → Sustainable wood
- → Oriented strand board

City/country:

Barcelona, Spain

Year:

2009

Plot size:

N/A

Building size:

140 m²

Number of rooms/residents:

1 bedroom/variable residents

Overall budget:

$690,000

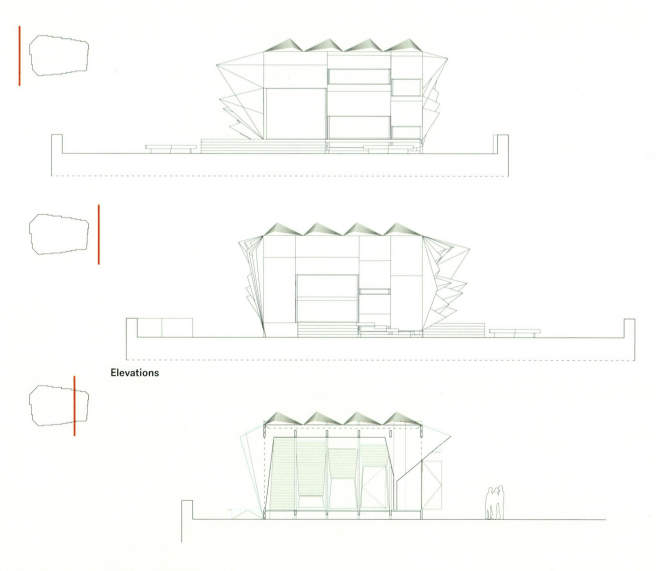

Elevations

Transverse section

Rural Urban Framework

Sustainable features

- Off-grid
- Biogas cooking system
- Insulating traditional materials
- Sunscreens
- Earthquake resistant
- Natural ventilation
- Thermal insulation
- Rainwater collection system

A House for All Seasons

Shijia Village, China

Simple and locally sourced materials reinvent the traditional Chinese courtyard house. Affordable and earthquake proof, the passive house provides a series of interior courtyards for circulating air, growing food, raising pigs for a biogas cooking system, and collecting rainwater.

Over the last 30 years, the mass migration of rural villagers into Chinese cities has had a dramatic effect on their rural homeland. The rural parts of China continue to undergo vast economic, social, and physical changes that only accelerate with time. These changes are particularly reflected in the transformation of China's vernacular architecture—a wholesale shift from regionally specific building typologies to generic, concrete structures. In the midst of such rapid industrialization, this self-sufficient residence acts as a humble return to tradition and ecology.

Near the city of Xi'an in the northern part of Shaanxi Province, the simple dwelling updates the formal language of the vernacular village house. The contemporary residential prototype initially began as an experiential learning workshop with students. These students interviewed various families in the village, collectively compiling a portrait of the modern Chinese village household. Their intimate findings revealed a portrait not only of building types, but also of an ancient lifestyle in transition.

As local houses transform from mud brick to concrete and tile, the construction process itself radically shifts. Now that most able-bodied villagers have left to work in cities, the hiring of outside labor and the reliance on imported materials replace collective methods for do-it-yourself construction. This physical deterioration of the village serves as a symptom of a larger movement from economic freedom into a system of dependency where the very concept of a rural livelihood becomes threatened. The prototype house resists the villagers' increasing dependency on outside goods and services. Built as a quiet and local manifesto, the home reminds the community of the importance of self-reliance.

By combining vernacular ideas from other regions of China with both traditional and new technologies, the design proposes a modern Chinese mud brick courtyard house. In a setting where the new rapidly replaces the old, the Shijia Village House forges a bridge between these two extremes and preserves the intelligence of local materials and techniques. More than just a classic courtyard house, the modest residence investigates and improves upon the modern village vernacular.

A multifunctional roof provides space for drying food, steps for seating, and a means to collect and store rainwater during the rainy season. This rainwater storage saystem keeps the water supply steady during the long and dry summers. Multiple courtyards are contained behind the brick perimeter walls. One of these courtyards hold a pig pen for raising farm animals on site and an underground biogas system that converts the animal waste into energy for cooking. Smoke from the stove channels through the traditional heated brick bed before exiting through the chimney. This efficient and ancient system ensures that none of the precious energy produced goes to waste.

Multi-purpose courtyards bring light and natural ventilation into the house while staging indoor/outdoor spaces for gardening, cooking, and animal farming.

The structure of the house brings together old and new. A concrete column and roof structure combines with mud brick infill walls. These mud brick walls stand as popular and time-tested methods of insulation in this continental climate. Unlike the typical mud structure, however, the new hybrid satisfies criteria for earthquake resistance. A supportive brick screen wraps the entire exterior wall of the house. This unifying wrapper not only protects the mud walls but also shades windows and openings. Gaps between bricks form an elegant pattern for light to filter through. These transitions between opaque and permeable areas maintain privacy while framing views of the surrounding landscape.

Completed on a budget of just $53,400, the residence embraces the domestic courtyard. Keeping within the village's 10 m x 30 m parcel grid, four multi-purpose courtyards behave as the social centers of the house. These semi-enclosed spaces are contained within the main perimeter walls. The protected gathering points set up an intimate visual and functional relationship between the courtyards and the interior rooms of the residence. Each courtyard plays a supportive role for the primary rooms of the house. Extending off the kitchen, bathroom, living room, and bedrooms, the courtyards prove spatially unique from one another while generating natural currents and climate control for the adjacent indoor areas.

From reinforced concrete to the naturally ventilating and insulative brick work, the earthquake-resistant home offers pragmatic and economical solutions to sustainable design. In a geographically remote area with few resources, the innovative yet uncomplicated house functions as a valuable reference to educate and inspire the local community. The cheaply sourced materials and streamlined construction process tap into the ecology of tradition.

Working with the Luke Him Sau Charitable Foundation and the Shaanxi Women's Federation, the program of the house continues to assert village independence. The dwelling now operates as a home for women and new center for women's handicraft, with a focus on straw weaving. A domestic and communal hybrid, the project links together the individual and collective identity of the village. Reinvigorating the local economy, the house supports and inspires independent strategies for village commerce and financial stability.

Sustainable features:
- Off-grid
- Biogas cooking system
- Insulating traditional materials
- Sunscreens
- Earthquake resistant
- Natural ventilation
- Thermal insulation
- Rainwater collection system

Sustainable materials:
- Mud brick infill walls
- Reinforced concrete

City/country:
Shijia Village, Shaanxi, China

Year:
2012

Plot size:
380 m²

Building size:
380 m²

Number of rooms/residents:
2 bedrooms/variable residents

Overall budget:
$534,000

Sustainable features diagram

1. Water heated by solar water heater
2. Roof used to collect rainwater
3. Summer sun is shaded by roof
4. Water filter
5. Chimney
6. Toilet
7. Biogas for cooking
8. Kitchen
9. Winter sun directly shines on greenhouse glass
10. Glazing material
11. Summer breeze passes through brick screen
12. Biogas pool
13. Biogas system
14. Dug out and used as fertilizer
15. Reed bed system for water filtration
16. Filtered water for irrigation
17. Grey water flows to reed bed
18. Water for washing and cooking
19. Water storage
20. Smoke passes underneath the bed
21. To provide heating Trombe wall heated through greenhouse glass; rammed earth construction acts as thermal mass
22. Heat radiation from Trombe wall

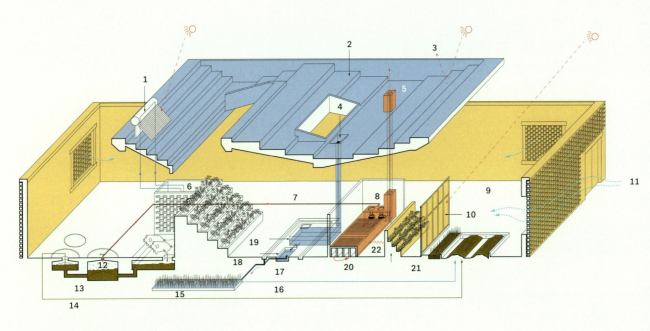

116

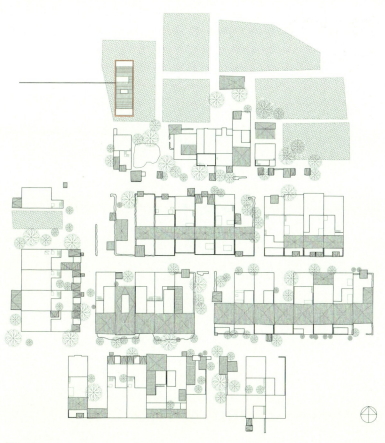

Site plan

Floor plan

1. Backyard with biogas system
2. Courtyard for pigs
3. Toilet
4. Courtyard for plants
5. Shelves for storage
6. Living room
7. Courtyard for washing
8. Kitchen
9. Bedroom
10. Greenhouse
11. Front courtyard
12. Front entrance

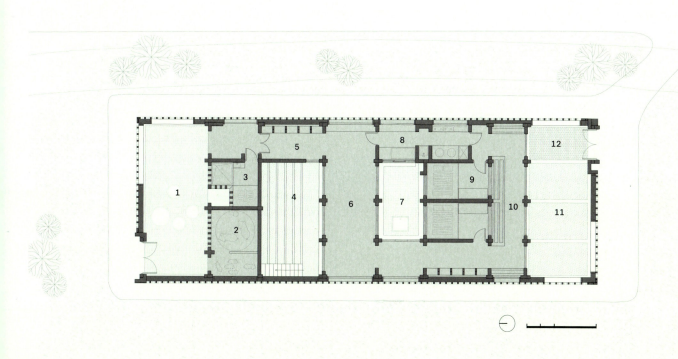

Floor plan

Jun Igarashi Architects

Sustainable features

- → Natural ventilation
- → Shading
- → Passive heating and cooling
- → Solar gain

A cluster of mysterious dark boxes form this energy-efficient house. The layout's many corners improve exposure to light and shade for passive heating and cooling throughout the year.

House O

Hokkaido, Japan

A series of rotated black boxes make up this striking, monolithic house. Built on a large 1,484 m² site in Northern Japan, the home resides in a small city of Eastern Hokkaido with just 7,000 residents. The area, known for its long-lasting forest industry, has experienced an increasing level of depopulation as the industry declines. With a very low building density in the area, the unique and energy-efficient house rests within an equally unique Japanese cityscape.

Quite a distance from its nearest neighbors, the unusual house crafts its own context. The first iteration of the interior layout consisted of a rational square plan. However, this approach resulted in extra circulation corridors, and oriented rooms and views in an irrational manner. The final layout instead cuts out each individual program and places it in a compact volume with a favorable location and orientation. For example, the kitchen enjoys a prominent placement looking out over the private garden while connecting back to the dining area. This considered location for the kitchen establishes a strong visual connection with the site. Through this layout method, the need for extra circulation corridors between hierarchical spaces is omitted alltogether.

Comprising a series of interconnected volumes, the main layout clusters around a private shared garden which directs light, breezes, and views of nature into the interior.

The two-bedroom house, built for a couple, ensures an ultra-private residential experience. Each volume, whether housing bedrooms, bathrooms, family spaces, or wash rooms, begins with a ten-meter-high ceiling. From this point, depending on the room function and location, the roof line either rises or lowers according to the particular needs of that space. This tailored approach allows for a range of visual and climatic atmospheres to coexist within a single house. The dark volumes decrease in height as they expand outwards from the tallest central living room cube. As the main communal space, the living room situates itself in the very center of the branching layout. This airy and inviting social space incorporates a large south-facing window to maximize solar gain and natural daylight. While increasing and decreasing in height, the floor level remains the same across the layout. From certain angles on the site, the house appears symmetrical, only to shape-shift and realign one step over.

Adding to the home's monolithic quality, the inward looking residence removes all apertures to the street except for a single, understated entry door. This decision to open up the house only in the back and garden area maintains a high level of privacy, away from the eyes of passersby. Wrapped inside this seemingly impenetrable shell, an ethereal and bright interior awaits. The white walled interior choreographs an interactive layout where spaces and nature frame and bleed into one another. Numerous openings, both low and high, let light into all corners of the house and generate a cross current to naturally cool the various spaces through the humid summer months. Low-lying windows capture unconventional views of the grass and exterior cladding. A sheer grey curtain runs across the main wall of the house that separates the living, dining, and kitchen areas. This generous curtain behaves as a flexible sunscreen to softly dampen the afternoon rays and add a further level of privacy to the house.

The residence, located in an area of Japan known for extremely cold winters, faces large fluctuations in temperature throughout the year. Compared to the original square plan, the home's current layout addresses these climatic challenges to ensure an efficient and stable temperature year round. The exterior form's various nooks and crannies optimize the exposure of each façade to light and shade. Responding to the path of the sun and the home's heating and cooling needs, these nooks act as buffer spaces for the windows to orient toward. The temperature difference between the façades which face the sun and those which face the shade keep the house well ventilated in the summer. During the winter, these nooks protect the windows from the cold wind and snow. The form of the house resembles a type of cactus which flourishes in the harsh desert climate. Applying a similar strategy to the building envelope, the cactus integrates folds along its surface for natural shading to keep it cool. By drawing from such a simple form in nature, the house not only achieves a comfortable passive climate and efficient energy strategy but also develops a starting point for a new architectural vernacular based on green design principles.

Protective and fortress-like from the outside and open and permeable from within, this one-of-a-kind residence becomes an ideal refuge. The clustering units embrace a personal garden as they rotate toward and away from each other. Introducing themes of contrast, simplicity, and complexity, the introverted house succeeds in sparking the imagination while addressing challenging climate conditions. With simple passive measures, the dwelling transcends local conventions in both architecture and energy efficiency.

Sustainable features:
- → Natural ventilation
- → Shading
- → Passive house strategies
- → Solar gain

Sustainable materials:

N/A

City/country:

Hokkaido, Japan

Year:

2008/09

Plot size:

N/A

Building size:

N/A

Number of rooms/residents:

2 bedroom/two residents

Overall budget:

N/A

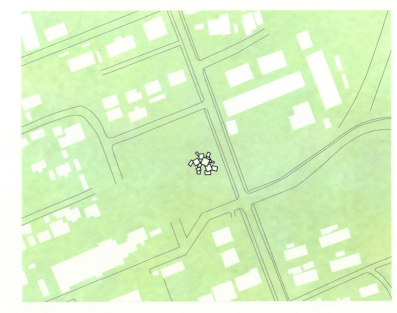

Site plan

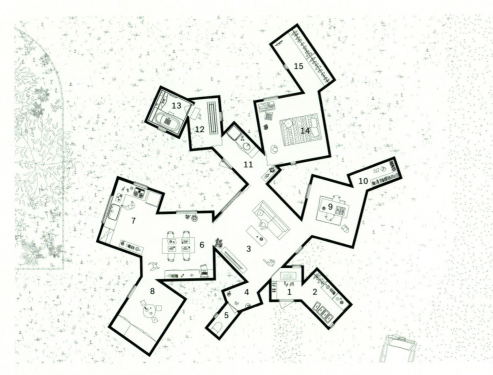

Floor plan

Floor plan
1. Entrance
2. Storage
3. Living room
4. Wash room
5. Toilet
6. Dining room
7. Kitchen
8. Japanese style room
9. Guest room
10. Storage room
11. Wash room
12. Utility room
13. Bathroom
14. Bedroom
15. Closet

Section

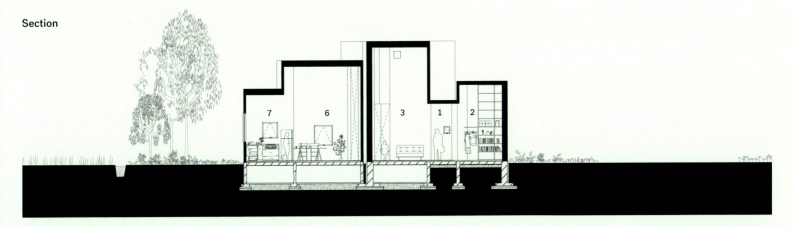

Arcgency

Sustainable features

- → Zero-emission, carbon neutral house
- → Recycled materials
- → Flexible building envelope
- → Green roof solutions
- → Solar energy, heating, and cooling systems
- → Photovoltaic and solar cells
- → Rainwater harvesting
- → Grey water system
- → Low-flow faucets and shower head
- → Dual flush toilets
- → Optimal solar orientation
- → Energy tracking system
- → LED lighting
- → Class A+++ appliances
- → Geothermal heating
- → Skylights

Through the innovative use of recycled shipping containers, energy-efficient appliances, and solar power for heating and cooling, this residential prototype surpasses Danish standards for energy efficiency by an impressive 50%. The flexible building envelope, skylights, and built-in energy tracking system stages a home that evolves to the changing demands of both its occupants and the climate over time.

WFH House — Sustainable Pre Fab House

Frederiksværk, Denmark

WorldFLEXhome (WFH) is a Danish consortium that develops modular, flexible homes for sale internationally. Based on Danish quality and technological innovation, these carbon neutral homes offer a basic housing concept that can be adapted to individual needs. The homes can be built as villas, townhouses, or residential clusters. Designed to produce more energy than they consume, these efficient dwellings also withstand earthquakes.

This model home meets the requirements of the international Active House cooperation, ensuring a healthy indoor climate. The crafted indoor experience features fixtures and appliances with low energy consumption as well as environmentally sound materials and insulation. Beginning in 2018, zero-energy buildings will be the standard for all public buildings in the European Union. By 2020, the same regulations will extend to all new buildings in Europe. Demonstrating a deep foresight, the carbon neutral home already lives up to these future energy directives.

An inspiring take on shipping container architecture, the prefabricated residence enjoys a short on-site construction period. The demountable structure makes for easy recycling or relocation. Additionally, the modular design allows for high-quality industrial production in large numbers, and distribution using standard container transport. Online customization tools give clients the opportunity to choose their own version of the house. A few of these personalization options deal with layout, size, façade solutions, and interior choices. These personal configurations happen within a predefined framework that maintains a high architectural value and quality of materials.

The modular housing concept works with 40-foot-high cubes as its structural system. This structure readily adapts to local climatic challenges and earthquake issues. The sloping prototype derives its silhouette from two stacked modules linked to a single module. This multi-level solution can also be downscaled to a single, open level depending on the clients' wishes. Kitchen elements built into the wall maximize floor space while simplifying water and plumbing connections.

Known as the "FLEX space", the social heart of the house contains a living room, kitchen, and multi-purpose area. Part of this communal space angles upward to form double-height ceilings, creating ideal lighting conditions. All other areas of the house link to this main space. True to its moniker, the flexible and shifting space provides numerous solutions within the same system. Each end of the public living area retains direct access to the outdoors and natural environment. Boundaries between inside and out disappear as the home's floor-to-ceiling glass doors fold open to the garden beyond.

A quiet landing provides access to the second floor. Expanding on the multi-purpose theme, this transitional area also doubles as a space for play, relaxation, or work. The pleasant nook affords an opportunity for personal retreat while still

remaining connected to the rest of the household. Above, each bedroom equals half of a module. The current configuration includes four bedrooms but can be rearranged into workspaces, children's rooms, and reading areas according to the evolving needs of the family.

Competitively priced in comparison with other green houses, this unique prototype's contemporary Danish design adds to the value of the project. The design showcases a variety of Nordic values including materials that age gracefully, access to nature and greenery, modern minimalism, and a distinctly playful spirit. The cheerful and airy white interior promotes strong visual relationships between rooms and from floor to floor via inwardly facing windows, walkways, and stairs.

The prefabricated home's structure comprises of stacked and recycled shipping containers that link together through an angled roof with built-in skylights.

Numerous sustainable features enhance these lifestyle values, resulting in a residence with an energy rating 50% lower than the standard requirements for new housing constructions in Denmark. The home's green aspects include the use of recycled shipping containers as the base module, an insulating green roof, a rainwater collection system, and a bamboo façade. Permeable paving, recyclable plasterboards, non-toxic oil treatments and paints further reduce the home's environmental impact. Photovoltaic panels generate all the energy needed to keep the residence off the grid. Multiple skylights illuminate the upper level of the house and circulate natural currents across the space. Rounding off the building's sustainable approach, dual flush toilets operated with water from the rainwater catchment system and low-flow faucets and shower heads mitigate excess water usage.

With the original pilot home tested and prototyped in Denmark, the first versions for sale will be built in China, just outside of Shanghai. Empowering rather than exploiting nature, this green house presents a universal model for design that lasts longer and creates less waste. This inspired cradle-to-cradle approach elegantly closes the gap between production, consumption, and reuse.

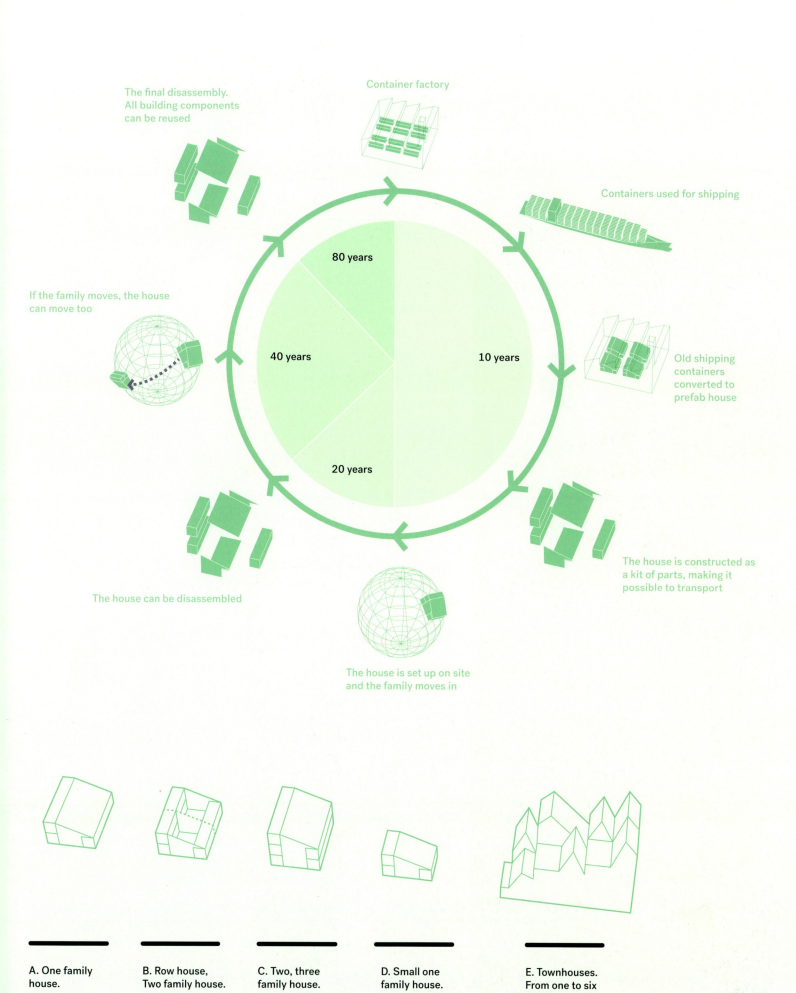

Sustainable features:
- → Zero-emission, carbon neutral house
- → Recycled materials
- → Flexible building envelope
- → Green roof solutions
- → Solar energy, heating, and cooling systems
- → Photovoltaic and solar cells
- → Rainwater harvesting
- → Grey water system
- → Low-flow faucets and shower head
- → Dual flush toilets
- → Optimal solar orientation
- → Energy tracking system
- → LED lighting
- → Class A+++ appliances
- → Geothermal heating
- → Skylights

Sustainable materials:
- → Recycled shipping containers
- → Green roof
- → Bamboo façade
- → Permeable paving
- → Recyclable plasterboards
- → Non-toxic finishes, sealers, and paints
- → Fiberglass insulation

City/country:

Frederiksværk, Denmark

Year:

2012

Plot size:

variable

Building size:

180 m²

Number of rooms/residents:

3 bedrooms/N/A

Overall budget:

N/A

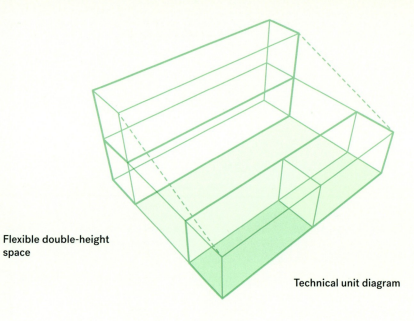

Flexible double-height space

Technical unit diagram

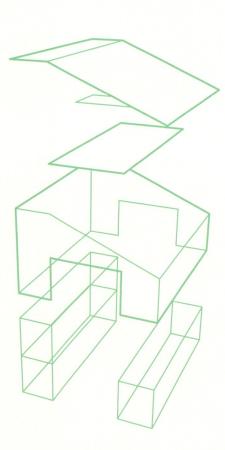

- → Solar cells, 30 m² (roof facing south)
- → Green roof
- → Rainwater is collected in underground storage
- → Skylights.

- → Highly insulated wall. 350Mm
- → Bamboo façade (Interchangeable façade system)
- → Windows that facilitate differentiated light

- → Containers or flexible steel frame system (can be transported as regular ISO containers)
- → Top class indoor climate
- → Durable, healthy materials

- → Heat pump
- → Water tank
- → Possible to connect to ground heating
- → Energy management system, online tracking of energy consumption/production

- → Paving that absorbes storm water
- → Large opening to the surroundings/nature

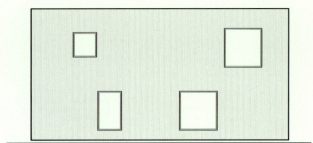
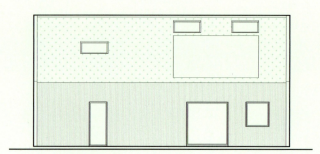

Elevations

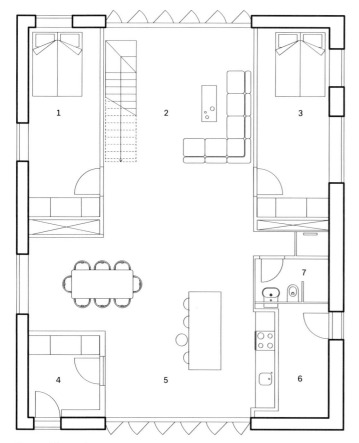

Ground floor plan

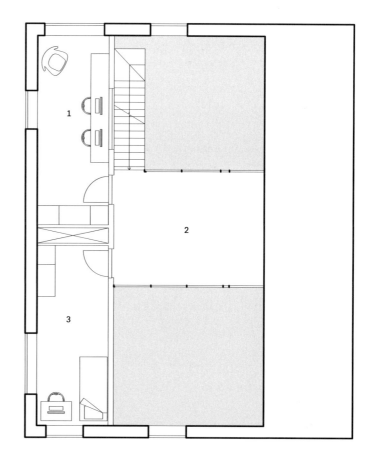

First floor plan

Ground floor plan

1. Bedroom
2. Living room
3. Bedroom
4. Entrance
5. Kitchen
6. Technical installations
7. Bathroom

First floor plan

1. Office or Children's room
2. Landing
3. Bedroom

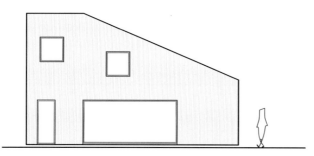
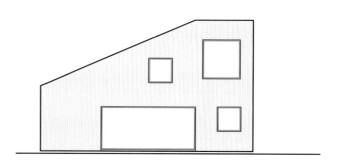

Elevations

131

Renzo Piano Building Workshop

"Diogene" Basic Shelter

Weil am Rhein, Germany

Sustainable features

- → Small footprint
- → Multi-purpose space
- → Sustainable materials
- → Natural ventilation
- → Energy-efficient glazing
- → Low-energy lighting fixtures
- → Off-grid
- → Photovoltaic and solar panels
- → Geothermal heat pump
- → Rainwater collection system
- → Low-water shower
- → Composting toilet
- → Mobile

This experimental shelter serves as a prototype for nomadic and off-grid housing. The tiny, mobile structure produces its own energy and integrates a composting toilet, a sustainable wooden structure, and geothermal heating.

Vitra's smallest building asks the biggest questions. Named after an ancient Greek philosopher famous for his ascetic lifestyle and living in a barrel, this self-sufficient hideout rethinks the modern dwelling. The micro unit oscillates between workspace, studio, and weekend home depending on the latest needs of its occupant. Far from its rag covered namesake, the streamlined habitat defines its spaces and supporting components in a more ergonomic, functional, and sustainable fashion.

The pitched roof housing prototype adopts an innovative and dynamic construction system that uses wooden panels to realize walls, floors, and partitions. These XLAM panels, an engineered wood product, consist of three layers of sustainable cedar wood boards, mutually intersecting and glued. By gluing together the intersecting boards, the resulting structure of the panel offers high-performance, full-dimensional stability and gives the product a rigidity that makes it suitable for the most demanding structural uses. Aluminum paneling clads the exterior and protects the dwelling from harsh weather conditions.

Transsolar, the widely respected climate engineering firm, has developed the necessary technology for Diogene in order to make it fully self-sufficient. The tiny residence features vacuum panels and triple-glazed windows for insulation, minimizing thermal bridges. Attached to the shell, these insulated vacuum panels guarantee maximum climatic comfort within an extremely thin element. Aided by the use of low-energy lighting fixtures, the off-grid unit also engages photovoltaic and solar panels for all its energy needs. Presenting an efficient and comprehensive approach to water management, the dwelling incorporates a geothermal heat pump, a rainwater collection system, a low-water shower, and a biological toilet. This composting toilet operates without consuming any water—a valuable alternative to flush toilets in areas without water supply or nearby waste treatment facilities. Smartly placed windows, doors, and skylights keep the one-room interior naturally ventilated.

Responding to the evolving needs of our contemporary and increasingly nomadic lifestyle, the cabin is designed as a mobile unit. Weighing just a few tonnes, the residence can be easily transported from place to place. Promoting a stripped-down approach to living, the surprisingly comfortable mobile home provides its users with all the basic creature comforts from any desired location. Placed freely in nature or right next to one's workplace, the unit is equipped to work in any and all settings.

The compact interior excels in its multi-purpose layout, where the main living space easily converts from a sleeping chamber to a basic workroom.

A marvel in multi-purpose design, the compact layout makes the most out of every precious square meter. The cheerful and bright interior evokes the language of a contemporary Scandinavian cabin. Developed piece by piece, the sophisticated floor plan stands as the result of rigorous analysis of how to maximize utility while minimizing the building footprint. Organized into kitchen, living, and bathing areas, these distinct programmatic spaces graciously link to one another.

Built-in storage boxes, located in a recessed partition wall between the living and service areas, optimize the limited space in the kitchen and bathroom. The cooking area integrates hanging aluminum plates for tableware and cutlery. Ventilation for the perforated aluminum shower plate and the toilet occur through an operable aluminum panel.

A crimson day bed lines the main wall of the living area. This sofa bed functions as a foldable element lined with two rows of thin pillows connected at the vertex. Allowing for easy packaging and further space-saving opportunities, this efficient furniture solution adapts to the daily needs of its user. The foldable structure comprises two wooden planks, the seat and back of which can be rotated into a double bed. Depending on the time of day and the work at hand, the sofa morphs from couch to bed to storage unit. A simple table lines the opposite wall of the living room. The wooden table divides into three different modules that can be opened and closed according to the wishes of the single occupant. Hidden behind the table panel when closed, a foldable steel profile supports these modules when in use. This flexible workspace generates a variety of spatial configurations that reflect the distinctive character of its modern inhabitant. Enhancing the flexibility of the living space, lightweight aluminum boxes hung from stainless steel hangers can be added and subtracted depending on the current storage demands.

Currently located on the experimental Vitra campus, the cabin serves as more of an ecological experiment than a finished product. The energy-efficient project, commissioned by Vitra chairman Rolf Fehlbaum, represents the most recent iteration of Renzo Piano's investigation of the minimalist home. According to Vitra, "Diogene is not an emergency accommodation, but a voluntary place of retreat." This straightforward statement underscores the heart of the project—a sustainable solution for living simply on the land.

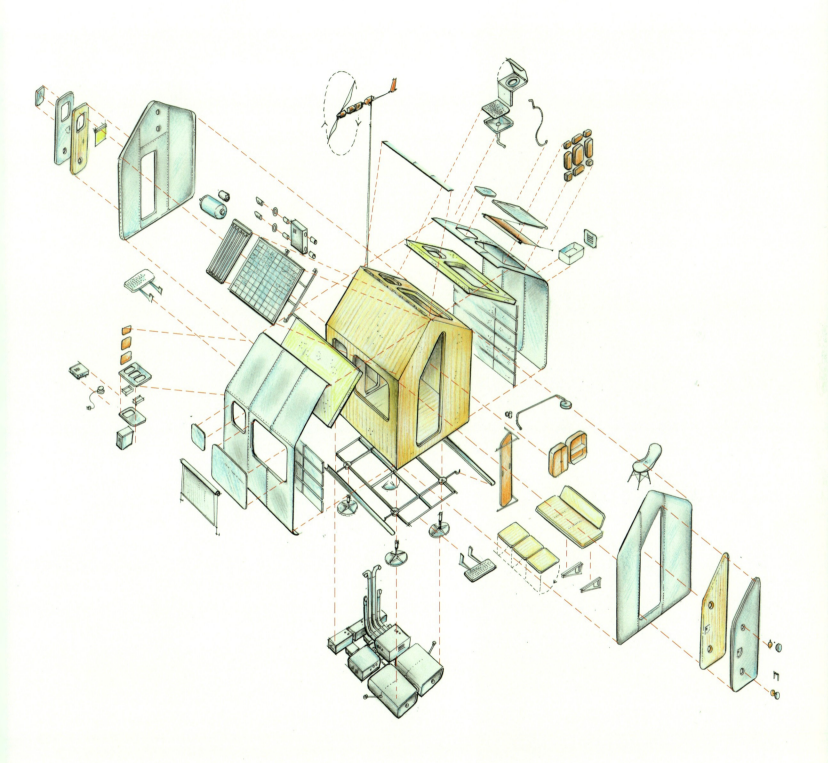

Exploded axonometric diagram

Sustainable features:
- Small footprint
- Multi-purpose space
- Sustainable materials
- Natural ventilation
- Energy-efficient glazing
- Low-energy lighting fixtures
- Off-grid
- Photovoltaic and solar panels
- Geothermal heat pump
- Rainwater collection system
- Low-water shower
- Composting toilet
- Mobile

Sustainable materials:
- XLAM cedar wood boards
- Vacuum panels
- Triple-glazed windows

City/country:

Weil am Rhein, Germany

Year:

2013

Plot size:

N/A

Building size:

7.5 m²

Number of rooms/residents:

1 bedroom/1 resident

Overall budget:

N/A

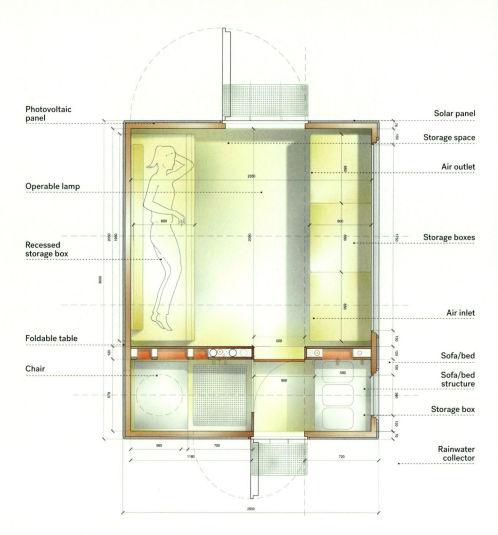

Floor plan

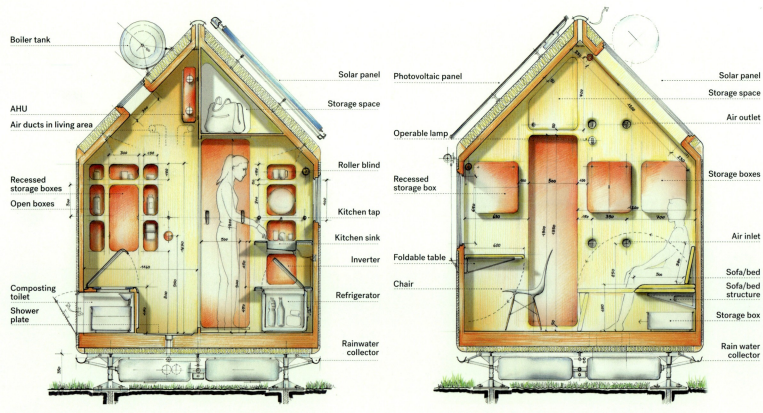

Sections

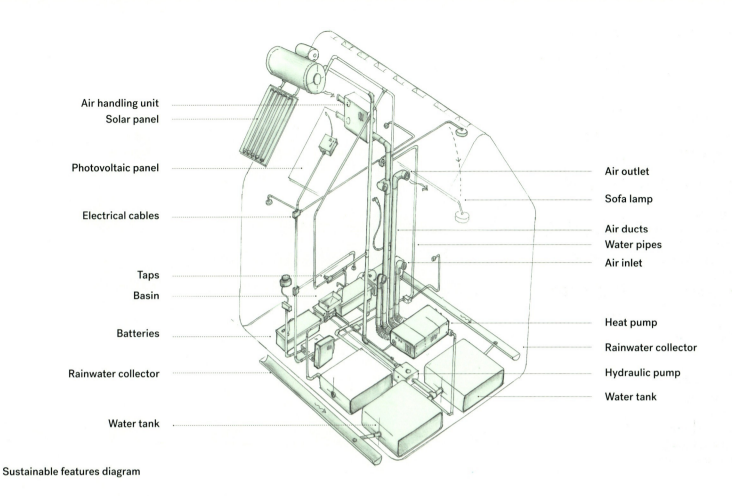

Sustainable features diagram

Elevations

Studio 1984

Sustainable features

- → Southern orientation
- → Compact footprint
- → Overhangs
- → Natural ventilation
- → Light foundations
- → Natural and locally sourced materials
- → Off-grid
- → Energy-efficient glazing

The Nest

Muttersholtz, France

Sustainable houses need not have hefty price tags. This modest structure uses locally available and recyclable materials to construct a passive and off-grid shelter.

Part of a sustainable housing exhibition in the Alsace region of France, this micro residence brims with ecological features. The nest-like dwelling develops an architecture that minimally impacts the natural environment. Inspired by the vernacular agricultural constructions in the area, the Nest's familiar shape and texture pay homage to traditional barns while capturing their discreet charm.

This pastoral inclination dictates the choice of widely available, locally sourced materials such as straw and wood. These readily available and sustainable elements allow the structure to maintain an extremely light touch on the land. Far from generating an archaic habitat, the project's references to its rural heritage are balanced by a number of technical innovations in terms of comfort, ambience, and energy efficiency. Due to the effort taken to seamlessly integrate the cabin into the landscape, several vernacular techniques receive valuable updates to make them more sustainable.

The mini habitat also stands as a reflection on the ephemeral nature of many rural constructions. Comprised of almost exclusively renewable materials, the structure can be easily deconstructed and recycled. Set on an elevated foundation, the eco cabin hovers over the site with only minimal connection points on the land. This slender foundation, made up of six driven piles of acacia wood, give the building the appearance of floating above the ground.

The micro building calls for a micro budget. Built with just $14,000, the simple structure features local, recyclable, non-toxic, and energy-efficient materials. Enhancing not just the local environment but also the economic fabric, this tiny house serves as model of sustainable, responsible, and ecological design. The comprehensive green building system never sacrifices architectural quality. Staying in tune to local and global needs, the micro dwelling achieves macro results.

Two hundred bales of packed straw become both the insulation and exterior cladding for the building. Held in place with a Douglas fir wooden structure and larch wood joinery, the tightly packed straw creates a wonderfully rustic and tactile exterior. From within, pinewood panels form an elegant finish material and a refreshing contrast to the wild nature of the outer surfaces. All the wood appearing in this residence is locally sourced, non-treated, and utilized to bring out the best of its natural qualities.

Applying several key passive house features, the endearing project presents a life off the grid. A floor-to-ceiling picture frame window and glass entry door capitalize on the building's southern orientation. Framing views of the serene meadow, these low-emissive, argon-filled, and double-glazed windows ensure a stable indoor climate throughout the year and changing seasons. The pitched roof includes prominent cantilevers on three of its four sides. With the largest overhang appearing toward the south, the building's north face stays intentionally uncovered to catch the weaker morning rays of sunshine. These strategic overhangs maximize comfort in both the summer and winter. The roof also introduces intentional gaps between itself and the main structure of the house to encourage ventilation and prevent overheating. Further supporting the off-grid energy strategy, a narrow, rectangular window on the west face of the structure provides natural cross ventilation.

Resonating with the most significant contemporary issues facing the architectural profession, the ambitious exhibition produces a committed, innovative, and environmentally friendly approach to green design. The carefully preserved site that hosts the exhibition promotes greater reflection on the relationship between manmade settlements and the natural

environment. Initiating a rediscovery of nature and its resources, the modest project builds upon the welcoming and understated characteristics of vernacular architecture.

Another goal for this exhibition reflects the urgent need to mobilize social energies in order to find innovative, efficient, and qualitative solutions for our current housing issues. The exhibition, and the Nest in particular, advocate for the design of moderately sized residential spaces. this compact dwellings offer a new way of living that responds to the changing social and ecological needs of our time. In accordance with the main concerns of the event, the Nest engages sustainably sourced, green construction elements designed for long-term use.

This tranquil pavilion behaves as an interactive lesson in architectural sustainability. Through sensitive concepts and energy-efficient technologies, the residence embodies a unique tranquility bolstered through its green design. A compelling demonstration of ecological and local thinking, the single-room shelter will transition into a small public facility for children canoeing on the nearby river. Adaptable to the changing needs of the local community, the fine cabin acts as a model example for reuse and the value of building with environmental and practical longevity in mind.

Untreated and locally sourced wood wraps around floor-to-ceiling, energy-efficient glazing located along the shelter's southern face.

Sustainable features:

- Southern orientation
- Compact footprint
- Overhangs
- Natural ventilation
- Light foundations
- Natural and locally sourced materials
- Off-grid
- Energy-efficient glazing

Sustainable materials:

- Low emissive, argon-filled, double glazing
- Local untreated Douglas fir, pine, and larch wood
- Acacia wood foundation piles
- Straw bale insulation
- Clay coating

City/country:

Muttersholtz, France

Year:

2012

Plot size:

N/A

Building size:

15 m²

Number of rooms/residents:

1 room/
0 residents

Overall budget:

$14,000

Floor plan and section

1. Corrugated steel plates
2. Douglas fir wood sections
3. VOC-free pine plywood panels
4. 200 bales of straw
5. Larch wood joinery / argon-filled, double glazed windows, with infra-red reflecting coatings
6. Foundations, six driven piles of acacia wood

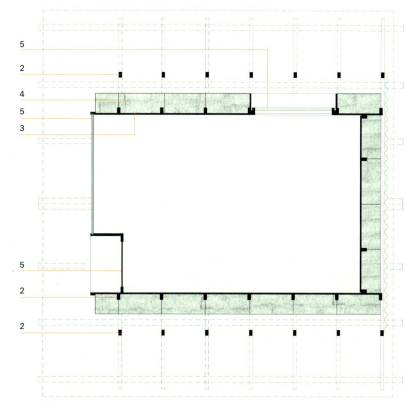

Floor plan

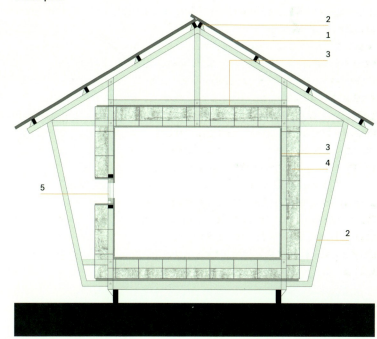

Transverse section

Elevations

H&P Architects

Sustainable features

- Regional and renewable materials
- Rainwater collection system
- On-site grey water collecting system
- Natural ventilation
- Flood protection
- Hanging garden
- Self-built in 25 days
- Mass-produced modules

Blooming Bamboo Home

Ha Noi, Vietnam

A bamboo house on stilts serves as an affordable prototype for flood-resistant housing. Made from renewable and locally available materials, the vernacular residence engages a range of passive features for climate control and incorporates a hanging garden on its façade for growing basic produce.

In a region of Vietnam plagued by severe natural phenomena including storms, floods, landslides, and drought, this unpretentious dwelling offers a sustainable and economical alternative to the vulnerable residential structures built in the area. Each year, these environmental disasters are responsible for the deaths of approximately 500 people and wreak havoc on the region's domestic assets and economic development. Designed to withstand these natural disasters, this simple bamboo home prototype presents an accessible residential solution for the millions of Vietnamese at risk of losing their homes to the forces of nature.

Simply assembled through bolting, binding, and hanging, residents can build the homes themselves. The bamboo modules come in two different sizes. Either 3.3 or 6.6 meters in length, these mass-produceable units enjoy a quick construction time that minimally impacts the land they sit upon. Built in just 25 days, the house can be completed with an impressively small budget of just $2,500. This modest building cost results in an accessible residential solution for even the region's poorest inhabitants.

The multi-purpose house, built from regional materials, sleeps up to six residents. In addition to the dwelling prototype, these units also promote a range of supporting uses. The adaptable structures can connect together or separate into individual modules to function as educational, medical, and community facilities.

Constructed with renewable materials, the home features a structure made from tightly packed bamboo cane, fiberboards, bamboo wattle, and coconut leaves. The fixed framing and geometric language of the dwelling establishes a new vernacular architecture for the region while remaining strong enough to withstand floods up to 1.5 meters high. A work in progress, future modules will be built to resist three-meter-high floods.

Efficient and pragmatic, the residence exudes a unique aesthetic sensibility in harmony with its tropical context. The humble house keeps its occupants warm throughout the most challenging environmental conditions. Similarly, the lightweight structure introduces built-in overhangs and skylights for further passive climate control. Overhangs prevent the lower level from overheating due to sun exposure during the warmest times of the year. The permeable bamboo walls and shutters fold outwards to naturally ventilate the building and generate cross breezes through the interior spaces.

Operable sections of the roof stand as an additional measure taken to maintain a comfortable, year-round indoor climate. These movable panel sections can be propped open or completely closed, depending on the weather and outside temperature. Venting hot air and replacing it with fresh currents, these panels enable effective and tailored customization of the interior climate.

The house, during the best times of year, merges with the natural surrounding landscape. Inspiring a seamless indoor/outdoor lifestyle, the fold-down terraces and framed swatches of sky become integral elements enhancing the residential experience. Whether opening up to the natural elements or purposefully keeping them out, the flexible enclosure remains in a state of flux as it negotiates the needs of its occupants with the demands of the environment.

Elevated on stilts, a small wooden ladder is the sole point of access to the house. This ladder leads to outdoor decks that wrap the perimeter of the structure. The area beneath the house can be used for keeping plants and animals, while allowing water to safely pass through in the event of a flood. Inside, communal living and sleeping areas occupy the main floor. Above, lofted mezzanines provide more intimate nooks for study or prayer. Ladders link these upper and lower levels together. Basic bamboo furniture blends into the interior, producing a textured and warm tapestry from the layered stalks.

Suspended sections of bamboo on the façade brim with plants, vegetables, and flowers to form an edible, vertical garden. This garden requires no additional land for cultivation and generates an independent source of produce for its occupants. On-site rainwater collection and grey water treatment irrigate the green façade and surrounding gardens. This recycled water also flushes the home's toilets. In the evenings, the home transforms into a glowing lantern as the interior lighting shines through the cracks of the bamboo walls.

Readily addressing current and future needs, the responsive prototype not only contributes to the area's ecological development over time but also to its gradual economic stabilization. The affordable and easily constructed shelter empowers the local community to take an active stance in combating natural disasters and poverty through sustainable and environmentally sensitive design. Suiting a variety of local climates and building sites, the modifiable housing system forges a tangible connection between vernacular culture and architecture.

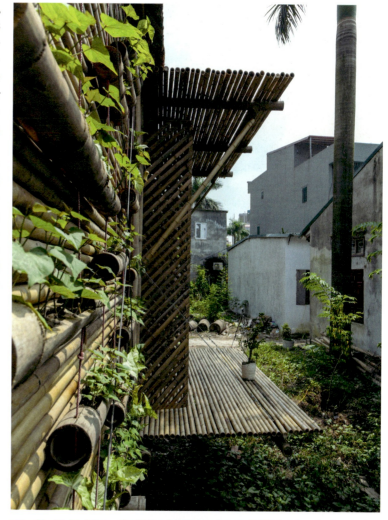

Operable bamboo panels circulate fresh air into the space when needed. These same panels can be shut tight during poor weather conditions.

Sustainable features:

→ Regional and renewable materials
→ Rainwater collection system
→ On-site grey water collecting system
→ Natural ventilation
→ Flood protection
→ Hanging garden
→ Self-built in 25 days
→ Mass-produced modules

Sustainable materials:

→ Bamboo
→ Fiberboard
→ Coconut leaves

City/country:

Ha Noi, Vietnam

Year:

2013

Plot size:

54 m²

Building size:

44 m²

Number of rooms/residents:

2 bedrooms/6 residents

Overall budget:

$2,500

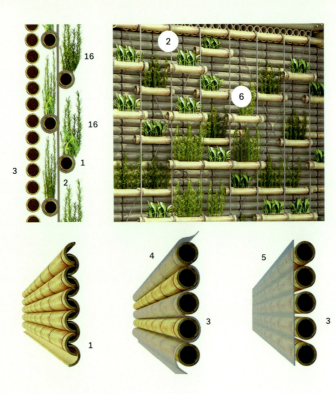

Wall materials

1. Bamboo of 8–10 cm diameter
2. Rope
3. Bamboo of 4–5 cm diameter
4. Nylon sheet (rain shield)
5. Polycarbonate sheet
6. Vertical garden (vegetable, plants, flowers etc.)

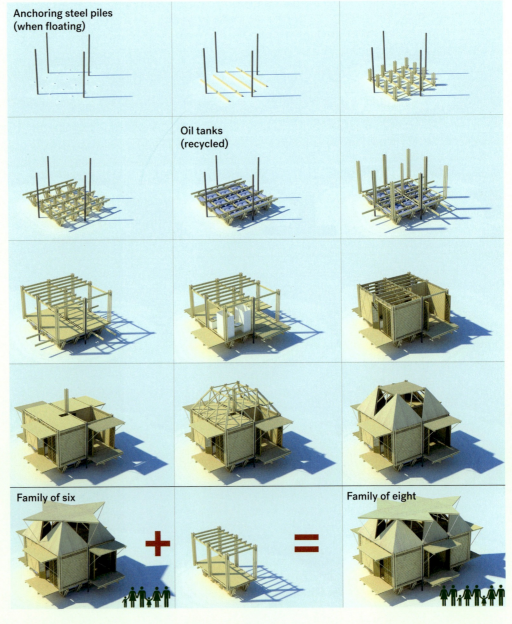

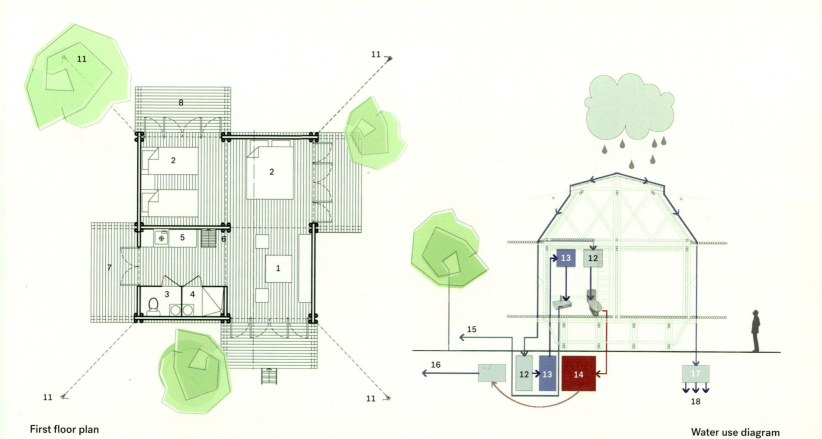

First floor plan

Water use diagram

First floor plan and section

1. Living room
2. Bedroom
3. WC
4. Bathroom
5. Kitchen
6. Stairs
7. Laundry and drying
8. Outdoor terrace
9. Indoor terrace (sleeping + learning + worship)
10. Area for animals/plants
11. Steel anchor

Wateruse diagram

12. Rain tank
13. Clean water tank (filtered)
14. Waste water tank
15. Water for gardening
16. Discharge site (after treatment)
17. Filter tank for rainwater
18. Rainwater cleaned and returned to the environment

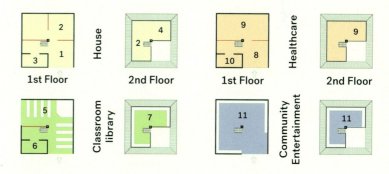

Flexible use of space

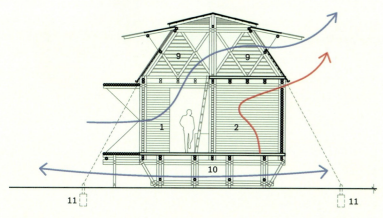

Section

Use of space

1. Living room
2. Bedroom
3. Kitchen + WC
4. Learning
5. Study room
6. Education
7. Library
8. Clinic
9. Medical treatment
10. For healthcare purposes
11. Community spaces

Tegnestuen Vandkunsten

Sustainable features

- Passive house strategies
- Local construction techniques
- Natural materials
- High-performance insulation
- Airtight construction
- Natural ventilation
- Heat recovery system and heat pump
- Energy-efficient glazing
- Negative carbon footprint
- Skylights
- Prefabricated elements

The Modern Seaweed House

Læsø island, Denmark

Reviving the ancient island tradition of seaweed houses, this project showcases the natural and renewable material's range of applications. Achieving a negative carbon footprint, the airtight and prefabricated house features seaweed cladding, roofing, and insulation.

On an island off the northern coast of Denmark, an ecologically inspired residence nestles into a forest clearing. The modern residence stands as a visual hybrid of the historical traditions of the region and modern Scandinavian design. Built as part of an ongoing project by Readania Byg to preserve, restore, and promote the island's seaweed thatched houses, the contemporary design reintroduces the overlooked organic material back into the discourse on sustainability.

This unusual yet charming residence's unexpected use of seaweed as an integral cladding and insulation element results in an extremely low-carbon building solution. Demonstrating the efficient and multi-purpose uses of seaweed in ecological design, the project encourages further exploration and integration of alternative and natural materials into contemporary construction practices. The packed seaweed and wooden construction generates a distinctive architectural identity particular to the remote island. By combining the insulating seaweed with a light wooden structure, the project dramatically reduces the home's carbon footprint.

A range of passive measures allow the house to maintain low operational costs and energy expenditure. These passive elements include a high insulation thickness, airtight assembly, heat recovering system, heatpump, and low-energy windows with triple glazing. The house lives up to the strictest standards for low-energy buildings in Denmark with an expected consumption of 20 kWh per year per square meter.

The residence complies with local planning restrictions. Influencing the general typology and orientation of the building, the restrictions keep the geometry simple and the structure detached. The shape of the lean one-story block with a high-pitched roof maximizes the surface area exposed to daylight for passive solar heating.

By choosing seaweed and wood instead of materials like concrete, steel, aluminum, bricks, and traditional insulation, the house generates significant energy savings. These efficient and ecological construction elements produce a negative carbon footprint in the building. Such sustainable material choices keep the house ahead of the energy consumption needed for its daily operation.

From an insulating material to interior and exterior cladding elements, seaweed plays a critical role throughout the house. The house is constructed with timber-frame panels stuffed with seaweed as an alternative to mineral wool insulation. Clad with firm, cylindrical cushions of seaweed, the roof and façades vary in density. For the pitched roof, the seaweed pillows stay thick and soft while the façades feature a smaller

and harder arrangement resembling battery packs in prefabricated panels. These innovative techniques, while produced as a work of craftsmanship, can also be developed industrially in larger volumes. Inside, the tactile ceiling consists of panels stuffed with seaweed and upholstered with linen fabric.

The house will enjoy the same lifetime as any other building. Even so, the unprecedented construction technique for the exterior cladding makes the exact life expectancy difficult to predict. As the seaweed does not rot, mold, or attract pests, it remains an extremely robust material. Over time, plants and birds are expected to inhabit the roof as part of its natural weathering process. A dense layer of roofing felt below the seaweed thatching helps ensure the technical integrity of the roof. Similar to wood, the seaweed turns a greyish silver with age.

A superior indoor climate is achieved thanks to the use of open and absorbent surface materials. These considered finish elements, including the upholstered ceiling and the shadowing canopy elements along the roof edge, provide outstanding acoustic qualities for the residence. Larch wood cladding runs up and over the floors and walls of the interior. This pale finish lends the home a modern accent while brightening the interior spaces with reflected sunlight. The inviting and simple interior organizes around a large, central living room. Equipped with three skylight windows across the roofline, this common social space also contains the kitchen. Situated at the end of the house, small sleeping lofts perch in the rafters above the bedrooms.

For the time being, the house functions as a holiday residence that can sleep eight. The home's ambitious low-energy performance, however, may soon convince its owners to stay for the entire year. Aside from its impressive energy savings, the seaweed components of the house require no maintenance. This relief from the standard upkeep of a typical house add to the attractiveness of engaging seaweed as a more common building material

Not only does sustainability take many forms, it also wasn't invented yesterday. Completed on a budget of approximately $371,000, the unpretentious home embodies a satisfying blend of old and new, tradition and innovation. A humble addition to a 5,251 m² plot of land, this residence broadens the dialogue on environmentally friendly and sustainable construction methods. Part country house and part seaweed revival, the efficient dwelling links together the past, present, and future faces of ecological design.

The interior of the pitched roof structure introduces ceilings filled with insulating seaweed and upholstered in linen fabric that reduce ambient noise in the house.

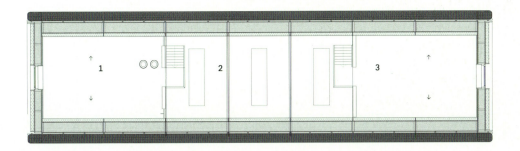

First floor plan

First floor plan

1. Recreation area
2. Bedroom
3. Living room

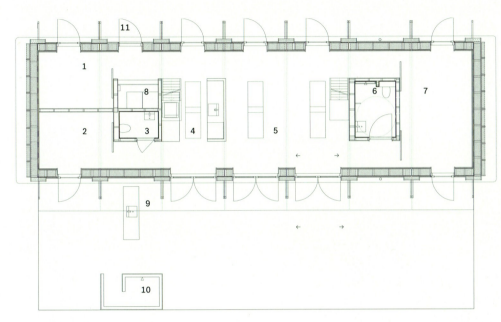

Ground floor plan

Ground floor plan

1. Reading room
2. Recreation room
3. Bathroom
4. Kitchen area
5. Sitting room
6. Bathroom
7. Bedroom
8. Wardrobe/technical units
9. Kitchen outside
10. Shower outside
11. Main entrance

Sustainable features:

→ Passive house strategies
→ Local construction techniques
→ Natural materials
→ High-performance insulation
→ Airtight construction
→ Natural ventilation
→ Heat recovery system and heat pump
→ Energy-efficient glazing
→ Negative carbon footprint
→ Skylights
→ Prefabricated elements

Sustainable materials:

→ Seaweed insulation, cladding, and roofing
→ Triple-glazed windows
→ Linen fabric
→ Knitted wool
→ Untreated larch wood
→ Prefabricated oriented strand board panels

City/country:

Læsø, Denmark

Year:

2013

Plot size:

5,251 m²

Building size:

119 m²

Number of rooms/residents

3 bedrooms / up to 8 residents

Overall budget:

$371,000

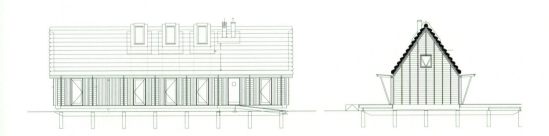

Elevations

Kraus Schönberg

Sustainable features

→ Prefabricated walls and floors
→ Recyclable materials
→ Geothermal power
→ Natural ventilation

Haus W

Hamburg, Germany

A prefabricated residence applies passive measures, inspired architectural solutions, and geothermal energy to achieve an efficient and attractive residential solution. The home's use of recyclable, CNC-cut timber framing keeps the dwelling insulated and within budget.

This affordable, prefabricated, and low-energy house accommodates a young couple and their two children. Capturing a classic modern aesthetic, the family house behaves as a connected space. Within this interconnected and shared interior, the floor plan also provides room for individual nooks and areas for personal retreat. Powered by geothermal energy and built for just $335,900, this budget friendly residence never sacrifices on attention to detail.

Set on a lush green plot bordered by mature trees, the house engages a relatively simple rectangular footprint. This regular volume gains complexity and a compelling identity as the façade cuts away in geometric steps to reveal generous glazing underneath. An assortment of operable square windows, both large and small, further erode the solid façade of the upper floor. This sprinkling of windows across the elevations brings sunlight into the house and inspires natural ventilation through the spaces.

The building separates into an upper and a lower level, one transparent and one opaque. Sustainable, CNC-cut timber panels form the walls and floors of the individual rooms on the upper level. These recyclable. multi-purpose panels not only help define space but also behave as finish surfaces. Keeping the building well insulated, the panels ensure a comfortable internal environment and a cost-effective building solution.

Edging along the exterior in stepped increments, the striated, painted timber façade cloaks the home's second story in a protective wrapper. A variety of rooms on the second floor orient toward the garden as well as an inner atrium. Corresponding to their individual functions, this upper level layout consists of bedrooms, bathrooms, a dressing room, and the children's rooms, each with its own distinctive height. The varied heights of these spaces project into the lower living areas. This common space below organizes around these staggered volumes without being interrupted by partitions. Such openness allows the family to combine rooms and functions in a myriad of ways.

Sunken into the ground, the lower floor features a band of continuous glazing that provides inspired views of the garden when moving through the space. This delicate lower level framed in glass visually contrasts with the solid timber above. The juxtaposition of materials and transparency levels dissolves the lower floor into the site, creating the illusion of the top floor hovering above the ground.

A gracious and bright open-plan living, kitchen, and dining room occupies the entire lower floor. In spite of being partially buried in the site, this lower level enjoys plentiful access to natural daylight. The industrial style kitchen looks out over a horizontal panorama of the forest grounds. When seated, this lofty yet cozy room offers a feeling of complete security as it burrows into the softly sloping landscape. The shifting heights of the ceiling above indicate the boundaries of the individual rooms on the upper level, generating a tactile awareness between the two floors. Compressing and expanding the spaces below, the multi-level ceiling demarcates unique areas within the open living room without the need for formal dividers. These offset volumes carve out a continuous yet personalized series of spaces over the two floors.

Glass doors open onto an intimate patio bordered by gardens. Blurring the lines between inside and out, this patio area becomes a vibrant gathering spot for enjoying al fresco

The partially buried and thermally insulated main living space incorporates a band of glazing on all sides to let natural daylight pass through.

meals in the summertime. When these doors stand open, they direct fresh breezes into the house for passive cooling. The floating timber façade reaches down toward the ground at the main entry. Still retaining a thin strip of glazing at the bottom, a precast concrete stair steps up to this elevated and discreet entry sequence.

A central atrium connects the upper and lower levels of the house. This luminous circulation space also channels light to the ground floor through large cutouts in its surfaces. These cutouts align with the perimeter windows, resulting in a layering of interior spaces and exterior views of nature. Promoting connection and a sense of togetherness, the apertures also introduce cross views between the different rooms and floor levels. A lemony wooden staircase set into the atrium corridor links the first and second floors. The outer wall of the atrium comprises a double-height bookshelf. Extending over both levels of the house, the two-story bookcase stands as the home's unifying centerpiece. A large square cutout in the bookshelf transmits light through the different spaces and levels.

Minimizing damage to the site due to an expedited construction schedule, the house adopts a responsive role to the surrounding ecosystem. Passive measures for heating and cooling enlist the help of solar gain and natural ventilation to maintain a consistent indoor climate throughout the year. Timeless and elegant, the three-bedroom house takes prefabricated components and transforms them into an extraordinary, bespoke residential experience.

Sustainable features:
→ Prefabricated walls and floors
→ Recyclable materials
→ Natural ventilation
→ Geothermal power

Sustainable materials:
→ CNC-cut timber panels

City/country:
Hamburg, Germany

Year:
2006/07

Plot size:
110 m²

Building size:
130 m²

Number of rooms/residents:
4 residents/3 bedrooms

Overall budget:
$335,900

Upper floor plan
1. Entrance
2. Atrium
3. Guest WC
4. Master bedroom
5. Dressing room
6. Children's room
7. Children's room
8. Bathroom

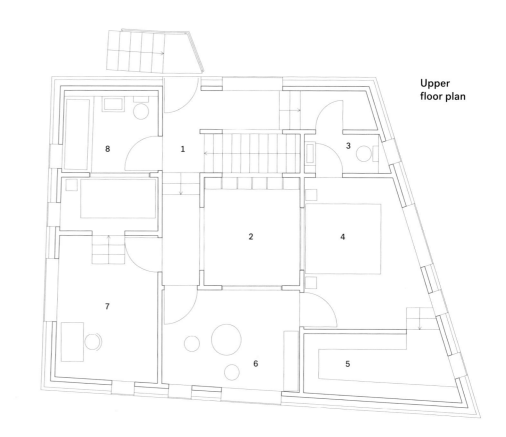

Upper floor plan

Lower floor plan
1. Living/kitchen/dining area
2. Storage and services

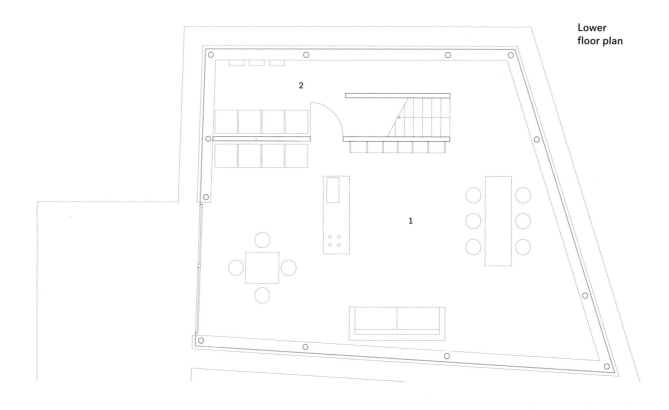

Lower floor plan

Lifethings

Sustainable features

- Zero energy house
- Passive house strategies
- Photovoltaic panels
- Solar thermal collection tubes
- Wood pellet boiler
- High-performance insulation
- Natural ventilation
- On-site food production

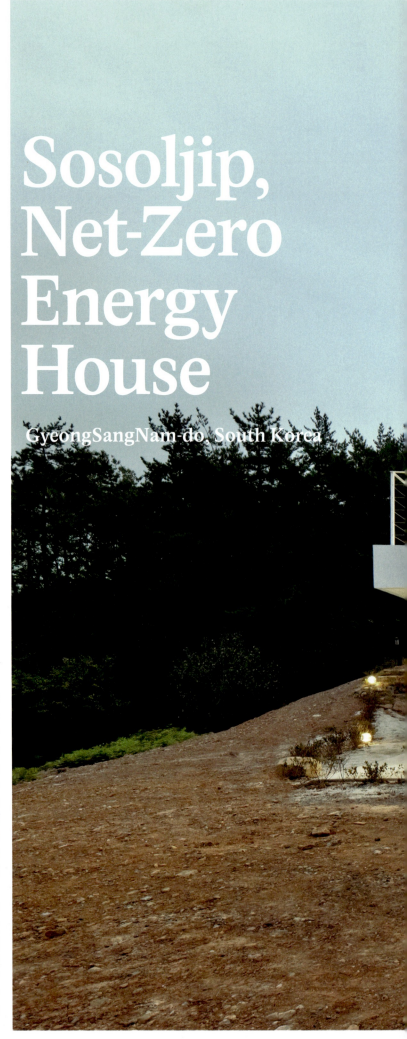

Sosoljip, Net-Zero Energy House

GyeongSangNam-do, South Korea

A home built for a client and her parents takes a proactive approach to ecology and rethinks our access to natural resources. The carbon neutral house not only produces all of its own energy through photovoltaic panels but also enables on-site food production.

A physical manifestation of a personal experience, this striking passive house in a remote countryside village responds to the convictions of its owner. A cultural curator and architectural educator, the owner studied in Milan during the local truck drivers' union strike against the soaring oil prices. Three days into the strike, the client found herself unable to find fresh groceries in the city. This experience brought her attention to the vulnerable nature of many of the food and supply systems we rely on each day. With the wish to one day build a self-sufficient community of her own, this sustainable residence represents the first step toward that dream.

Architect and client worked together to develop a home sensible in design, construction, and budget. Built into the sloping terrain, the house features a number of sustainable elements including photovoltaic panels, solar heat collection tubes, and a wood-burning boiler. Keeping the construction costs at a reasonable level, the residence stands as proof that an environmentally conscious house with renewable energy production can be achieved with a modest budget.

Consisting of three flexible spaces, the layout accommodates the client, her parents, and guests. The main volume holds the parents' individual living room, bedroom, kitchen, and dining space. Independent yet connected, the owner's private studio and living space on the mezzanine level link to the parents' quarters via a porch. The multi-purpose studio also functions as a library and a classroom for architecture workshops. In time, the guest spaces will transition into temporary housing for friends and extended family.

Taking advantage of the village's characteristic landscape of stepped agricultural fields, the house burrows into the hillside of the 600 m² site. Guest rooms cluster on the lower level of the residence while the family spaces appear on the floor above. All of these areas enjoy direct access to the outside. The parents' rooms connect to the guest space through an interior stair, which allows the guest rooms to transform into extra bedrooms as needed. Sharing a flexible wall, these two guest rooms can open up into a large single room whenever desired. The roof of this guest space doubles as a garden, overlooking a magnificent view of the sea.

The owner's more separate living areas sit under a sloped roof, angled to receive the best sun exposure year round. Fitted with 3 kW photovoltaic panels and solar heat collection tubes, the roof produces the majority of the home's energy. A wood-burning boiler acts as the secondary heat source to avoid fossil fuel usage. Thoughtfully placed windows facilitate natural cross ventilation and are carefully sized to minimize heat loss.

In constructing a net zero energy house, the management of energy proves more important than producing it. This passive energy approach means that insulation becomes the most important element in the house. For this case, external insulation blocks heat or cold before it even enters the structure. Unless a window or door opens, not a single centimeter of the building experiences direct exposure to the external climate. To further protect against harsh weather conditions, 20-centimeter-thick styrofoam insulation wraps the reinforced concrete structure. During the summer, the building relies on this high-performance insulation layer and natural ventilation for cooling without air conditioners. Aside from the damaging environmental effect of heavy reliance on air conditioners, the electricity consumption required to run such appliances cannot be met with photovoltaic production.

Panels or shingles are intentionally absent on the exterior. Opting for a clean, white finishing system, this simple choice minimizes damage to the external insulation during installation. Polyurea, a spray-on finish often used in water parks, gives the exterior a unified and contemporary appearance. The resilient and waterproof material delicately covers the insulation underneath. This efficient material also eliminates the need for classical roofing, dramatically speeding up the overall construction process. Simple, functional, and easily understandable, the wall section frames the interior spaces. Composed of reinforced concrete, styrofoam insulation, polyurea, and paint, these walls effectively protect from all adverse weather conditions. The inside surfaces of these walls stay refreshingly bare. With no gypsum boards, wallpaper, or paint used, the interior exudes an atmosphere of simplicity while celebrating the inherent qualities found in raw materials.

Promoting indoor/outdoor living and a life untethered to the grid, this inspiring residence provides a fresh perspective on how we relate to both family and nature. The project also raises awareness of our precarious relationship to natural resources and the increasing value of self-sustaining solutions. No longer at the mercy of fluctuations on the global energy market and in food supply chains, this house demonstrates the pricelessness found in true independence.

The roofs of the strategically angled house are filled with photovoltaic panels that generate all of the home's energy requirements.

Sustainable features:
- → Zero energy house
- → Passive house strategies
- → Photovoltaic panels
- → Solar thermal collection tubes
- → Wood pellet boiler
- → High-performance insulation
- → Natural ventilation
- → On-site food production

Sustainable materials:
- → Styrofoam insulation
- → Polyurea finish

City/country:

GyeongSangNam-do, South Korea

Year:

2012

Plot size:

600 m²

Building size:

230 m²

Number of rooms/residents:

4 bedrooms/ 3 residents

Overall budget:

$296,000

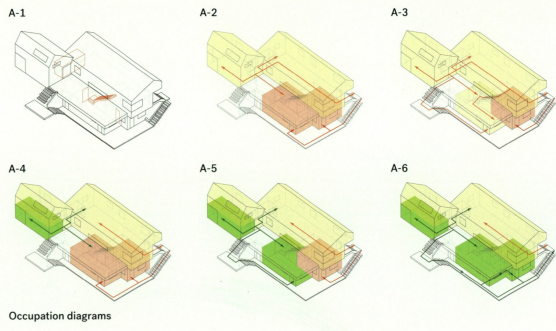

Occupation diagrams

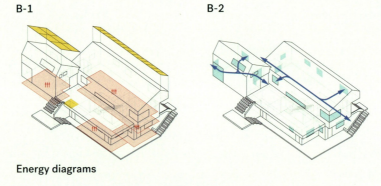

Energy diagrams

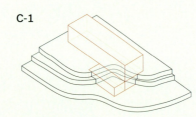
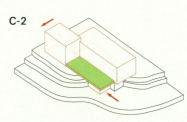
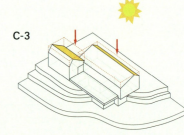

Massing diagrams

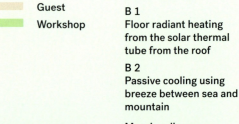

Family
Guest
Workshop

Energy diagrams

B 1
Floor radiant heating from the solar thermal tube from the roof

B 2
Passive cooling using breeze between sea and mountain

Occupation diagrams

A 1
Parts/elements of the house with semi-connections that allows flexible occupation (in red)

A 2–6
occupation of different residents and their circulation

Massing diagrams

C 1
Use trace of stepped agricultural fields

C 2
Shift upper mass for access, view, roof garden

C 3
Recline roof for solar collection

Sectional model

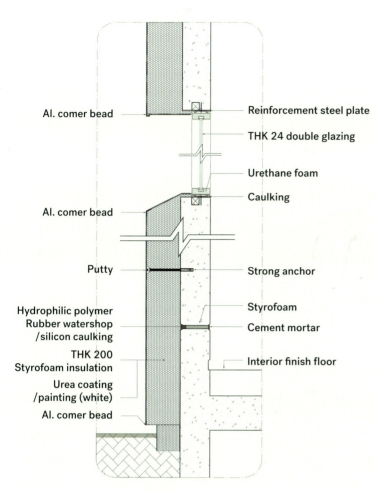

Wall detail

- Al. corner bead
- Reinforcement steel plate
- THK 24 double glazing
- Urethane foam
- Al. corner bead
- Caulking
- Putty
- Strong anchor
- Styrofoam
- Hydrophilic polymer
- Rubber watershop /silicon caulking
- Cement mortar
- THK 200 Styrofoam insulation
- Interior finish floor
- Urea coating /painting (white)
- Al. corner bead

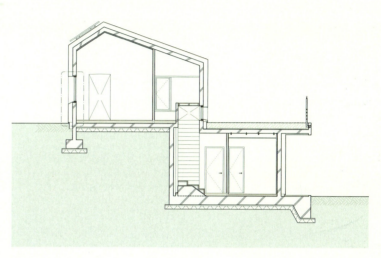

Elevation

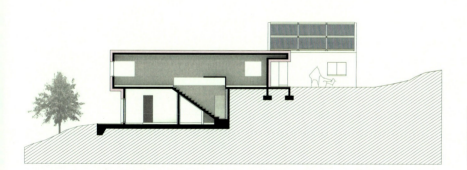

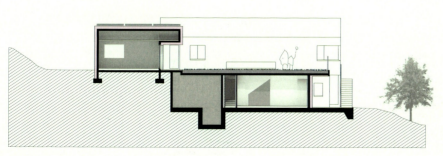

Sections

Paul Archer Design

Sustainable features

- Carbon neutral house
- Motorized façade panels
- High-performance insulation
- Solar orientation
- Passive house strategies
- Airtight construction
- Heat recovery ventilation system
- Natural ventilation
- Thermal and photovoltaic solar panels
- On-site food production
- Green roof solutions
- Recycled materials
- Energy-efficient glazing

Green Orchard

South Gloucestershire, UK

Interweaving passive and active sustainable principles, this carbon neutral house introduces a mirrored and reactive façade. The motorized exterior panels develop a flexible relationship to the exterior climate while the rest of the house incorporates recycled materials, efficient glazing, airtight construction, a green roof, and an outdoor garden to grow one's own food.

A unique carbon neutral house sits within 2,675 m² of landscaped gardens in the green belt of South West England. The house replaces a dilapidated, single-story dwelling with a contemporary, low-rise, four-bedroom home. Due to the site's sensitive location, the volume of the new house only expands to a footprint 40% larger than the original residential structure. This same consideration for preserving the pristine site informs the decision to partially sink the ground floor into the inclining landscape. Benefiting from spectacular views over the Severn Estuary, all four elevations take advantage of the surrounding views and access to the garden.

The living spaces engage an open floor plan. A wood-burning stove rests at the heart of the interior layout while a nursery appears on the floor below. This considered spatial organization results in a greater sense of openness that maximizes views and sunlight throughout the house. In addition to promoting the enjoyment of the surrounding landscape and views, the interior arrangement of the home also benefits from diagonally opposed window positions to promote natural cross ventilation. Oriented to catch the sun at different times of the day, two external wooden terraces connect to the garden and encourage a harmonious relationship with the outdoors.

The metallic outer skin of the building is made of bespoke, handcrafted, full-height panels. These electronically motorized panels slide open based on the needs of the home's two occupants. The highly insulated panels allow the residents to control and vary the thermal performance of the house depending on the time of day and year. By introducing a shifting façade system, the house boasts a flexibility that enables it to constantly shift its orientation and overall appearance.

With a project brief calling for a Californian Case Study House with green credentials, the novel residence choreographs seamless indoor/outdoor living while delivering a zero carbon agenda. The design of the house uses the Passivhaus principles of superinsulation and super airtightness. These efficient strategies manifest in the installation of a heat recovery ventilation system on the roof. Produced by Vent-Axia, the heat-exchanger mechanism transfers heat from the stale air being drawn out of the house to the fresh air, which is then redistributed back inside. The roof also features a mix of thermal and photovoltaic solar panels which produce more energy than needed to operate the house. This excess energy flows back into the public grid, generating additional cost savings for the home.

A wood-burning stove serves as both the social heart and main source of heating in the house. This centrally placed stove has a back boiler that connects to radiators that efficiently distribute the heat across the interior. In the summer months, the stove's electric component stays powered by the rooftop photovoltaic panels.

The house and surrounding landscape are designed with the specific intention to reduce the consumption of and dependency on energy. With this commitment to ecology in mind, a large section of the garden remains reserved for the cultivation of fruits and vegetables. Now, the residence and its surrounding gardens can produce not only all of the home's energy but also the majority of its food supply.

Filtering out pollutants from the air, a green roof embeds the property into the landscape. This green roof acts as an effective form of insulation. Keeping the building cool in summer and warm in winter, the roof further reduces the requirement for excessive energy production.

Out of a $846,485 budget, approximately 20% of the home's costs consist of sustainable features and materials. A timber structure on the upper floor offers effective insulation above while the use of a concrete structure below generates thermal storage for the lower level. Walls insulated with recycled newspapers further support an efficient and stable indoor climate year round. Understanding that proper insulation is the primary key to a sustainable structure, the project also showcases thermally efficient glass. These locally sourced, sealed unit windows are double glazed and filled with argon gas. Finally, the building's cladding integrates insulated window panels that oscillate between black boarding and polished honeycomb aluminum.

The gleaming home responds to the changing needs of its older occupants. Most domestic activities take place on the ground floor of the house. With all the living spaces concentrated on this main level, the lower floor makes room for guest accommodation, service equipment, and a workshop space. The crisp, clear lines of the exterior volume softly fade into the natural backdrop thanks to the high-performance, reflective cladding. This memorable home manages to stay both unabashedly contemporary and environmentally sensitive. Acting as both a protective enclosure and a mirror to the wild, the residence exposes the elegance and peace of mind awaiting the sustainably inclined.

Perhaps the home's most compelling feature, motorized exterior panels grant the residents the flexibility to frame their own views and tailor the interior's solar exposure.

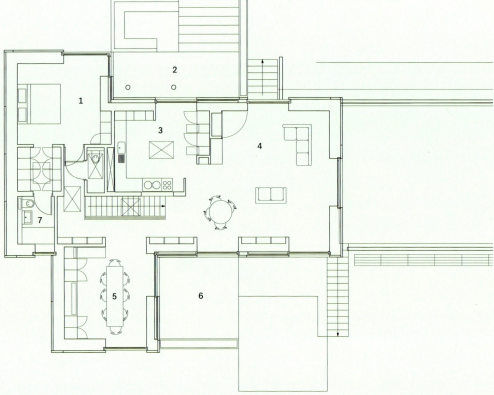

Ground floor plan

Ground floor plan

1. Bedroom
2. Patio
3. Kitchen
4. Livingroom
5. Diningroom
6. Patio
7. En-suite bathroom

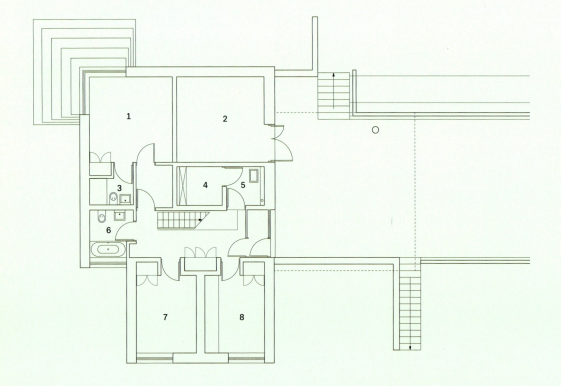

Basement plan

Basement plan

1. Bedroom
2. Workshop
3. Shower room
4. Nursery
5. Utility room
6. Bathroom
7. Bedroom
8. Bedroom

Sustainable features:

→ Carbon neutral house
→ Motorized façade panels
→ High-performance insulation
→ Solar orientation
→ Passive house strategies
→ Airtight construction
→ Heat recovery ventilation system
→ Natural ventilation
→ Thermal and photovoltaic solar panels
→ On-site food production
→ Green roof solutions
→ Recycled materials
→ Energy-efficient glazing

Sustainable materials:

→ Green roof
→ Recycled newspaper insulation
→ Timber structure
→ Double-glazed, argon-filled windows

City/country:

South Gloucestershire, UK

Year:

2011

Plot size:

2,675 m²

Building size:

200 m²

Number of rooms/residents:

4 bedrooms/2 residents

Overall budget:

$836,000

Northeast elevation

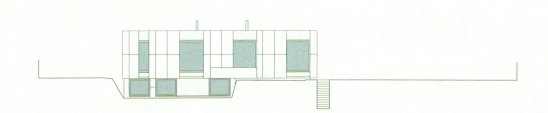

Southwest elevation

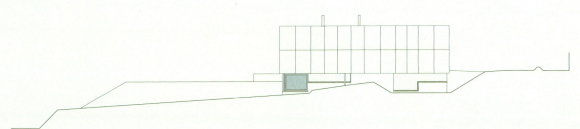

Northwest elevation

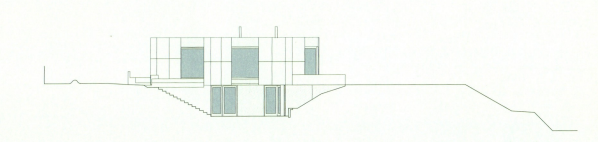

Southeast elevation

Powerhouse Company

Sustainable features

- → Solar panels
- → Solar hot water
- → Geothermal heating
- → High-performance insulation
- → Energy-efficient glazing
- → Natural ventilation
- → Skylights
- → Locally sourced materials

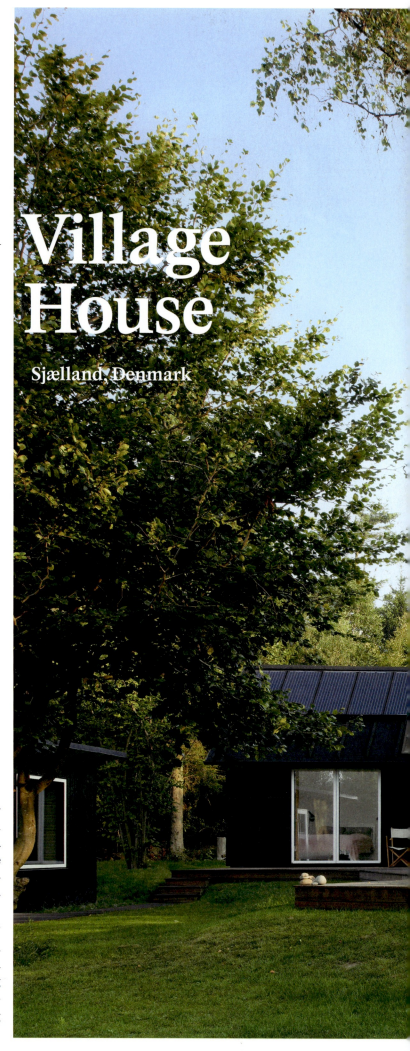

Village House

Sjælland, Denmark

Sustainably harvested and locally sourced materials form this energy-efficient summer cabin. Solar panels and geothermal heating warm the structure during the winters and natural ventilation maintains a fresh and temperate indoor climate throughout the summer.

Village House masterfully rethinks the classic Scandinavian summer cabin. Built for a young family in northern Denmark, this weekend house represents a thoughtful exploration of the Danish vacation home typology. While keeping the cabin's footprint small, the residence presents a diverse range of spatial and sustainable possibilities through the use of a five-fingered floor plan.

The house consists of a cluster of five wings on a 1200 m² plot—each its own miniature cabin. These distinctive units fan out like a hand spreading its five fingers over the site. Such a unique and varied layout generates a variety of views, lighting effects, and outdoor areas for the home. This compelling variation enables the house to provide an enjoyable and engaging environment year round and at all times of day.

Operable skylights and energy-efficient glazing promote natural currents through the interior, circulating fresh air during the warmer times of year.

While summer houses are traditionally thought of as family spaces, when children grow older they need more independence from their parents. With this consideration in mind, a built-in sensitivity to the family's changing privacy needs over time influences the home's 'village of cabins' organization. In this format, individual spaces unite in a shared central core. A large window set above the living room allows sunlight to bathe the dining table at midday. This star-shaped social center connects the living room and kitchen. Complete with enticing loft spaces, the communal area still offers pockets of seclusion for time alone within the family circle. From here, each member of the family has the option of further privacy when needed. This flexible spatial solution faithfully reflects the rather different desires of the family members. With one person wanting a picturesque, cozy, and archetypal summer house, another craves a spacious and contemporary feeling. The beauty of the home's final design rests in its uncanny ability to tastefully unify these seemingly oppositional aesthetic agendas.

A mix of classic Danish cabin design with modern conceptions of space gives this residence an appealingly timeless yet contemporary ambiance. Achieving an archetypal residential silhouette, the elementary wooden structure incorporates a pitched roof. The home's primary material, spruce wood planks, are certified by the Programme for the Endorsement of Forest Certification (PEFC). This sustainable material is locally sourced from the Nordic region. The blackening of these timber boards grants the home a streamlined and refreshingly modern appearance.

The all black exterior, accented in white, embraces its discreet color palette—another dark shadow in the surrounding woods. By contrast, the uniform white interior surfaces maximize the impact of the northern light throughout the house. Light wood flooring, furniture, framing details, and plentiful skylights further enhance the ethereal quality of the bright interior.

Sustainability plays an equally important role in the home's design. Twelve solar panels integrated in the roof generate all the electricity for the house. Two solar collectors, also roof mounted, keep a steady supply of hot water flowing year round. Geothermal energy sourced from the garden heats the floors of the entire residence. In addition to producing these renewal resources, the home's use of high-performance insulation makes sure none of this energy goes to waste. The cabin's roof, walls, and foundation are all secured with 400 mm-insulation. This thick insulation results in very deep window casings. Made from strong oak, these window sills double as shelves or seating nooks, elegantly framing the landscape. The windows themselves utilize a triple-glazing system to make them as efficient as possible. During the hottest summer months, eight skylights open up to promote natural ventilation through the interior.

Located on a rather standard site with neighbors on all sides, the home's context inspires a more introverted approach. Instead of opting for a typical compact dwelling, which would make the garden feel small and produce dark spaces in the house, the project instead cracks the home open to let the light shine in. The arrangement of all the rooms benefits from ample sunlight exposure directed in from both the garden and the sky. By bringing in light from the sides and top of the house, an even solar gain ensures a stable indoor climate during the sunny times of year. Small terraces facing south, east, and west encourage sunbathing. These warm patches remain even in the wintertime when the sun is low.

Rustic yet modern, the sustainable residence achieves a highly utilitarian and low-maintenance update to the classic holiday home. Rather than offering an abundance of interior space, the house instead develops a close relationship to its natural context. The summer cabin purposefully contrasts with the clients' everyday home, both in terms of daily rituals and efficiency. By choreographing a completely separate lifestyle for retreat and respite, the house exudes a holiday atmosphere while remaining at the forefront of sustainability.

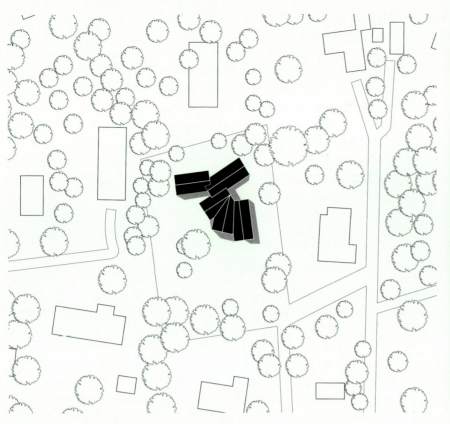
Site plan

Floor plan diagram

Sustainable features:	Sustainable materials:	City/country:	Plot size:
→ Solar panels	→ Triple-glazed windows	Sjælland, Denmark	1200 m²
→ Solar hot water	→ Locally sourced spruce wood planks	**Year:**	**Building size:**
→ Geothermal heating		2012	110 m²
→ High-performance insulation			**Number of rooms/ residents:**
→ Energy-efficient glazing			3 bedrooms/ N/A
→ Natural ventilation			**Overall budget:**
→ Skylights			N/A
→ Locally sourced materials			

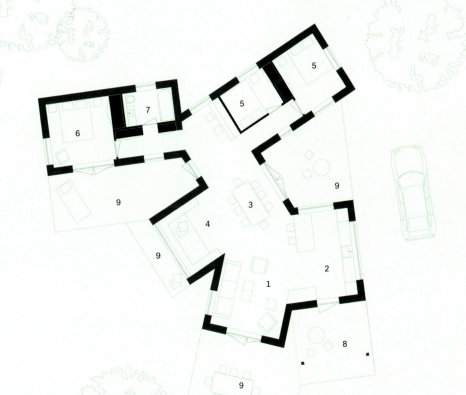

Ground floor plan

Ground floor plan

1. Living room
2. Kitchen
3. Dining room
4. Alcove
5. Bedroom
6. Master bedroom
7. Bathroom
8. Covered terrace
9. Open terrace

Section

Kjellgren Kaminsky Architecture

Sustainable features

- → Passive house
- → High-performance insulation
- → Reduced thermal bridges
- → Airtight connections
- → Natural ventilation
- → Latent heating
- → Insulating walls, foundations, and ceilings
- → Overhangs
- → Solar orientation
- → Solar panels

Villa Nyberg
Borlänge, Sweden

Built from sustainably harvested pine boards, this ecologically sensitive home exceeds Swedish passive house standards. The airtight residence integrates solar panels to produce its own energy and engages overhangs and solar orientation to optimize the indoor climate.

A charming, sustainably minded house takes up residence in a pine forest clearing next to a pristine lake in central Sweden. The original design of the light wooden dwelling began as a conceptual project and later adapted to suit the needs of the client. Creating a house like an analog clock, the circular floor plan introduces a central courtyard that allows the occupants to experience different parts of the house at different times of the day. In addition to showcasing the passage of time, the project also serves as a model of sustainable design. This enticing passive house integrates specific design criteria and efficient technology to achieve record-breaking residential energy savings.

Highlighting the changing of the seasons and the passage of time, the home inspires a fluid and evolving relationship to one's surroundings. Over the course of a day, one can move from room to room around the building and continually experience new views and daylight conditions. The more public and socially inclined living room and kitchen areas open up toward the impressive views of the lake. All the more private areas of the house, on the other hand, exude a more introverted atmosphere. Situated on the back of the house, these bedrooms and bathrooms offer smaller windows with intimate views toward the forest. An ethereal atrium space at the center of the floor plan holds a slender staircase that links to the second floor. This serene, connective area draws daylight down and into the interior core of the house.

Clad in sustainably harvested pine boards, the exterior of the house will gradually weather into a grey patina over time. This muted hue will help the house continue to blend in with the tree trunks of the surrounding forest—a subtle camouflage that improves with age. Stepping up the hill, the outline of building echoes the natural incline present on the 1100 m² site. Over time, the natural vegetation will grow up to the building edge, allowing the building to settle and relax into the landscape.

In contrast to the serenely wild exterior setting, the interior retains a bright yet neutral modern quality. Exceeding Swedish passive house standards, Villa Nyberg functions as an extremely well-insulated building. The residence is mainly heated by the latent energy generated from body heat and household equipment. Thick, insulating walls, foundations, and ceilings combined with the use of high-performance glass ensure that none of this latent energy goes to waste. Further reducing heat loss, the round shape of the house eliminates cold-bridges and limits the number of wall enclosures and points where heat can escape. Projections of the home's energy consumption for heating come to just 25 kWh per square meter each year. This particularly positive energy rating stems from the project's overall airtightness.

Proper sealing and insulation play a critical factor in the reduction of heat loss for this passive house. Raising the bar for Swedish passive house standards, the residence outperforms the previous airtightness record of 0.07 liters per square meter with an impressive rating of 0.3 liters per square meter. This dramatic improvement in airtight construction results in considerable savings in energy used for heating during the long Scandinavian winters. A large overhang extends out and over the main entry. This cleverly positioned overhang blocks the harsh rays of the sun during the peak summer months while still inviting in the low-lying sun during the winter. Keeping the home bright and warm throughout the winter, and cool and protected during the summer, the overhang provides a simple yet effective method for added climate control.

The roof, clad in zinc, affords the residents the opportunity to bask in the exhilarating views of the lake and nearby nature from a terrace on the second level. This semicircular rooftop level welcomes in daylight through floor-to-ceiling glazing and glass doors. When open, these apertures generate a cooling current that spreads throughout the house. By exchanging the hot air that gets trapped at the ceiling level with a fresh breeze, the house benefits from this refreshing natural ventilation technique over the course of the warm summer months. Above, two solar panels perch on the highest point of the house. These solar panels link to a solar hot water heater that produces the hot water for the home, further mitigating the reliance on conventional energy supplies and natural resources.

This lakeside getaway represents a new prototype for the genre of sustainable retreats. The environmentally friendly dwelling was completed on a budget of approximately $650,000. Opening up to the sea and the forest, the house develops a more harmonious and ecological way to live in and with nature. The unconventional circular layout not only shifts one's attitude about how to relate to different residential spaces but simultaneously embeds lessons of ecology and respect for the land within each of its design choices.

Setting a new record for airtight construction, the house is composed of sustainably harvested pine boards that are sealed and insulated to reduce thermal bridges.

Sustainable features:
- Passive house
- High-performance insulation
- Reduced thermal bridges
- Airtight connections
- Natural ventilation
- Latent heating
- Insulating walls, foundations, and ceilings
- Overhangs
- Solar orientation
- Solar panels

Sustainable materials:
- Sustainably harvested pine boards

City/country:
Borlänge, Sweden

Year:
2010

Plot size:
1100 m²

Building size:
156 m²

Number of rooms/residents:
2 bedrooms/ 2 residents

Overall budget:
$671,000

Siteplan

Floor plan
1. Entrance
2. Kitchen
3. Dining room
4. Living room
5. Bathroom
6. Storage
7. Bedroom
8. Bedroom
9. Toilet

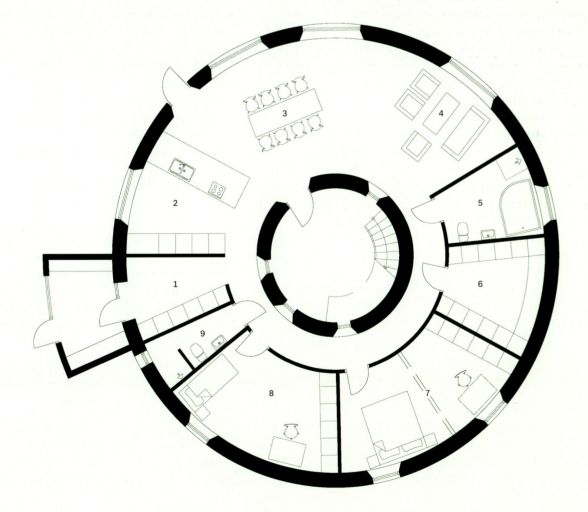

Floor plan

181

Tham & Videgård Arkitekter

Sustainable features

- → Southern orientation
- → Natural ventilation
- → Winter garden
- → Energy-efficient glazing

Garden House

Viksberg, Sweden

This triangular home does away with its shady northern face, bringing the rest of the house out into the path of the sun. Covered in a wooden trellis, the home's double-height sunroom and winter garden occupies the point of the triangle. The warm space, clad in high-performance glazing, allows the residents to grow their own food throughout the year.

A house needn't always have four walls and a roof. In some instances, three walls can work even better. This imaginative triangular residence challenges preconceptions of what a house can and should look like. Driven by the desire for a garden and the fatigue of city life, the owners of the striking residence gave up their urban duplex apartment in central Stockholm to reconnect with nature. Like the vines that surround it, this new dwelling grows out of a scenic countryside location at Lake Mälaren to the west of the city of Stockholm.

The wooden residence functions as an integrated vertical addition to the garden. Wrapped in a latticed grid of slender wooden members, the indoor and outdoor spaces gradually blend into and interact with one another. The triangular footprint stands as the formal response to a steep slope that diagonally crosses the site. In order to avoid creating a shady northern side of the house that would make gardening problematic, the residence instead only faces east, west, and south. Thoughtfully oriented to maximize sun exposure throughout the year, one of the two long façades faces south. The design invests in this climatically valuable side with large apertures to welcome in the sun. This considered placement on the site eliminates the pure northern façade and its weak winter light from the floor plan entirely, allowing the garden to thrive and merge with the house.

Such a bold building footprint further encourages the garden's plants and vines to climb high on the oversized trellis that covers much of the façade. Over time, the house will become more and more hidden within the greenery. Behind this trellis, the home appears to gradually dissolve as it transitions from an opaque shelter to a transparent greenhouse at its tip. An open kitchen and dining area connect to this winter garden via glass sliding doors. Not only making it an easy trip to pick homegrown herbs and vegetables, the physical and visual proximity of the indoor garden to the rest of the house further erases the boundaries between the natural and the manmade. During the warmer parts of the year, the glass doors that separate the house from the winter garden and the outdoors swing open to stage a seamless path from inside to out and vice versa.

The exhilarating winter garden occupies the point of the triangular layout. Here, the double-height greenhouse also functions as a natural technique for preheating the crisp fresh air before it enters the residence. Catching and warming the precious rays of sunshine over the long Scandinavian winter, the indoor garden serves as the home's most valuable space. The winter garden, complete with two inviting wicker chairs, masterfully captures the refreshing quality of an outdoor experience and brings it indoors. Ample glazing backed by the exterior trellis inspires a visceral connection to nature and the outdoors, even during the harshest winter months. This bright and alluring interstitial space between the inside and outside establishes a needed outlet for the pent-up energy and winter malaise that comes from staying indoors too long.

A roof terrace transforms into a vibrant social gathering spot during the warmer times of year. This outdoor lookout area offers a 360° panoramic view over the nearby hills toward Lake Mälaren. Extending over the roofline by several feet, the multipurpose trellis doubles as a guardrail for the rooftop terrace.

Both structure and finishes are made from a light wood. In addition to providing a soft touch over the delicate land, the use of a light-colored wood adds to the overall brightness of the house. Minimizing the need for electricity during the daytime, the wooden surfaces reflect sunlight into the deepest corners of the home. Large, rectangular windows on all sides flood the interior with light throughout the day. Framing captivating scenes of the wild landscape, these picture windows cultivate a constant and rich connection to nature. A central stair leads up to the rooftop terrace. Again, a glass door linking the two areas introduces yet another brilliant way for light, views, cool breezes, and solar gain to transmit indoors. Rethinking the typical dark stairwell, this luminous staircase acts as a highly effective transmitter of sunlight into both levels of the house. The stair features a loose mesh screen that behaves as both a safety partition and a clever, low-cost solution for letting the light shine in.

This dwelling demonstrates that efficiency and ecology can take many forms. In this instance, the simple triangular gesture of its floor plan not only lends the home an iconic quality but also produces substantial energy savings by maximizing the solar gain present on the site. Promoting themes ranging from natural ventilation to indoor/outdoor living and gardening, the residence utilizes fundamental ecological principles to achieve tangibly sustainable results. The further this one-of-a-kind retreat disappears into its wild setting, the more power it commands. As the vines grow taller, a noble lesson for respecting the land remains.

Sliding glass doors expose the house to cool breezes in the summer while a winter garden heats the house in the winter and provides space for year round gardening.

Sustainable features:

→ Southern orientation
→ Natural ventilation
→ Winter garden
→ Energy-efficient glazing

Sustainable materials:

→ Low-energy windows
→ Wood structure and lattices

City/country:

Viksberg, Sweden

Year:

2008

Plot size:

N/A

Building size:

180 m²

Number of rooms/residents:

3 bedrooms/N/A

Overall budget:

N/A

Roof plan

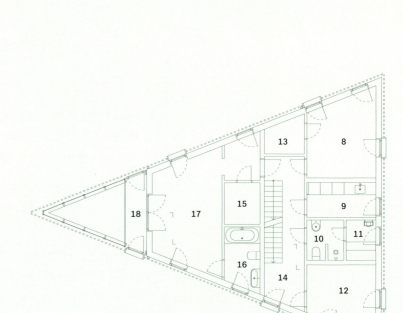

First floor plan

Ground floor plan

1. Entrance
2. Kitchen
3. Library
4. Living room
5. Winter garden
6. Bathroom
7. Technical room

First floor plan

8. Bedroom
9. Laundry room
10. Bathroom
11. Sauna
12. Bedroom
13. Closet
14. Hallway
15. Closet
16. Master bathroom
17. Master bedroom
18. Balcony

Roof plan

19. Roof terrace

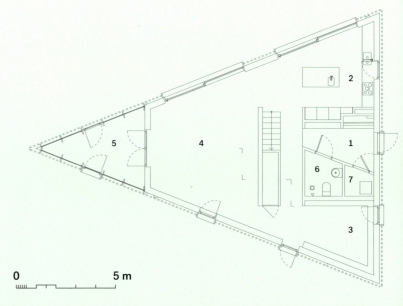

Ground floor plan

0   5 m

Site plan

Djuric Tardio Architectes

Eco Sustainable House

Paris, France

Sustainable features

- → Prefabricated structure
- → Two-week assembly
- → Sustainable materials
- → Reduced on-site construction pollution
- → High-performance insulation
- → Reduced thermal bridges
- → Radiant heating
- → Energy-efficient glazing
- → Solar gain
- → Sunscreens
- → Natural ventilation
- → Shutters
- → Rainwater collection system
- → On-site food production

Prefabricated and assembled on site in just two weeks, this wooden house masters a passive approach to energy efficiency and a proactive approach to ecology. In addition to sunscreens, shutters, and high-performance insulation to control the interior climate, a rooftop garden fed by an on-site rainwater collection system empowers the family to grow their own food at home.

Deserving of a closer look, this charming two-story residence rethinks how to design for sustainability and the complex needs of the modern family. A wooden pergola over the rooftop terrace gives the home a classic, pitched roof silhouette. Resembling an unfinished roof, the pergola references the formal language of the surrounding residential context. This clever compositional decision grants the house the freedom to experiment without disrupting the urban rhythm. Built on a $900,000 budget, the building's open rooftop subverts suburban and ecological conventions. The classic domestic shape instead activates a typically wasted part of the home and transforms it into a social outdoor space for family gatherings, gardening, and personal reflection.

Large glazed apertures on the northern façade open onto the street. These rectangular windows integrate customized shutters designed from stainless steel mirror. The unusual material choice for the shutters reflects scenes of nature and nearby vegetation into the house and onto the street. The microclimates from room to room are regulated by the opening and closing of the mirrored shutters. These sunscreens allow the family to control the amount of ventilation and light penetration reaching each room. Acting as a type of subtle camouflage, the movement of the shutters keeps the façade in a state of ongoing aesthetic flux. Piece by piece, the house gradually disappears and reappears as each mirrored shutter panel swings open to reflect the outdoors.

Prefabricated in a workshop and delivered to the site, the home offers a fresh interpretation of the modular housing concept. The final assembly of the residence was completed in just two weeks. Set onto an elevated foundation, the prefab residence is made entirely from Finnish larch wood panels. Granting the home a unified and polished appearance, these wood panels originate from the sustainably managed cooperatives of small private forest owners. The pre-cut panels, supplemented by wood fiber insulation and non-treated siding, arrive at the site almost finished. With the building plot already located in a very dense suburb of Paris, these ecological, prefabricated choices reduce on-site pollution during construction. An efficient exterior insulation system completely eliminates thermal bridges to achieve effective climate control for the interior. This well-insulated wooden structure succeeds in making the built-in radiant heating almost superfluous.

Deliberately oversized, the double-glazed, argon-filled windows protecting the patios and the southern façades capture the sun in the winter. During the summer, the open canopy and pergola structure shelters the generous glazing from excessive solar gain. This imaginative pitched roof structure behaves as an efficient analog method of year-round climate control. Circumventing the need for intensive air conditioning or heating, this pergola system welcomes in the sun and natural ventilation as needed.

The flexible and modular design responds to the lifestyle and unique values of its owners. Focusing on flexibility and adaptation within the everyday living spaces, this tailored outcome produces two distinct areas for the blended family unit. With very few adjustments, these two areas can become one larger, combined space when desired. Giant sliding walls on each floor divide into two day spaces. Separate but overlapping, the current organization creates an office and library on the ground floor and a cinema on the first floor that can be quickly readjusted at any time. The walls of the skylight illuminating the ground floor can be optionally removed to form a visual link between the two levels. Finally, a sideboard on wheels slips between the kitchen and the terrace on the ground level to move the dining area outside on sunny days.

According to the different seasons, the spatial organization of the house can shift considerably. In the summer, the interior seeps into the outdoors. During these warmer months, the large backyard and rooftop terrace add to the open and spacious reading of the layout. A fireplace acts as the second heart of the house throughout the cold winter months, encouraging the family to gather and linger.

A rainwater recovery system adds further ecological support to the environmentally sensitive residence. This recycled water supply allows the homeowners to cultivate aromatic plants and a lush garden without the risk of overwatering. Intimate and sunny, the rooftop terrace doubles as a vegetable garden. Affording the residents the urban luxury of growing much of their own food, the pergola shades the vegetables below while becoming a hanging garden for kiwis, squash, and grapes above.

In an area shaped by outdated zoning regulations, the sustainable and cheerful dwelling serves as a breath of fresh air for the neighborhood. The simple and straightforward approach to ecology promotes a metropolitan lifestyle that remains respectful of nature and its precious resources. An urban oasis and model of efficiency, this house showcases the joy found in sustainable living.

A shaded rooftop terrace provides space for the family to cultivate their own food. These fruits and vegetables are irrigated by a rainwater recovery system.

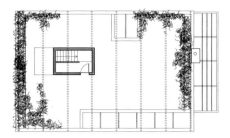

Roof plan

First floor plan

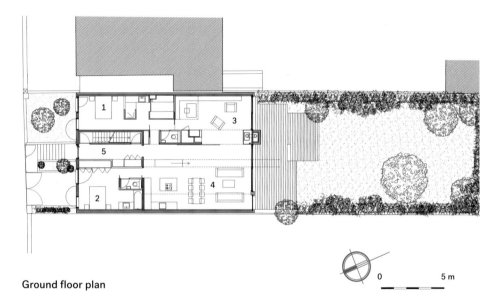

Ground floor plan

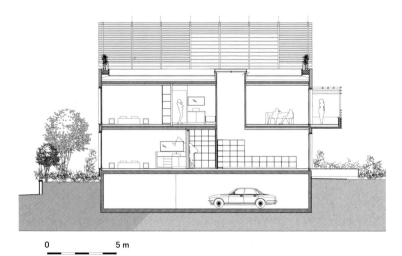

Section

Sustainable features:	Sustainable materials:
→ Prefabricated structure	→ Finnish wood panels
→ Two-week assembly	→ Wood fiber insulation
→ Sustainable materials	→ Non-treated siding
→ Reduced on-site construction pollution	→ Double-glazed, argon-filled windows
→ High-performance insulation	
→ Reduced thermal bridges	**City/country:** Paris, France
→ Radiant heating	**Year:** 2012
→ Energy-efficient glazing	**Plot size:** 648 m²
→ Solar gain	**Building size:** 246 m²
→ Sunscreens	**Number of rooms/residents:** 2 rooms/2 residents
→ Natural ventilation	
→ Shutters	**Overall budget:** $900,000
→ Rainwater collection system	
→ On-site food production	

Ground floor plan
1. Bedroom
2. Bedroom
3. Library
4. Living room
5. Entrance

First floor plan
1. Bedroom
2. Bedroom
3. Library
4. Living room

UUfie

Lake Cottage

Bolsover, Canada

Sustainable features

- → Local materials
- → Local contractors and artisans
- → Traditional construction methods
- → Charred cedar to prevent fire and termites
- → Insulating walls and roof
- → Natural ventilation and lighting
- → Southern exposure

Built with local materials by regional artisans, a small family cabin presents a refreshing interpretation of ecological design. An insulating pitched roof stands as one of the cottage's most striking features. Clad in a charred cedar, this natural roofing technique prevents fire and termites.

Lake Cottage reinterprets life in a tree house, where nature plays an integral part in the experience of the building. In a forest of birch and spruce trees along Canada's Kawartha Lakes, the intriguing cottage functions as a two story, multi-use addition to a woodland family house. The small but spacious residence sits a distance from the water's edge, camouflaged in the foliage of the encircling trees. Combining seemingly unrelated techniques of both illusion and ecology, the unconventional forest retreat captures the imagination and a swatch of the natural world

A steeply sloping, seven-meter-high, A-frame pitched roof covered in black steel and charred cedar siding comprises the structure of this appealing residence. Accented by polycarbonate mirrors that promote the illusion of the building containing the forest inside, a protected outdoor terrace and entry area connects the interior to the landscape. This transitional and reflective terrace, formed by a deep cut in the building volume and wrapped in mirrored panels on both sides and ceiling, initiates an atmospheric and spatial blurring between nature and building that continues into the interior. The main rectangular living area operates as a self-contained, double-height interior volume, supported by several supporting rooms along its periphery.

Fourteen openings into this grand living area reveal both inhabited spaces as well as glimpses of sky and trees. Each of these equally treated apertures are further articulated by edge finishes of interior birch plywood panels, kept raw to show the inherent nature of the material. This abstract and slightly surreal quality of the interior spaces provokes the imagination, transforming an otherwise domestic setting into a playful space of wonder and curiosity. A solid timber staircase with white inset treads leads to a bright loft. This circulation passage inspires the feeling of ascending into the tree canopies, as sunlight softly falls on a feature wall covered in fish-scale shingles stained in light blue. Intimate and irregular, the luminous loft above nests into the sharply angled pitched roof. The tiny room, set between two sloping planes, integrates multiple windows and skylights to keep the hidden space bright and well ventilated year round.

Using local materials and traditional construction methods, the whimsical cottage incorporates numerous sustainable principles. A technique of charring cedar appears on the black wood cladding of the exterior. This eye-catching surface treatment acts as a natural agent against termites and fire. Thick walls and roof provide a high insulation value and a central wood hearth keeps the house warm during the colder times of year. The central fireplace, built into the main wall of the living room, playfully references the home's classic silhouette. Deep recessed windows and skylights introduce natural ventilation and soft lighting into the space throughout the spring and summer months.

The unique and ecological cottage fluidly connects interior and exterior spaces, choreographing a protected experience of life inside the tree branches. Through the creative use and sourcing of local materials, contractors, and artisans, the dwelling achieves high levels of detail and finishing. The exterior wood cladding of charred cedar, a technique originating from Japan, generates a visual richness and texture to the monochromatic surface. The cottage also strategically orients toward views of the lake, with the majority of windows capturing the southern exposure.

Adapted for life in all four seasons, the modestly sized cabin contains flexible and inviting spaces for living, dining, and sleeping. The extension, designed in a way to deconstruct the traditional ideas of interior and exterior space, develops a gradual transition between these two living states. Just off the main living area, a modern white dining room evokes the sensation of eating al fresco among the tall forest trees. Floor-to-ceiling glazing on the dining room's two main walls frames up-close views of the surrounding nature. To further enhance this forest dining experience, abstract cutouts of dark tree silhouettes interrupt the glass walls. These minimalist, branching trees add a sense of enclosure and privacy to the open dining space. After a heavy snowfall, this abstract forest forms a point of contrast between the white interior and exterior spaces. Two open windows visually link this dining area to the living room and create natural cross ventilation for this lower level.

The layered and ethereal cabin crafts an exceptional hideout in balance with its natural context. Resembling a building within a building, this supporting structure now takes on a main role in the family's residential complex. Exercising a light touch both environmentally and visually, a large portion of the cabin all but disappears behind the wall of mirrors enclosing the terrace. In its place, the mirrored façade becomes a reflective extension of the natural surroundings, underscoring the project's poignant yet sustainable philosophy.

Plentiful skylights and windows bring natural daylight and breezes into the space. A simple wooden stove provides the heating for this shared family room.

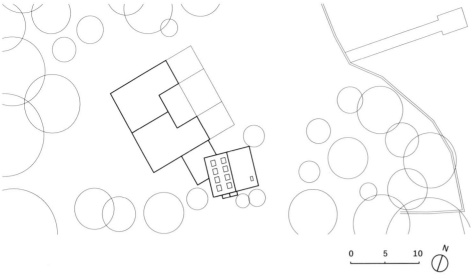

Site plan

Sustainable features:
- Local materials
- Local contractors and artisans
- Traditional construction methods
- Charred cedar to prevent fire and termites
- Insulating walls and roof
- Natural ventilation and lighting
- Southern exposure

Sustainable materials:
- Charred cedar
- Birch plywood
- Cedar shingles
- Maple log
- Raw steel

City/country:
Bolsover, Canada

Year:
2013

Plot size:
1675 m²

Building size:
65 m²

Number of rooms/residents:
3 bedrooms/variable residents

Overall budget:
N/A

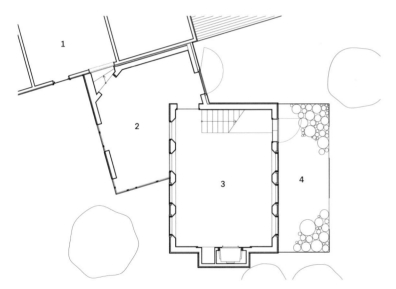

Ground floor plan

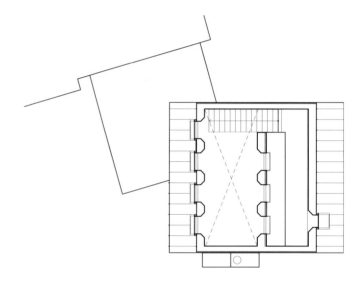

First floor plan

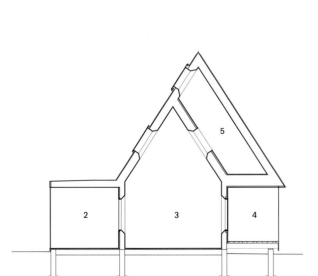

Section

Ground floor plan and section

1. Existing building
2. Dining area
3. Living area
4. Terrace
5. Loft

Kengo Kuma & Associates

Sustainable features

- → Radiant floor heating
- → Insulating tatami mat flooring
- → Solar orientation
- → Airtight sealing
- → High-performance insulation
- → Recycled materials
- → Wooden insulated window sash
- → Natural daylighting

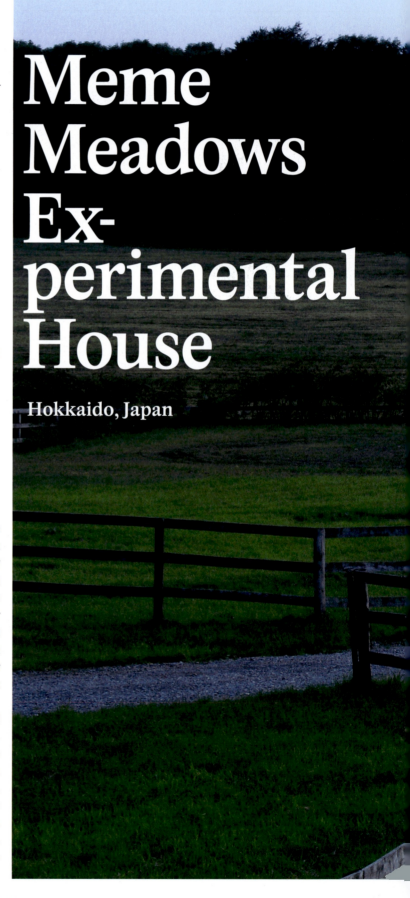

Meme Meadows Experimental House

Hokkaido, Japan

Part of an ongoing project for developing sustainable housing, this humble structure embeds ancient and contemporary techniques for achieving energy efficiency. Heated by a central hearth and tatami mat floors, an airtight polyester membrane cloaks the wooden structure in a translucent wrapper that welcomes in the sunlight while keeping out the cold.

This experimental house derives its aesthetic language from the traditional housing style of the Ainu people in the region. Known as 'Chise', this vernacular typology consists of an insulated house built with earth, clad in bamboo or sedge grasses, and elevated above the ground to promote ventilation and prevent humidity. To heat the interior and radiant floors, these homes feature a central fireplace that is never allowed to go out. This translucent dwelling on the main island of Hokkaido combines these traditional methods for winter proofing with modern materials to achieve an efficient residence in sync with nature.

Located in northern Japan in one of the country's coldest regions, the house pays special attention to its climatic context. In this area, the temperature can drop as low as -25°C. Despite this cold, the Ainu people have succeeded in living here with the warmth from the hearth as their sole source of heating. Learning from this local wisdom, Kengo Kuma's project proves that technology need not be the only solution for leading a modern life. By merging ancestral wisdom with new techniques for energy efficiency, this simple dwelling stands as a 21st-century update to the archetypal housing of Hokkaido.

The design rejects the tendency to insulate a home through thick walls and small windows, as these techniques often cut off inhabitants from their surroundings. Instead, this house crafts an environment where nature can be felt across the interior. The structure of the house comprises a wooden frame made of Japanese larch. Spanning this frame, a membrane material made of a polyester-fluorocarbon coating creates an airtight seal from the outdoors. A removable glass-fiber cloth membrane covers the interiors, forming an ethereal lining that transmits daylight into the house. Between the two membranes, a polyester insulation made from recycled PET bottles ensures the penetration of light through the inner and outer layers. The composition of these layered membranes creates a pocket of warm air in between that keeps the internal environment at a comfortable temperature year round.

Taking a broad approach to insulation and climate control, the dynamic environmental engineering for the house also includes a radiant heated floor as part of its heating strategy. However, due to the efficient insulation and weatherproofing present throughout the house, many winter days require no additional heating. In one part of the house, a wooden insulated window sash is installed on the exterior of the membrane. This added device monitors the living environment of the house and can be alternated with other types of sashes according to the current climatic demands. Similarly, the interior's glass-fiber cloth lining is removable. This built-in flexibility affords researchers the rare opportunity to test how a range of efficient components will impact the thermal performance of the residence.

Translucent membrane walls, insulated with recycled bottles, allow daylight to illuminate the interior. The space is heated by a central hearth and radiant floors.

Staging a life enveloped in sunshine, the thin membrane surfaces naturally illuminate the interior without relying on a supporting electrical system. This analog, but surprisingly effective, approach to lighting calls for a lifestyle synchronized with the rhythms of nature. The semi-transparent walls of the house grant the occupants the rare opportunity to track the movements of the sun throughout the day without ever leaving the comforts of the enclosure. Rising at daybreak and retiring to bed after dark, the back-to-basics house only utilizes electricity to help warm the water for the floor's radiant heating system. In time, a large solar panel will be added to the site to eventually take the home completely off the grid.

Currently used as a guest house for scholars and researchers studying sustainable design, the residence takes on a rich glow in the evenings. A beacon in the snow, the translucent skin of the house transmits a warm light into the countryside. From within, a thick tatami mat lines the floor. This rougher floor covering references the coarse cattail mats developed by the Ainu people. Transmitting the radiant heat, the tactile mat foundation encourages a humble life close to the ground.

The luminous house takes into account the history and locality of the site. Responding to the client's wishes for a home that does not focus exclusively on technology, the dwelling synthesizes old and new techniques for green design into a real-life environmental experiment. The client holds an international competition every year for architecture students, and the winning plan gets realized on the site. So far, two houses are already completed. Both projects integrate natural heating systems: one from fermented grass and the other from horse manure. Kengo Kuma, acting design director for the entire site, also serves as the chief judge of this competition. His residence behaves as a harmonizing force between the different structures, broadening the discussion of vernacular sustainability.

Sustainable features:
→ Radiant floor heating
→ Insulating tatami mat flooring
→ Solar orientation
→ Airtight sealing
→ High-performance insulation
→ Recycled materials
→ Wooden insulated window sash
→ Natural daylighting

Sustainable materials:
→ Straw and rush flooring
→ Polyester insulation from recycled bottles
→ Removable glass-fiber cloth lining

City/country:
Hokkaido, Japan

Year:
N/A

Plot size:
N/A

Building size:
N/A

Number of rooms/residents:
1 bedroom/variable residents

Overall budget:
N/A

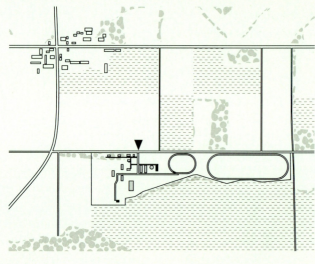

Site plan

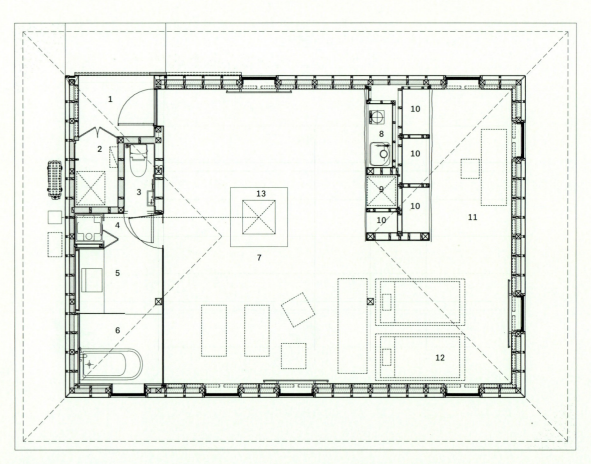

Floor plan

Floor plan

1. Entrance
2. Storage/machine room
3. Toilet
4. Washing machine
5. Dressing room
6. Bathroom
7. Living/dining room
8. Kitchen
9. Refrigerator
10. Storage
11. Study room
12. Bedroom
13. Chimney

1. Dressing room
2. Living/dining room
3. Bedroom

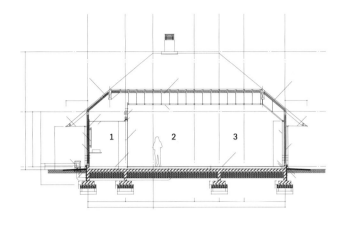

1. Bathroom
2. Dressing room
3. Toilet
4. Entrance

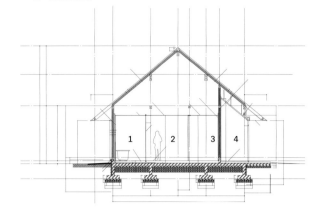

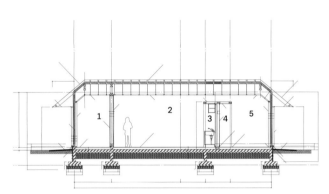

1. Entrance
2. Living/dining room
3. Kitchen
4. Storage
5. Study room

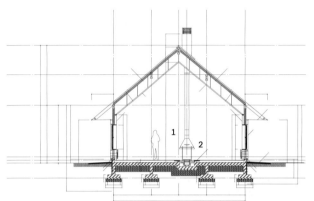

1. Living/dining room
2. Fire pit

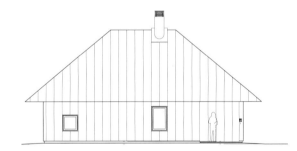

North elevation

South elevation

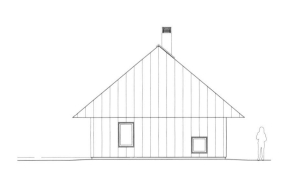

East elevation

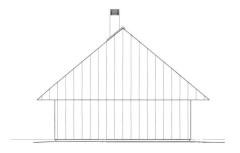

West elevation

Lode Architecture

Sustainable features

- Passive house principles
- East-west orientation
- Southern exposure
- Natural shading and solar strategy
- Thermal insulation
- Airtight connections
- Low thermal mass
- Prefabricated structure

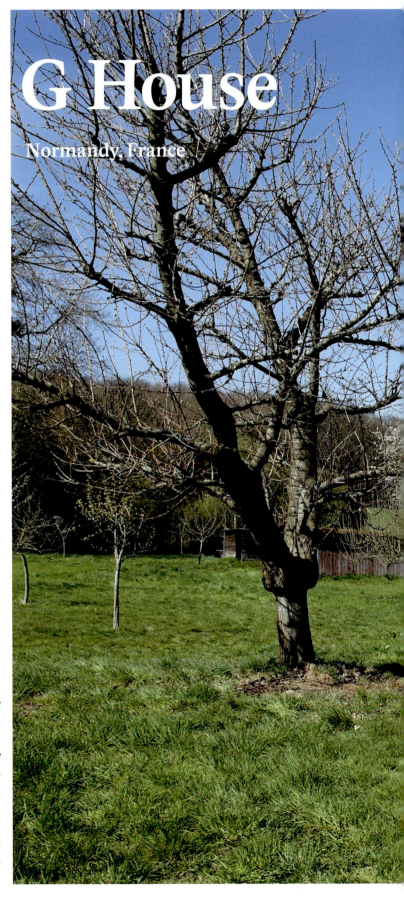

G House
Normandy, France

Archetypal and accessible, this classically shaped house utilizes a prefabricated structure. The airtight construction embeds passive approaches for heating and cooling through southern orientation, natural ventilation, and efficient insulation.

Near the Seine estuary, between woods and orchards, this holiday home appears at first like a dark silhouette highlighted against a green background. The simple monochrome volume incorporates a smooth front façade and sharp connective edges. Referencing the simple language of local structures in the area, the house settles quietly into its landscape. In the daylight, the sheen of the slate cladding softly reacts to the changing skies of Normandy.

Inside, one discovers a hollow volume free of columns and structural supports. A series of load-bearing walls, made of wooden panels, carve out the interior space. Openings cut into the wooden walls and panels let light and air circulate through the floor plan. These apertures of varying sizes form points of egress, frame interior views, and invite the outdoors inside. By using the effects of superimposition and gaps, these picture windows present a kaleidoscopic vision of the home and its inhabitants. These same apertures cast a glow out into the neighborhood during the evening. Picking up the warm tones of the interior wood panels, the alluring glow transforms the house into a welcoming beacon.

At the center of the layout, the bright livingroom extends out onto a spacious terrace. Large glass sliding partitions, oriented to maximize solar gain, join these two spaces together. Benefiting from the shade cast by a big cherry tree, the inviting terrace becomes an active gathering spot on warm days. A spacious kitchen sits adjacent to this shared, indoor/outdoor family area. The second floor houses the family bedrooms. Each intimate bedroom enjoys impressive views of the picturesque country setting.

Built as a holiday home, the intermittent use of the house strongly influences its environmental approach. The final design prioritizes passive devices and architecture, enhancing both energy performance and the comfort of the occupants. Optimizing exposure, the longitudinal organization of the house tracks the arc of the sun. Oriented east to west, an oversized opening on the south captures the afternoon sun. Roll-down shades prevent overheating and add a level of privacy when needed. On the pitched roof, a series of reflective conduits complement the light supplied from the north side. Improving the average exposure to sunlight across the house, the layout remains sensitive to the cycle of days and seasons.

Thermal insulation also represents a key focus for the residence. The choice of wood slab and a wood paneling structure insulated from the outside achieves high levels of airtightness. This wooden structure produces a low thermal mass building, perfect for a weekend home that needs to heat up quickly over short periods of time. Within this built-in thermal framework, a wood stove suffices to comfortably heat the home during the chillier parts of the year.

The simple building engages a dry process framework with prefabricated elements. This streamlined construction system allows for swift assembly, minimized site impact, and a highly efficient final product. The structure stacks the wooden slabs on top of one another to build up the ground floor's three levels. Topped with linoleum, the lower level surface treatment requires little maintenance and casts an appealing sheen over the living room. Following the natural slope of the land, these floors rest on shallow foundations. Such minimal foundations insure ventilation from below, while making sure not to impede the drainage of rainwater.

Above these floors, solid wood panels make up the entire structure that covers the 12-meter length of the house. The load-bearing walls, made in two pieces, connect together with a median joint. Cutting down on on-site material waste, all left over wood pieces are repurposed as doors, steps, or fixed furniture. In order to highlight the clean structure, and to allow the passage of plumbing and electicity, the side walls and the roof ceilings feature a white plaster finish and gypsum fiberboards. These plastered surfaces offer a visual contrast against the load-bearing walls that showcase both of their wooden sides.

In order to obtain a more direct expression of the original plan, the outdoor cladding takes on an added importance. Carefully implemented, the exterior façade embeds flush windows and seamless roof details. The extensive use of synthetic slate within a continuous layout demonstrates a commitment to durability and contemporary aesthetics while staying anchored in local building traditions.

Perched on a 2,760 m² plot, the three-bedroom, two-story house provides a tranquil and energy-efficient interpretation of the weekend home. The pared-down layout and material finishes inspire an equally simple approach to daily life. Evoking a classic outline through advanced methods for prefabrication, the vacation house embodies a sustainable update to the vernacular architecture of the region. This humble residence subtly nudges a timeless archetype into the realm of green design.

Enjoying natural ventilation and solar gain, glass sliding doors connect the main living area to a generous southern facing terrace.

Sustainable features:
→ Passive house principles
→ East-west orientation
→ Southern exposure
→ Natural shading and solar strategy
→ Thermal insulation
→ Airtight connections
→ Low thermal mass
→ Prefabricated structure

Sustainable materials:
→ Laminated timber panels
→ Synthetic slate
→ Gypsum fiberboards

City/country:
Normandy, France

Year:
2011

Plot size:
2,760 m²

Building size:
72 m²

Number of rooms/residents:
3 bedrooms/ N/A

Overall budget:
N/A

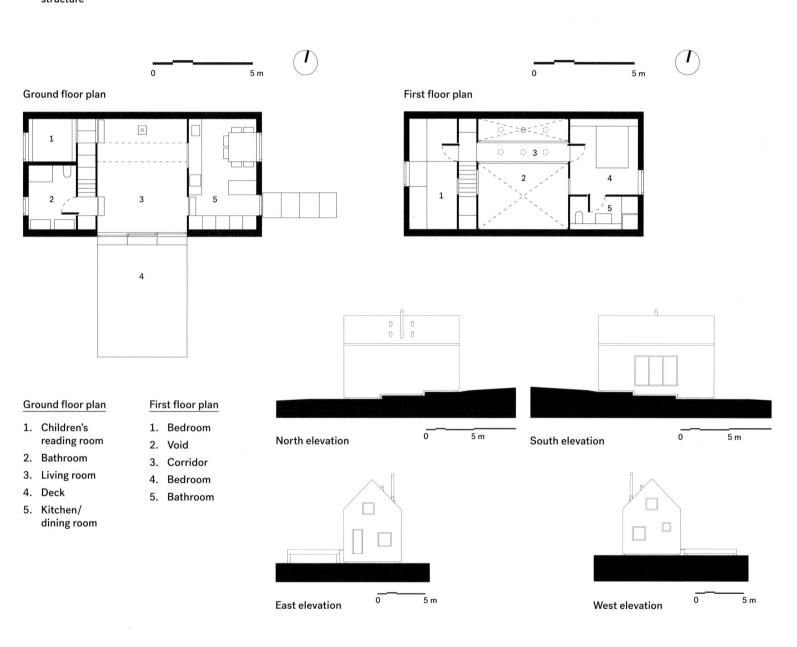

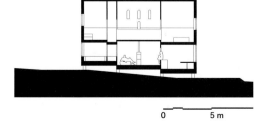

Ground floor plan
1. Children's reading room
2. Bathroom
3. Living room
4. Deck
5. Kitchen/ dining room

First floor plan
1. Bedroom
2. Void
3. Corridor
4. Bedroom
5. Bathroom

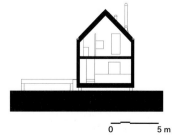

BME-Odooproject

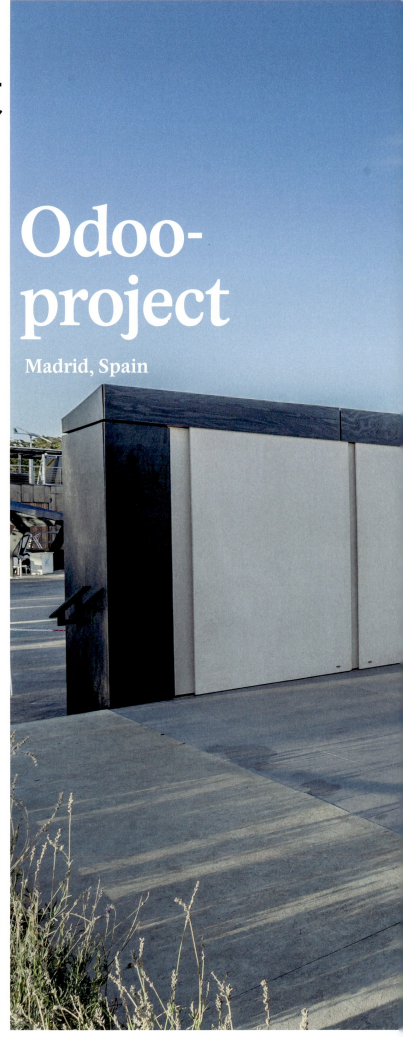

Odooproject
Madrid, Spain

Sustainable features

- → High-performance insulation
- → Airtight construction
- → Energy-efficient glazing
- → Active and passive climate conditioning systems
- → Built-in shading
- → Solar gain
- → Southern orientation
- → Thermal mass
- → Radiant floor heating
- → Solar cells

An indoor/outdoor, carbon neutral home built for Europe's Solar Decathlon, produces more energy than it consumes. Applying a comprehensive approach to sustainability, the prefabricated project fuses an efficient energy automation system and photovoltaic panels with techniques for passive heating and cooling.

Built for the 2012 Solar Decathlon Europe competition in Madrid, this innovative residence stands as the realization of a student project from the Budapest University of Technology and Economics. The comprehensive dwelling brings together students from five different departments of the university to form a multidisciplinary team. This team consists of both electrical, environmental, and building service engineering and architecture students as well as students from the areas of management, logistics, public relations, and communications. Demonstrating that sustainability is not just a technological issue, this residential prototype offers an inventive approach to both ecological living and architecture.

The house features a new type of outdoor living, combining the advantages of traditional and modern lifestyles. A summer wall, the home's characteristic component, influences the general design of the house and hosts a number of different features. These multipurpose exterior units consist of a summer kitchen and resting area where the daily activities of cooking, eating, relaxing, and working can be carried out with the greatest level of comfort. The summer wall defines the space of the terrace and incorporates the blocks necessary for the flexible functionality of the outdoor kitchen and living area. The spaces of the house are activated in variable intensities according to the current season. During the winter, the heated interior spaces become the social heart of the house while the outdoor terrace takes on a prominent role throughout the warm summer months. The transitional periods of spring and autumn, and the cooler summer evenings, transform these two parts of the house into a single, united living area.

Defining the appearance of the project, integrated solar panels on the roof and the façade represent the project's most dominant aesthetic and architectural elements. These vertically installed solar panels produce energy mainly in winter and complete the home's roofing system. Accordingly, the electrical switchboard, mechanical units, and large tanks for the passive cooling system are placed here as well.

The residence features a unique passive surface heating and cooling system. This efficient system compensates for the lack of thermal mass by adding insulated water tanks filled with collected rainwater. The rainwater tanks connect to the piping running through the floor and ceiling with a heat exchanger device. In the winter, the thermal load extracted from the floor transmits to the buffer tank for use as nighttime heating. To take full advantage of the advanced mechanical system, a specially developed automation system engages existing and freely configurable tools to program a unique application for the house.

Striving to realize the most energy-efficient building possible, the house achieves a positive energy balance through the minimization of energy consumption and the maximization of energy gain. Utilizing passive design strategies and systems, the home dramatically reduces energy consumption. Some of these passive techniques include optimal building orientation for solar gain, a high-performance building envelope with cellulose thermal insulation to mitigate heat loss and thermal bridges, natural daylighting, and sufficient thermal mass. With optimized usage guaranteed by the intelligent building automation system, the home is outfitted with efficient appliances. This flexible and easily upgradeable automation, into which new devices can be integrated, allows for reconfiguration at any time, according to current demands. An effective HVAC system applies several methods for generating a comfortable interior climate condition, all of which finds the most efficient solution for heating and cooling possible. Finally, a future-oriented electrical system—compatible with smart-grid systems—will be able to charge electric cars and make preventive decisions depending on the weather forecast.

Sliding wooden panels reveal a built-in outdoor kitchen that extends the floor plan out onto a central patio with integrated shading.

Flexibility serves as one of the most important aspects impacting the home's design process. A fundamental aspect of sustainability, this flexibility results in a project that can not only function as a two-person home, but also as an Expo pavilion and learning tool in different cities. Developed in accordance with one another, the home's architectural details and mechanical and electrical system work together to establish an integrated energy solution for complex and changing needs. The summer wall and patio, the integrated solar panels, and the suspended ceiling with built-in lighting, surface cooling, and acoustic panels comprise the key aspects of this sustainable, wood paneled house. Built in Budapest, transported to and exhibited in Madrid, and finally relocated back to Budapest, the home readily adapts to a range of climates. Executed on a budget of $414,600 and assembled in just twelve days, the prefabricated, single-room building promotes flexibility in terms of layout, energy consumption, and location.

Sustainable features:
- High-performance insulation
- Airtight construction
- Energy-efficient glazing
- Active and passive climate conditioning systems
- Built-in shading
- Solar gain
- Southern orientation
- Thermal mass
- Radiant floor heating
- Solar cells
- Natural daylighting
- Intelligent building automation
- Twelve day assembly
- Transportable structure

Sustainable materials:
- Triple-glazed glass
- Cellulose thermal insulation

City/country:

Madrid, Spain

Year:

2012

Plot size:

N/A

Building size:

N/A

Number of rooms/residents:

1 bedroom/variable residents

Overall Budget:

N/A

Longitudinal section

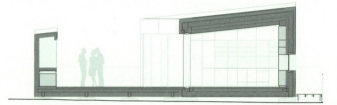

Transverse section

Summer wall elevation

1. Summer kitchen
2. Movable fireplace
3. Timber sliding door
4. Outdoor living

Summer wall elevation

North elevation

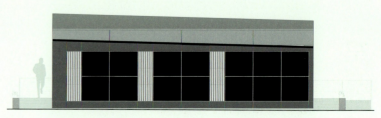

South elevation

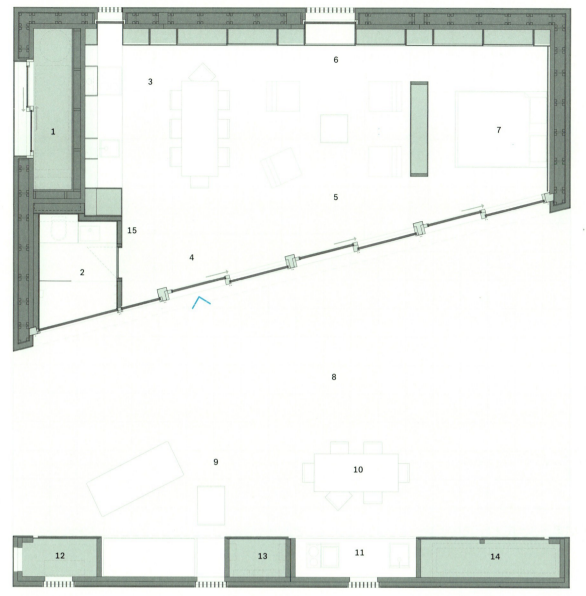

Floor plan

1. Mechanical room
2. Bathroom
3. Cooking/ dining area
4. Entrance
5. Living area
6. Work area
7. Bedroom
8. Terrace
9. Outdoor living area
10. Outdoor dining area
11. Summer kitchen
12. HVAC outdoor closet
13. Electric controls
14. Thermal mass
15. House controls

Floor plan

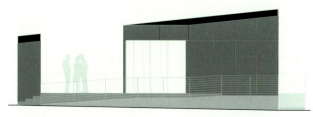

East elevation

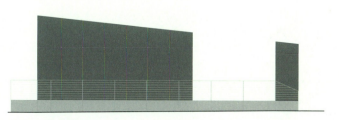

West elevation

217

Parsonson Architects

Sustainable features

- → Solar orientation
- → Overhangs
- → Natural ventilation
- → Energy-efficient glazing
- → Adjustable louvers
- → Insulating foundation and roof
- → Reduced thermal bridges
- → Ventilated roof cavities
- → Solar hot water
- → Solar panels
- → Raw, locally sourced, and recyclable materials
- → High-performance insulation

Shoal Bay Bach

Aramoana, New Zealand

Inspired by the farming structures of the region, this understated wooden dwelling crafts an energy-efficient residential experience that remains respectful to the sensitive coastal landscape. Natural ventilation, insulation, and finishes complement the home's use of solar power, while double-glazed windows and built-in overhangs and louvers maintain a stable year-round climate.

A scenic residence makes the most of its breathtaking farmland surroundings. Part of a remote settlement, the house sits on the rugged eastern coastline of southern Hawkes Bay. The simple and sustainable wooden structures serve as a holiday retreat for a large family and their guests—a place to enjoy the long summer holidays in this unique part of the world.

The three-bedroom house, built for a family of seven, arranges itself along a north-south axis parallel to the coast. Designed as an extension of the rural setting, the home rests on an elevated foundation alongside the original wool shed, which has served the bay since the early 1900s. The residence consists of two slightly off-set pavilions, one housing the bedrooms, bathroom, and garage and the other accommodating the main living space. Sun decks at the north and south end of the living pavilion follow the arc of the sun throughout the day.

This configuration allows the sun to penetrate and warm the heavily insulated interior while framing views of both sunrise and sunset. A built-in window seat along the edge of the kitchen continues out onto the southern sun deck, erasing perceived boundaries between inside and out. Disappearing behind the kitchen bench, a sliding glass door converts the space into an indoor/outdoor cooking area.

Sliding screens of cedar slats at the north-west end of the structure provide adjustable shelter for the site's variable wind conditions. Doubling as walls for outdoor sleeping, these screens introduce a layer of added privacy for the house, away from the eyes of neighboring campers. This more intimate deck affords a ventilated place to relax in hot weather.

Oriented to optimize solar gain, the home applies a number of passive energy saving methods. The layout of the house and its overhangs are configured for maximum sun penetration in the winter, and shade and ventilation in the summer. Double-glazed windows reduce fluctuations in the indoor temperature throughout the changing seasons. In hot summer weather, sliding doors enable the living pavilion to be fully opened up to the outside and promote cross ventilation through the house. The settlement relies on communal water collection to meet its needs. Solar panels, mounted on the bridge between the two living pavilions, generates the hot water heating for the home.

Double layered for extra insulation, the two interconnected gabled roofs successfully prevent thermal bridging through their steel structure. Fully recyclable, the roof consists of aluminum and corrugated iron. A slot designed into the roofing keeps the roof cavities well ventilated. The home's insulated floors, raised above the ground, also include space for ventilation. These elevated floors maximize interior space by creating extra room below for storing kayaks, bikes, and beach equipment. Wool insulation, a natural and high-performance material, is used to protect the interior from shifts in temperature caused by the hot summer days and cool winter nights. A wood-burning stove warms the interior during the colder times of year.

Built on a 500 m² plot of land, the wooden structure features sustainable and untreated materials. The residence's exterior timber, left natural to weather over time, exudes a rugged quality reflective of its wild context. As the years go by, the developing rustic patina will gradually camouflage the house further and further into the landscape. Pinus radiata plywood, a regional pine tree with a warm color tone, clads the entire interior. Sourced and grown on local plantations, the wood cladding grants the interior spaces a light and airy quality. These open and inviting spaces do without any painted or plastered wall finishes. Instead, the pure wood interior utilizes natural wood oils to maintain its rich and luminous appearance.

The bedroom pavilion integrates a standard truss roof while the main living pavilion finds a structural solution to craft an open and generous space. By adding a series of supporting exterior posts, the living pavilion remains free of the visual and physical weight of the interior trusses. This shift in structural solutions from one building to the next produces a layered and evolving internal atmosphere. Sliding glass doors connect the open living, kitchen, and dining pavilion to the outdoors. When open, these flexible partitions naturally ventilate the interior space and bring in cool breezes.

Fitting for the windswept region, the wooden structure gives the home a delicate and almost temporary reading upon the land. A contemporary interpretation of the classic farm buildings in the area, the energy-efficient house embraces a pared-down and modest approach to living. This bucolic summer residence acts as a welcome respite from the family's more complex daily life. Rugged yet welcoming, the dwelling offers unpretentious shelter within a framework of approachable green design—a place to kick off one's shoes and not worry about tracking in sand through the house.

Covered terraces bring light and air into the interior. Operable wooden slats shield these indoor/outdoor spaces from harsh winds and excess solar gain.

Sustainable features:
- → Solar orientation
- → Overhangs
- → Natural ventilation
- → Energy-efficient glazing
- → Adjustable louvers
- → Insulating foundation and roof
- → Reduced thermal bridges
- → Ventilated roof cavities
- → Solar hot water
- → Solar panels
- → Raw, locally sourced, and recyclable materials
- → High-performance insulation

Sustainable materials:
- → Double-glazed windows
- → Steel structure
- → Untreated wood
- → Natural wool insulation
- → Locally sourced pinus radiata plywood
- → Recyclable aluminum roof

City/country:
Aramoana, New Zealand

Year:
2008

Plot size:
500 m²

Building size:
150 m²

Number of rooms/residents:
3 bedrooms/ 7 residents

Overall Budget:
N/A

Floor plan
1. Living room
2. Dining room
3. Kitchen
4. Morning deck
5. Afternoon deck
6. Passageway
7. Study
8. Bedroom 1
9. Bathroom
10. Bunk room
11. Bedroom 2
12. Stairs to attic overflow area
13. Garage
14. Outdor shower

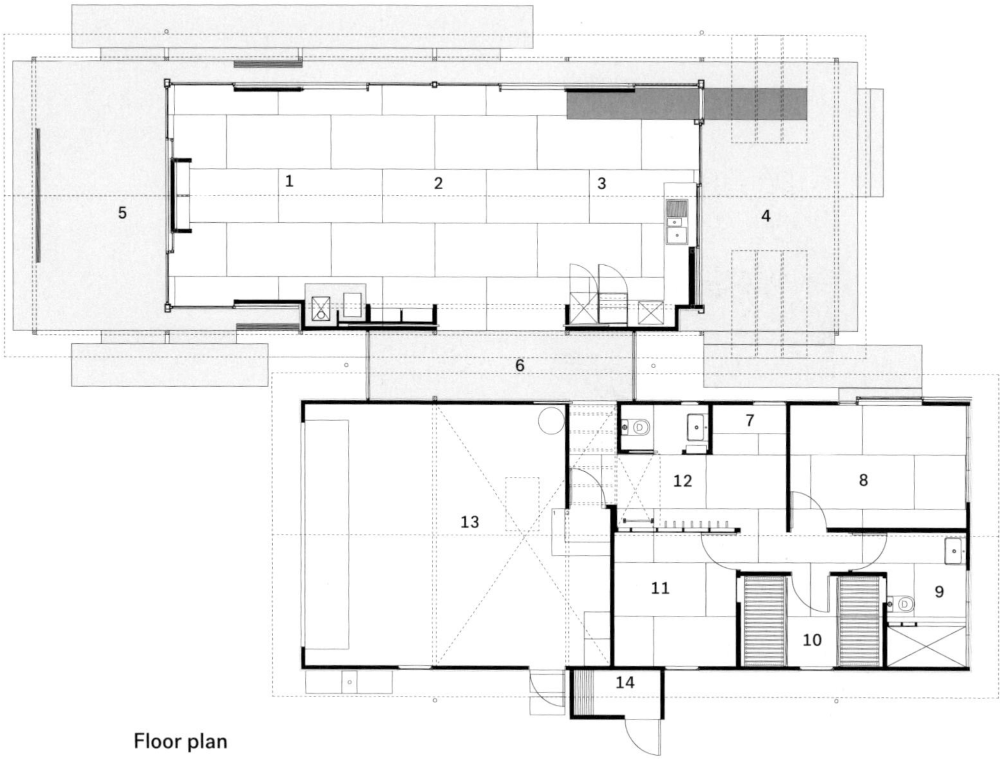

Floor plan

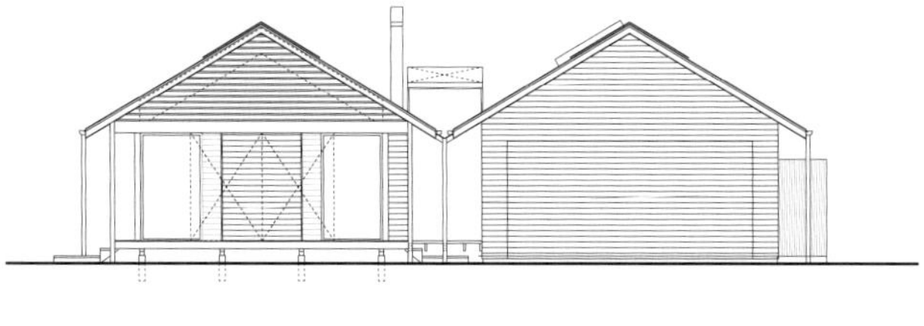

North elevation

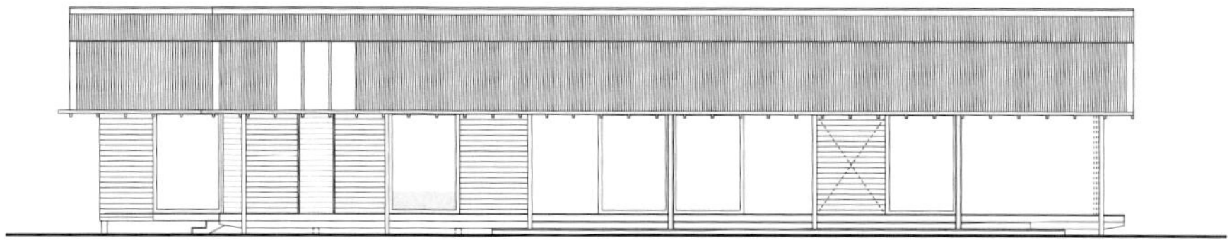

East elevation

South elevation

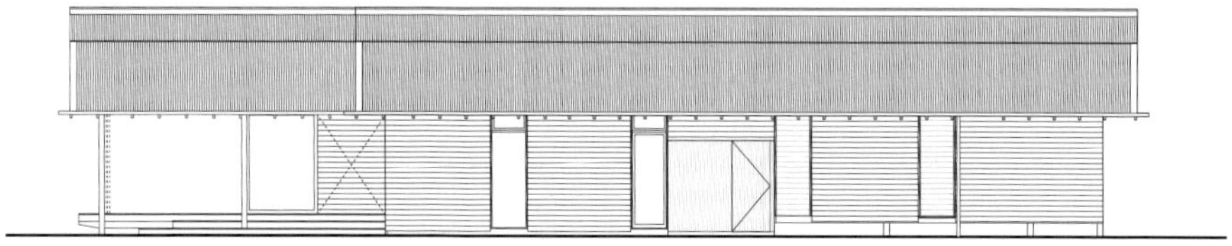

West elevation

221

Ryall Porter Sheridan Architects

Sustainable features

- Passive and active strategies
- Salvaged wood
- Photovoltaic panels
- Energy recovery ventilator
- Thick exterior walls
- High-performance insulation
- Reduced thermal bridges
- Energy-efficient glazing
- Thermal mass
- Airtight construction

Orient House IV and Artist Studio

Orient, NY, USA

This home renovation and new artist studio serve as two of the most energy efficient structures on Long Island. Built according to the International Passive House standards, the carbon neutral project utilizes reclaimed wood cladding, high-performance insulation and glazing, and produces more energy from solar power than it consumes.

A home and artist studio composed of two wood buildings resides on a bluff overlooking the Long Island Sound and Connecticut. The project consists of a complete renovation of an existing modern house built in the 1960s and a new freestanding artist studio. With updated and efficient windows, air and moisture barriers, high-performance insulation, and mechanical systems, the remodeled two-bedroom home now meets the International Passive House (PHI) standards.

Taking advantage of new construction opportunities, the goal of the artist studio creates an energy-efficient building with annual net-zero energy use. By adhering to passive house standards, the studio ranks among the first dozen structures in the United States to be certified by PHI. With a total annual energy demand of 2,200 kWh, offset by rooftop photovoltaic panels producing 5,605 kWh per year, the studio generates more than twice the electricity it uses. This impressive excess energy production achieves the American Institute of Architects' sustainability goals for the 2030 challenge, eighteen years ahead of schedule.

The project integrates both high and low-tech environmentally friendly materials to minimize its environmental impact. Salvaged pine and Douglas fir wood from demolished New York City buildings clad each structure in a protective rainscreen. This aged timber framing conceals a double-wall insulation system sealed by taped sheathing. Such an airtight barrier effectively prevents heat loss in the wintertime. During seasonal peaks and dips in temperature, a 90% efficient energy-recovery ventilator (ERV) brings fresh air into the space when windows are closed. An air-source heat pump supplies the home's heating and cooling needs year round.

In spite of retaining the existing 2 x 4 wood framing system, steel radically transforms the home's building envelope to comply with new hurricane zoning requirements for the area. Thick exterior walls packed with dense cellulose insulation minimize thermal bridges. To visually soften the construction's thick walls, thin aluminum extensions transition into deeply recessed triple-pane, operable casement windows. These low-emissive windows serve as some of the most energy-efficient glazing examples manufactured today. This glazing reduces both heat loss and heat gain, resulting in a comfortable and stable interior environment

The studio interior, illuminated by north-facing clerestory windows, satisfies the artist's requirement for a minimalist and luminous space, without the glare of south-facing glass. This gracious and timeless structure accommodates a large and bright painting studio with an art storage space, office, private bathroom, and screened porch area. Perhaps the structures

Bright sun terraces create protected indoor/outdoor spaces for the studio and main house. The terraces bring daylight and cool breezes into the interior.

most alluring feature, the screened porch introduces an indoor/outdoor shelter surrounded by nature on all sides. This contemplative space lets light into the interior during the winter and becomes an outdoor workplace throughout the summer.

In order to fully comply with passive house standards, the studio successfully captures the winter sunlight. Two-thirds of the building's heating load is supplied passively with a south-facing wall of translucent insulated panels. These panels, laminated onto a masonry wall, store and radiate heat into the space. The exterior façade panels direct the low winter sun's rays onto the masonry wall. In the summer, this same system deflects the high, penetrating sun while keeping the building well insulated and cool. Solid mahogany appears on the exterior decking and screen porch flooring for both the main house and the studio.

Perched on a 646 m² plot, the multi-level house connects to the landscape with an elevated wooden deck. This entry procession to the residence highlights the home and studio's rustic, aged timber skin. Oriented toward the north, the home enjoys scenic waterfront views. The slope of the site influences the stepped form of both structures. Working its way down the hillside, the home transitions from a one-to three-story building at its lowest point. An operable skylight set into the roof on this upper level directs sunlight and natural ventilation into the hardest to reach areas of the house.

The layout promotes access to the outdoors. Supported by generous glazing and framed views across all levels, large screened porches and sun decks expand the building footprint into the natural landscape. The home's split-level layout comprises a stepped open kitchen, living, and dining sequence, and a private studio placed off to one side. Above, the bedrooms and more intimate living spaces look out over the treetops. Contrasting with the dark and rugged exteriors, the home and studio feature light-filled interiors with clean and simple finishes. The residential restoration and new supporting building overcome site and structural challenges to achieve a carbon neutral footprint and a life enhanced by both nature and creative practice.

Sustainable features:
- Passive and active strategies
- Salvaged wood
- Photovoltaic panels
- Energy recovery ventilator
- Thick exterior walls
- High-performance insulation
- Reduced thermal bridges
- Energy-efficient glazing
- Thermal mass
- Airtight construction

Sustainable materials:
- Reclaimed heart pine and Douglas fir
- Solid mahogany
- Packed cellulose insulation
- Triple-glazed windows

City/country:
Orient, NY, USA

Year:
2012

Plot size:
646 m²

Building size:
232 m² (house)
111 m² (studio)

Number of rooms/residents:
2 bedrooms/
N/A

Overall budget:
N/A

Site plan

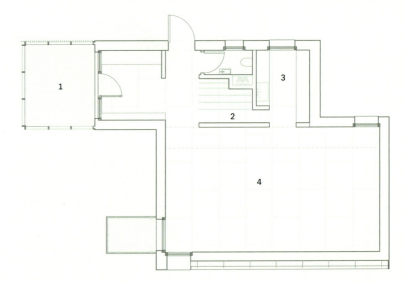

Studio floor plan
1. Screen porch
2. Painting storage
3. Utility room
4. Painting studio

Studio floor plan

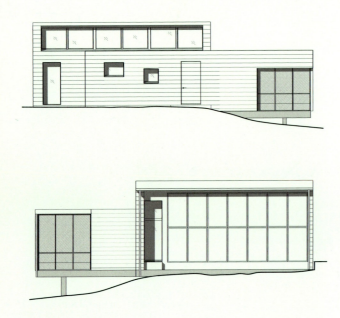

Studio elevations

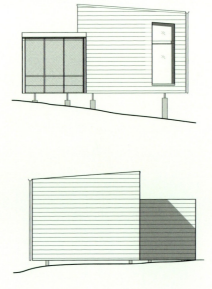

First floor plan

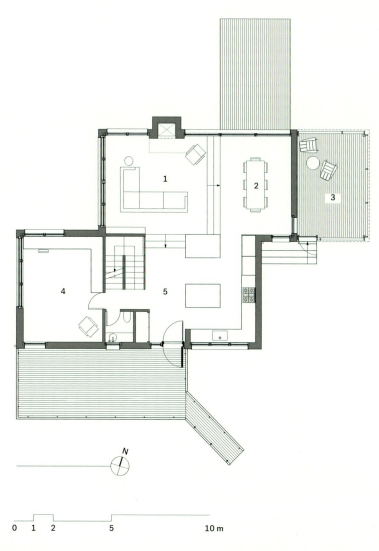

Ground floor plan

Ground floor plan	First floor plan
1. Living room	1. Bedroom
2. Dining room	2. Open to ground floor
3. Screened porch	3. Bathroom
4. Studio	4. Dressing room
5. Entrance/kitchen	

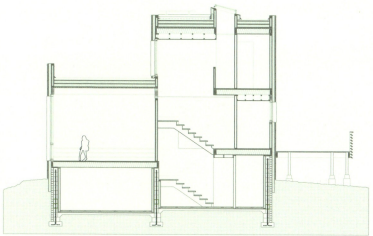

Main house section

Unsangdong Architects Cooperation

Kolon e+ Green Home

Yongin, Gyeonggi-do, South Korea

Sustainable features

- → Negative carbon footprint
- → Green roof solutions
- → Solar gain
- → Passive house certified
- → 95 green technologies
- → High-performance insulation
- → Energy-efficient glazing
- → Airtight construction
- → Photovoltaic panels
- → Cooling radiator
- → Natural daylight system
- → Natural ventilation
- → Rainwater collection and purification system
- → Recycled materials
- → Energy management system
- → CO_2 concentration monitoring

Introducing more than 95 sustainable technologies, this mountain-like dwelling achieves an energy + and carbon negative rating. The house, certified by the Passivhaus Institut in Germany, features a sophisticated green wall and roof system with built-in irrigation from rainwater catchment.

On a sweeping site of nearly 5,600 m², this futuristic home utilizes more than 95 green technologies. The angular dwelling covered by green walls and roofs produces and exceeds all of the home's energy needs. Certified by the Passivhaus Institut in Germany, the visually and ecologically experimental residence stands as the result of an active collaboration between the architects and the Kolon Institute of Technology.

A prototype for the future, the house combines principles of landscape architecture and sustainable architecture. The environmentally friendly housing model stimulates its occupants' commitment to both design and ecology. Implementing various high-performance insulation systems for the façade, solar power, purified rainwater recycling, and smart ventilation strategies, the iconic home inspires a contemporary and responsible lifestyle. The synthesis of dozens of optimized green technologies work together with intelligent energy-saving systems to keep the dwelling energy independent and carbon neutral.

Tiered landscaping with integrated solar panels and rainwater collection make up the home's iconic and ecological identity.

The fluid relationship between architecture and nature becomes an integral part of the family of four's daily life in the house. Exuding an unusual charm, the rational and emotional dwelling derives both its shape and ecological systems from nature. Arguably the home's most prominent feature, the network of sloping green walls and roof structures, demonstrate the home's commitment to a comprehensive, eco+ approach. This green roofing system minimizes energy loss in the winter while maximizing solar energy gain in the summer. Solar photovoltaic panels mounted on the rooftop sections produce the home's energy+ rating. These solar panels liberate the home from the public energy grid, allowing it to operate exclusively from the power generated by the sunlight collected during the day. The photovoltaic system also provides the domestic hot water for the house.

Evoking the language of an abstracted mountain or terraced landscape in silhouette, the angled surfaces of the green walls and roof promote rainwater catchment and irrigation. The rainwater collection and harvesting system irrigates the plantings and green surfaces while also doubling as water for flushing the home's toilets. These collection pools also create adiabatic cooling for the interior in the warmer times of year. Efficiently capturing the natural resources found in the sun, wind, and rain, this tapestry of green blanketing the interior facing walls of the residential complex achieves a visual harmony between the surrounding nature and the unconventional architecture.

Applying numerous passive and active energy-saving strategies, the airtight construction successfully maintains a stable year-round indoor climate. High density, triple-glazed windows appear throughout the house. In the summer, these inset windows prevent direct sunlight from overheating the interior. This same glazing transmits radiant heat from the sun during the winter months. New technologies, including a cooling radiator and natural lighting system with ventilation, ensure maximum comfort for the residents across the seasons. Environmentally friendly wallpapers and CO_2 concentration monitoring systems are used throughout the building. A total of 450 installed sensors monitor the home's various technologies. An energy management system saves, combines, and controls all information on energy output and input by connecting with each electrical element, such as the lighting fixtures, outlets, and switches.

Separated by a shared garden, the house decreases in height from a two-story main unit to a smaller single-level detached supporting unit. The roof of this smaller residential volume bends down to merge with the garden. A simple, built-in stairway invites the family onto the roof, crafting a continuous indoor/outdoor experience. Furniture made from recycled plastic and lumber adorns the minimalist interior spaces. The main residential unit integrates storage systems developed by

the Kolon Institute of Technology to improve the utility and openness of the floor plan. Clerestory windows illuminate the lofted second floor and naturally ventilate the space.

The goal for this project interweaves state-of-the-art green technologies with experimental architecture in a subtle and appealing way. Contrasting with the typical structures found in Korea, the house instead adopts the chaotic, fractal, and folding shapes found in nature and transfers them into a dynamic architectural expression. A reinforced concreted structure painted white supports the home's gestural roof gardens. The striking contrast of colors and materials initiates an engaging dialogue between the natural and manmade elements of the house. Reacting against modern civilization's tendency toward over-industrialization, the house argues for a more balanced coexistence with the land and its resources. Through a holistic approach to sustainability, the dwelling embodies an extension of the nature that surrounds it.

Site plan

Sustainable features:		Sustainable materials:	City/country:
→ Negative carbon footprint	→ Cooling radiator	→ Triple-glazed windows	Yongin, Gyeonggi-do, South Korea
→ Green roof solutions	→ Natural daylight system	→ Recycled plastic and wood furniture	Year: 2011
→ Solar gain	→ Natural ventilation		Plot size:
→ Passive house certified	→ Rainwater collection and purification system	→ Environmentally friendly wallpapers	5,525 m²
→ 95 green technologies	→ Recycled materials	→ Green walls and roof	Building size: 957.40 m²
→ High-performance insulation	→ Energy management system		Number of rooms/ residents:
→ Energy-efficient glazing	→ CO_2 concentration monitoring		3 bedrooms/ 4 residents
→ Airtight construction			Overall budget:
→ Photovoltaic panels			N/A

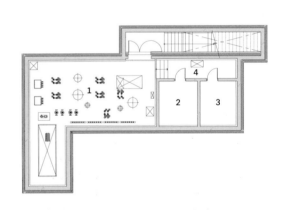

Basement floor plan

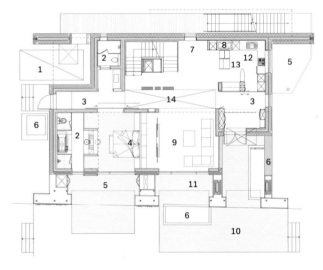

Ground floor plan

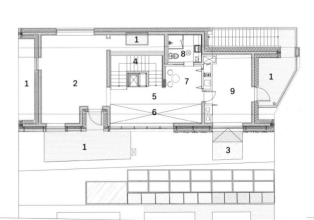

First floor plan

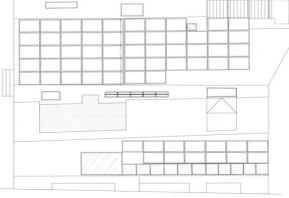

Roof plan

Basement floor plan

1. Mechanical room
2. Electrical room
3. Mechanical room
4. Shaft

Ground floor plan

1. Garage
2. Bathroom
3. Entrance
4. Bedroom
5. Terrace
6. Cistern
7. Stair hall
8. Laundry chute
9. Living room
10. Main entrance
11. Balcony
12. Kitchen
13. Dining room
14. Corridor

First floor plan

1. Terrace
2. Gallery
3. Cistern
4. Stair
5. Corridor
6. Atrium
7. Family room
8. Bathroom
9. Bedroom

Sections

1. Gallery
2. Terrace
3. Garage
4. Corridor
5. Bathroom
6. Mechanical room
7. Terrace
8. Stairhall
9. Corridor
10. Living room
11. Terrace
12. Mechanical room
13. Skylight

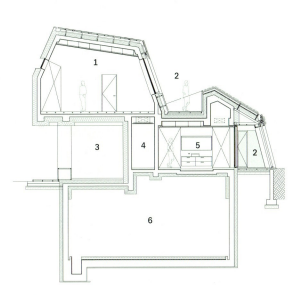
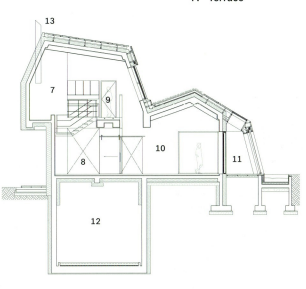

Sections

Guilhem Eustache

Sustainable features

- → Solar gain
- → Built-in shading
- → Natural ventilation
- → High ceilings
- → Double walls
- → Light color palette
- → Adiabatic cooling
- → Local materials
- → Native tree plantings

Fobe House

Tassoultante, Morocco

A modern home applies ancient methods for cooling desert structures. Built with local materials, the elegant residential compound features double walls for insulation, a light color palette, strategic shading, and water elements for adiabatic cooling.

This cluster of ethereal white residences appears just outside of the vibrant city of Marrakech. Built for a Belgian film producer and his Egyptologist mother, the project consists of a private residence, a small caretaker's dwelling, a free-standing garage, a pool house, and a totemic fireplace. The project establishes a close dialogue with the land, the vegetation, and the Atlas Mountains on the horizon. Located on a 2.5-hectare plot, the modestly sized residential grounds strike a dynamic equilibrium with the land in spite of the dramatic difference in scale.

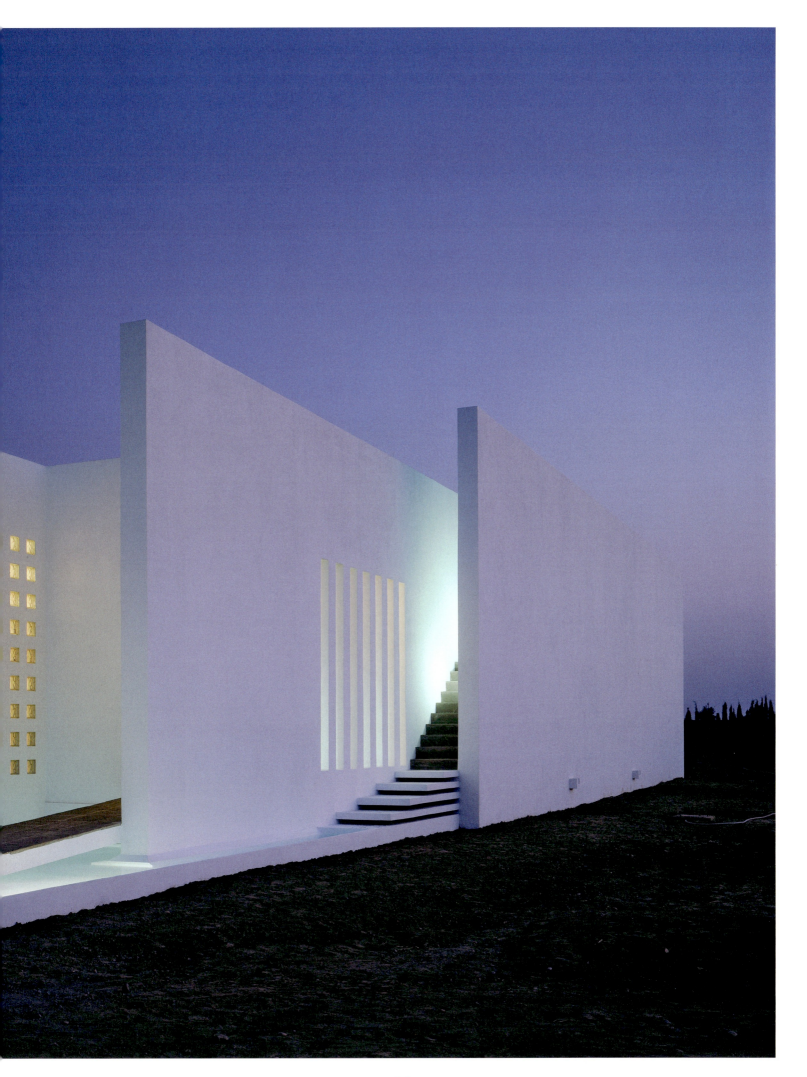

The overall design of the project grew out of the topology of the terrain. With simple and iconic lines, the house gracefully adapts to desert life. Rejecting the temptation to transplant Western lifestyles to Morocco in the form of sprawling lawns and elaborate watering systems, the residence instead engages architectural solutions adapted to the arid climate, cultural values, and economic conditions of the area. The main residence sits on the center of the plot while the caretaker's house and garage stand on the edge of the site closest to the road to Marrakech. Two overlapping white planes mark the main entrance of the house and contain a discreet staircase that leads to a rooftop terrace.

Sophisticated plays of light and shadow enhance and strengthen the different volumes. Patterned cutouts add a sense of rhythm to the project, breaking up the monolithic quality of the heavy white masses. The apertures also bring light into the more private areas of the house while still protecting against the harsh desert sun. Following extensive analysis of the site, the orientation of each building minimizes solar gain while maximizing views of the Atlas Mountains, breezes, and access points on the plot. A compromise between climatic and aesthetic considerations, each structure keeps within a strict height restriction to preserve the wildness of the land.

Temperature control represents a key challenge when building in the desert. With summer temperatures hovering around 40° Celsius in the shade, the heating and cooling concept plays a critical role in the home's ecological success. To combat the heat, the rooms feature high ceilings and double walls. An air pocket between the two walls increases the number of openings to the outside. These slender corridors introduce welcome drafts into the interior. The two bedrooms are the only rooms with air-conditioning. This reversible system, which also allows for heating during the coldest winter nights, only gets used during the ten through fifteen hottest days of the year. During the cold January evenings, two fireplaces warm the main residence and the caretaker's house.

The home incorporates a winter living space and a summer lounge, so the residents can engage with different parts of the house according to the season. Concrete sun screens are positioned in front of most of the openings. These protective buffers efficiently shield the home when the sun is at its highest position in the sky, and throughout the warmest season of the year. The use of light colors and the placement of narrow pools of water by the entrance further add to the project's natural cooling systems. A stately swimming pool aligned with the center of the house and accented by a dramatic stepped diving board also generates a consistent cool breeze for the interior.

Access to water becomes another important consideration with desert construction. There is, on average, between ten and twenty days of rainfall per year in the region. The chance of flooding during these times leads to the elevation of all the buildings on the complex 50 cm above the ground. Accessible via a well on the land, all water supplies for the house originate from glaciers on the nearby Atlas Mountains. The careful preservation of the wildness of the land has been enhanced by the planting of more than 500 trees on the site. A total of 23 olive trees, 10 palm trees, 450 eucalyptus trees, 200 mimosa trees, and 20 fruit trees make up the rich assortment of regional plantings.

While decidedly modern in its aesthetics, the home adopts numerous local and traditional techniques to respond to the harsh climate of the region. In addition to weaving in vernacular methods of climate control, the project also works with carefully chosen sustainable materials. All materials are sourced locally and require minimal maintenance. These elements include local clay, tadelakt, and stones from the Ourika valley. Tadelakt, the finish of choice throughout the project, is a completely waterproof, polished plaster made from lime and finished with olive oil soap. The humble components of this finish lend the house a tactile and timeless quality. By applying simple, regional principles of heating, cooling, and ecological construction techniques, the project shows that energy efficiency can be as traditional as it is technological. This residence demonstrates the vernacular side of sustainability—a beacon and a place of reverie.

Serene pools of water at both the front and back of the dwelling create adiabatic cooling for the house, where gentle breezes can waft through.

Sustainable features:

→ Solar gain
→ Built-in shading
→ Natural ventilation
→ High ceilings
→ Double walls
→ Light color palette
→ Adiabatic cooling
→ Local materials
→ Native tree plantings

Sustainable materials:

→ Local clay
→ Tadelakt plaster

City/country:

Tassoultante, Morocco

Year:

2014

Plot size:

2.5 hectares

Building size:

170 m²

Number of rooms/residents:

2 bedrooms/
2 residents

Overall budget:

N/A

Ground floor plan

1. Bridge
2. Basin
3. Corridor
4. Guest bedroom
5. Guest bathroom
6. Kitchen
7. Pantry
8. Summer living room
9. WC and sink
10. Winter living room
11. Master bathroom
12. Dressing room, walk-in closet
13. Master bedroom
14. Terrace
15. Swimming pool
16. Outdoor shower
17. Pool house

Ground floor plan

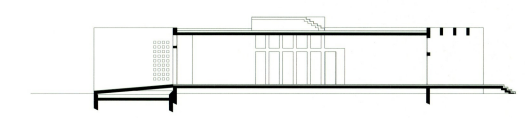

Longitudinal section

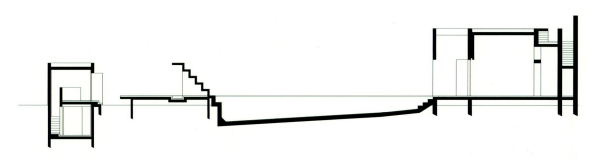

Transverse section

Andrea Oliva

Sustainable features

- → Natural ventilation
- → Rainwater collection
- → Overhangs to protect from solar gain and winter winds
- → East-west orientation to maximize solar performance
- → Energy-efficient glazing
- → Radiant heating
- → Solar hot water
- → Photovoltaic panels
- → Home automation (domotics)

House on "Morella"

Castelnovo Sotto, Italy

A pavilion-like house combines passive and active strategies to achieve an energy-efficient residential experience. The home's most prominent and sustainable feature consists of a grid of mobile façade panels that slide open and closed according to the level of desired sun exposure and natural ventilation.

Evoking the language of a classic modern pavilion, this minimalist two-story residence stands out against a landscape characterized by channels, shrubbery, and gardens. The experimental dwelling, framed by villas and agricultural houses in the distance, rests between the rural landscape and a nearby road. Applying an assortment of energy-saving techniques, the home integrates a commanding visual presence with a commitment to environmental sensitivity.

Elevated off the ground to create a minimally invasive approach, the house consists of two volumes nested inside one another. An oversized and open white rectangle protects the smaller, insulated residential volume set inside. The exterior band forms a covered walkway and a large porch that serves as a climatic buffer for the home's interior. With an orientation of 18° toward the west, the dwelling aligns for maximum solar benefit.

A simple stair links the elevated house to the expansive 16,000 m² grounds. The main entry occurs through a bright and tastefully appointed living room. Adding to the luminous quality of this space, a narrow cut out from the floor above floods the primary wall with extra light. The residence's use of white walls reflects daylight into all parts of the interior, even during the darkest months.

The thoughtful geometry of the porch and the appearance of ample glazed surfaces along the home's southern façade anticipate the arc of both the summer and winter sun. This spatial organization enables the house to open up to capture the winter sun while remaining protected from penetrating rays of the afternoon summer sun. By studying how the sun moves across the site, a system of integrated horizontal shutters and mobile panels afford the family the flexibility to curate the desired amount of daylight exposure and privacy for the interior. These grey panels produce a shifting façade that varies in permeability. When open, the light glass façade and interior levels are revealed. When closed, these geometric panels turn the house into a mysterious monolith protected from the natural elements.

Combining certain characteristics found in the agricultural houses of the region, the modern design embeds vernacular elements into its floor plan. These local techniques include a circulation route that also promotes ventilation, overhangs for protecting the vertical masonry, and a portico for sheltering the open and exterior spaces of the building. The residence's structure avoids the presence of thermal bridges through the use of porous brick walls coated in an insulating finish on the exterior. An attic space made from tiles and reinforced concrete enjoys a high insulation level that keeps heat from escaping through the ceiling. Seamlessly detailed and hidden from view above the attic, a rainwater catchment system of corrugated iron and drainage pipes connect to a storage tank.

In addition to the home's more passive energy strategies, numerous efficient technologies assist in the structure's day-to-day performance. Framed in plywood, the generous windows appearing throughout the dwelling consist of low emissive glass filled with argon gas. This high-performance glazing aids in interior climate stabilization year round and minimizes the home's reliance on extra heating and cooling. For general heating, radiant panels fed by a low condensation boiler keep the interior warm through the winter. Endowed with a mechanized system for air recycling, this additional method of climate control reduces the family of four's yearly energy usage to approximately 5.19 kilowatt hours per square meter. Solar panels from a photovoltaic array generate 6kW of energy to accommodate all of the home's hot water needs.

A home automation system, known as domotics, further curbs energy consumption. This efficient energy-saving system supports precise temperature controls from room to room, monitors the performance of general electrical appliances, and automatically turns off the lights in empty places. Additional features of this system check warm water production for the bathrooms and regulate operation times for each electric appliance.

The main rooms of the house orient along its southern face to ensure access to solar gain at all times of year. Service rooms and corridors cluster along the structure's northern side. With living spaces below and bedrooms above, the gracious but pared down interior inspires a tranquil and evolving relationship to the outdoors. As the gridded façade panels slide open or closed, the home's interior atmosphere and exterior appearance continuously evolve. Whether framing views of a favorite country vista or blocking out the harsh summer rays, these panels contribute to the house's ability to react to and remain efficient during dramatic shifts in season and overall climate. Built on a budget of $553,000 the iconic residence presents a streamlined blend between active and passive, traditional and high-tech methods of energy efficiency.

Sliding panels in varying sizes allow for the continued customization of the façade according to the desired amount of natural daylight and ventilation.

Sustainable features:

→ Natural ventilation
→ Rainwater collection
→ Overhangs to protect from solar gain and winter winds
→ East-west orientation to maximize solar performance
→ Energy-efficient glazing
→ Radiant heating
→ Solar hot water
→ Photovoltaic panels
→ Home automation (domotics)

Sustainable materials:

→ Exterior insulation
→ Low emissive, argon-filled glass

City/country:
Castelnovo Sotto, Italy

Year:
2009

Plot size:
1.6 hectares

Building size:
350 m²

Number of rooms/residents:
3 bedrooms/4 residents

Overall budget:
$553,000

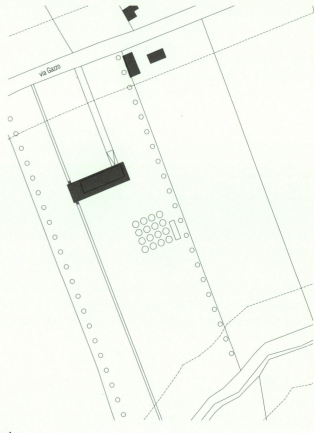

Site plan

Sun map longitude 44° 48'

Direction of prevailing winds

Orientation

Rainwater

Natural ventilation

Summer 70°

Winter 20°

Rainwater tank

Sustainable strategies diagram

Basement floor plan

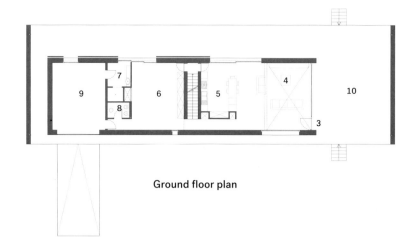

Ground floor plan

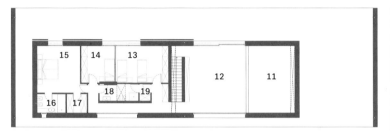

First floor plan

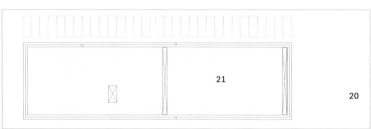

Roof plan

Basement floor plan	Ground floor plan	First floor plan	Roof plan
1. Cellar	3. Main entrance	11. Atrium	20. Green roof
2. Technical room	4. Living room	12. Study room	21. Aluminum corrugated sheeting
	5. Kitchen	13. Bedroom	
	6. Play room	14. Bedroom	
	7. Laundry	15. Bedroom	
	8. Guest bathroom	16. Bathroom	
	9. Garage	17. Closet	
	10. Porch	18. Bathroom	
		19. Closet	

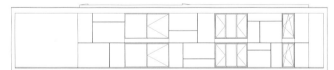

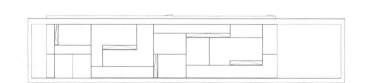

South elevation

North elevation

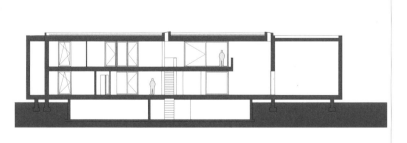

Longitudinal section

Transverse section

Vo Trong Nghia Architects

Sustainable features

- → Natural ventilation
- → Green façade for sun and noise protection
- → Rainwater collection system
- → Automatic irrigation pipes
- → Porous façades
- → Skylights
- → Passive house strategies

Stacking Green

Ho Chi Minh City, Vietnam

A narrow townhouse develops an efficient passive cooling strategy by stacking layers of plants along its front and back façades. These permeable partitions, irrigated with rainwater collected on site, shield the interior from direct sunlight and noise while promoting cross ventilation.

A slender residence in the heart of Ho Chi Minh challenges the city's current trend toward urban sprawl. As many newly developing Asian cities open up to investment and the global marketplace, they are quickly losing the regional characteristics that make them special. This erosion of local vernacular has hit Ho Chi Minh City particularly hard, as quality of life and access to greenery rapidly declines. True to its name, this narrow but tall, multi-level dwelling brings greenery back to the city. Taking the form of a tight and densely packed residential experience, the home's greenery can be enjoyed from both inside and out—a vertical and visual oasis for the neighborhood.

The layered townhouse builds upon the local fondness for streets, balconies, and courtyards filled with plants and flowers. Even in this modernizing city, the people still unconsciously desire a substitute for the rampant tropical forest. The house translates this custom into architectural expression through the creation of a façade composed of planters filled with lush vegetation. These planters act as horizontal louvers, directing light and air into the house. In addition to contributing to the visual comfort of the inhabitants, this green façade also upgrades the indoor thermal environment. This passive method of climate control saves energy typically spent on cooling, reducing the structures carbon footprint. Culminating in an intimate rooftop garden, the residence functions as a serene oasis in the center of the city.

Designed for a couple in their thirties and one of their mothers, the house rises out of a compact plot just four meters wide and twenty meters deep. The front and back façades are composed of layers of concrete planters cantilevered from two sidewalls. Automatic irrigation pipes installed inside the planters keep the plants hydrated while minimizing maintenance and excess water usage. Rainwater collected in a storage tank and pumped up to this irrigation system closes the resource gap between production and consumption, lessening the home's impact on the environment.

The four-story house disguises itself behind twelve levels of greenery. Spaced according to the height of the plants which varies from 25 cm to 40 cm, these minimalist white planters give the façade a rhythmic and playful quality that bleeds into the jungle-like interior. Semi-open, the permeable green screen maintains a high level of privacy and security for the residents. Unlike the typical and often aggressive methods used for achieving privacy in the city, the home's stacked green plantings instead offer a friendly and environmentally beneficial alternative for separating public and private life.

such a tropical and humid climate, the residents scarcely rely on their air conditioner. With an electricity bill of just $25 per month, the house predominately utilizes natural ventilation and passive design methods to meet its cooling needs.

Within a restrictive building footprint, the home choreographs a gracious use of space. The ground floor accommodates the main entry, parking, storage, and private bedroom for the mother. Above, the layout unifies into a single open living and dining space illuminated by a light well. The third level of the house comprises the couple's tranquil sleeping and bathing quarters. Culminating in the secluded rooftop garden, the final residential level features a study room and prayer room that open out onto nature. Advocating for a simple life between the leaves, this exhilarating final layer provides the ultimate vantage point for admiring the chaos and complexity of the city below.

Layers of plants allow fresh currents to circulate through the open air stairwell while shielding the circulation space from the eyes of the city.

At the rear of the house, an exterior staircase and courtyard nestles between the planters and the back wall. This indoor/outdoor staircase connects the upper levels of the house while ventilating and filtering the fresh air supply. Gratings on the rooftop vent the hot air up and out of the house. The insulating roof garden doubles as a climatic buffer for the bedroom below. Toward the street, a glazed partition subtly separates the entry parking space and front of the house from the plants. Inside, the layout engages as few partitions walls as possible to maximize views of the green façades and encourage ventilation. The skylights also allow natural light to penetrate deep into all levels of the house. In the mornings and afternoons, sunlight peaks through the leaves of the plants lining both façades to cast dappled shadows over the interior granite walls. These elegant and striated walls are composed of strictly stacked stones, 2 cm thick.

Inspired by the bioclimatic principles found in traditional Vietnamese courtyard houses, the residence applies a number of passive cooling features. Both the green façade and roof garden protect its inhabitants from direct sunlight, street noise, and pollution. The indoor environment enjoys refreshing natural currents throughout the house generated by the porous façades and two strategically placed skylights. Even in

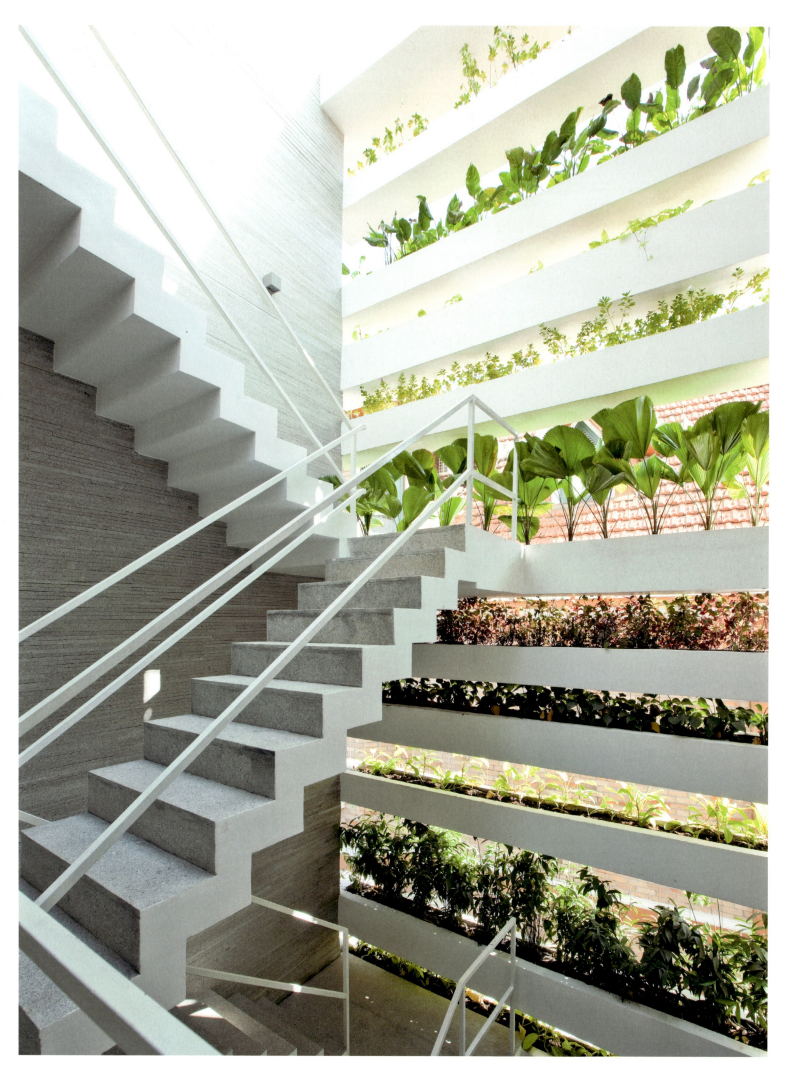

Sustainable features:
→ Natural ventilation
→ Green façade for sun and noise protection
→ Rainwater collection system
→ Automatic irrigation pipes
→ Porous façades
→ Skylights
→ Passive house strategies

Sustainable materials:
→ Green façade and roof garden
→ Concrete planters

City/country:
Ho Chi Minh City, Vietnam

Year:
2011

Plot size:
80 m²

Building size:
215 m²

Number of rooms/residents:
2 bedrooms/ 3 residents

Overall budget:
N/A

Site plan

Elevation

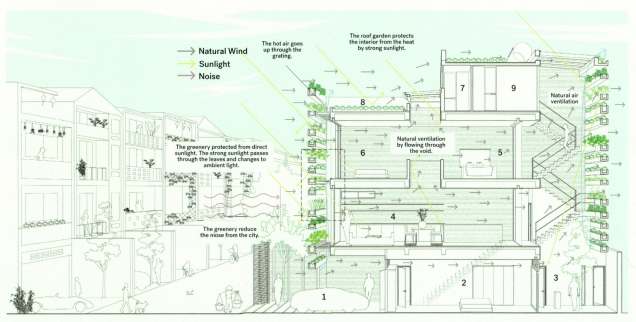

Section diagram with sustainable features

Section
1. Parking
2. Bedroom 1
3. Courtyard
4. Living space
5. Bathroom
6. Bedroom 2
7. Worship room
8. Roof garden
9. Study room

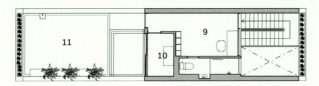

Third floor plan

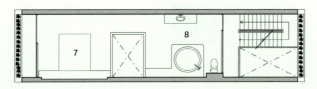

Second floor plan

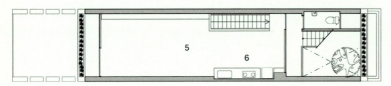

First floor plan

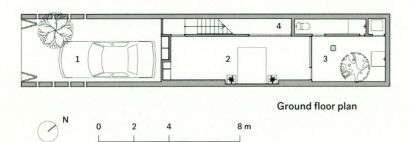

Ground floor plan

Ground floor plan
1. Parking
2. Bedroom 1
3. Courtyard
4. Storage

First floor plan
5. Living space
6. Kitchen space

Second floor plan
7. Bedroom 2
8. Bathroom

Third floor plan
9. Study room
10. Worship room
11. Roof garden

Longitudinal section

Elevation

Index

A

Ábaton Arquitectura
Spain
www.abaton.es

Off Grid Home
Architect/designer:
Camino Alonso, Ignacio Lechón, Carlos Alonso
Photo credits:
Belén Imaz and Ábaton
www.pepepisa.com
Additional credits:
Interior Decoration & Furnishing: Batavia.

→ Page: 28

Acme
United Kingdom
www.acme.ac

Hunsett Mill
Architect/designer:
Friedrich Ludewig, Stefano Dal Piva and Karoline Markus, Nerea Calvillo, Chris Yoo
Photo credits:
Cristobal Palma
www.estudiopalma.cl;
Friedrich Ludewig
Additional credits:
Contractor:
Timber Structure:
Willow Builders / Eurban, Flood
Defense:
Nuttall;
Structural engineer:
Adams Kara Taylor (Gerry O'Brien, Gary Lynch);
Services engineer:
Hoare Lea (Phil Grew);
Quantity surveyor:
Philip Panks & Partners / Cyril Sweett;
Sustainability:
Hoare Lea (Phil Grew).
Landscape:
ACME (Julia Cano, Kelvin Chu, Stefano Dal Piva, Deena Fakhro, Michael Haller, Friedrich Ludewig).

→ Page: 56

Andrea Oliva
Italy
www.cittaarchitettura.it

House on "Morella"
Architect/designer:
Andrea Oliva
Photo credits:
Kai-Uwe Schulte-Bunert
www.kaiuweschultebunert.de
Additional credits:
Luca Paroli, David Zilioli.

→ Page: 240

Aray Architecture
Japan
www.asei.jp

Shirasu
Architect/designer:
Asei Suzuki
Photo credits:
Daici Ano
www.fwdinc.jp

→ Page: 68

Arcgency
Denmark
www.arcgency.com,
www.lendagerark.dk

WFH House– Sustainable prefab house
Architect/designer:
Arcgency
Photo credits:
Jens Markus Lindhe
www.jenslindhe.dk,
Mads Møller.
Additional credits:
Manufacture:
worldFLEXhome, Nordisk Staal;
Collaborators:
Danish Technological Institute;
Technical engineer:
Henrik Sørensen;
Construction engineer:
Sloth Møller.

→ Page: 124

Architecten de Vylder Vinck Taillieu
Belgium
www.architectendvvt.com

House Rot-Ellen-Berg
Architect/designer:
Architecten de Vylder Vinck Taillieu
Photo credits:
Filip Dujardin
www.filipdujardin.be
Additional credits:
Design team:
Jan De Vylder, Inge Vinck, Jo Taillieu, Sebastian Skovsted, Olivier Goethals, Indra Janda;
Structural engineering:
Arthur De Roover Structureel Ontwerp, Gent;
Contractor carpentry:
Gebroeders De Clercq, Lochristi;
Contractor roofing:
Ducla, Beernem;
Contractor finishing:
Van Eeghem,Sint-Amandsberg Alumetal, Wingene client themselves

→ Page: 62

B

Barton Myers Associates
United States
www.bartonmyers.com

Montecito Residence
Architect/designer:
Barton Myers Associates
Photo credits:
Ciro Coehlo
www.cirocoelho.com
Additional credits:
General contractor:
Caputo Construction Corporation;
Structural engineer:
Norman J. Epstein;
Landscape architecture and interiors:
Rios Clementi Hale Studios;
Mechanical and plumbing engineer:
AG Mechanical Engineers;
Electrical engineer:
Smith Engineering Associates;
Civil engineer:
Penfield & Smith.

→ Page: 76

Bercy Chen Studio
United States
www.bcarc.com

Edgeland House
Architect/designer:
Bercy Chen Studio
Photo credits:
Paul Bardagjy
www.bardagjyphoto.com

→ Page: 34

BLAF Architecten
Belgium
blaf.be

Passive House with Textile Skin
Architect/designer:
Barbara Oelbrandt
Photo credits:
Stijn Bollaert
www.stijnbollaert.com
Additional credits:
Façade illustrations:
Chalkboard artist Eva Mouton;
Structural engineer:
Frank Haentjens.

→ Page: 46

BME-Odooproject
Hungary
www.odooproject.com

Odooproject
Architect/designer:
BME-Odooproject
Photo credits:
Balázs Danyi
www.danyibalazs.com

→ Page: 212

C

Carl Turner Architects
United Kingdom
www.ct-architects.co.uk

Slip House
Architect/designer:
Carl Turner Architects
Photo credits:
Tim Crocker
www.timcrocker.co.uk

→ Page: 82

D

Desai/Chia Architecture
United States
www.desaichia.com

LM Guest House
Architect/designer:
Desai Chia Architecture
Photo credits:
Paul Warchol
www.warcholphotography.com
Additional credits:
Structural engineer:
Ove Arup & Partners;
Mechanical/electrical/plumbing engineer:
Tucker Associates (Salamone Group);
Geotechnical engineer:
GeoDesign;
Civil engineer:
Paggi Martin DelBene;
Landscape architect:
Michael Van Valkenburgh Associates;
Building envelope consultant:
James R. Gainfort AIA Consulting Architect;
Lighting consultant:
Christine Sciulli Light + Design;
Construction manager:
Daniel O'Connell's Sons.

→ Page: 88

Djuric Tardio Architectes
France
www.djuric-tardio.com

Eco Sustainable House
Architect/designer:
Djuric Tardio Architectes
Photo credits:
Clément Guillaume
www.clementguillaume.com

→ Page: 188

F

FRPO Rodriguez & Oriol
Spain
www.frpo.es

MO House
Architect/designer:
Fernando Rodríguez, Pablo Oriol
Photo credits:
Miguel de Guzmán
www.imagensubliminal.com,
Process images: FRPO.

Additional credits:
Collaborators:
Pastora Cotero, Inés Olavarrieta, Cornelius Schmitz, Cristina Escuder;
Contractor:
Alter Materia, Grupo Singular;
Consultants:
KLH, Alter Materia, Miguel Nevado;
Furniture:
Paredes & Pino. Schneider & Colao Studio Gallery, Volumen Mobiliario, La Pluma Verde.

→ Page: 94

G

Guilhem Eustache
France
www.guilhemeustache.com

Fobe House
Architect/designer:
Guilhem Eustache
Moroccan correspondent:
Hicham Belhouari (architect)
Photo credits:
Jean-Marie Monthiers
www.jm-monthiers.fr

→ Page: 234

H

H & P Architects
Vietnam
www.hpa.vn

Blooming Bamboo Home
Architect/designer:
H & P Architects
Photo credits:
Doan Thanh Ha

Additional credits:
Architect in charge:
Doan Thanh Ha, Tran Ngoc Phuong;
Team:
Chu Kim Thinh, Erimescu Patricia, Nguyen Van Manh, Nguyen Khanh Hoa, Nguyen Quynh Trang, Tran Quoc Thang, Pham Hong Son, Hoang Dinh Toan, Pham Quang Thang, Nguyen Hai Hue, Nguyen Khac Phuoc.

→ Page: 142

I

Institute for Advanced Architecture of Catalonia
Spain
www.iaac.net

Endesa Pavilion
Architect/designer:
Institute for Advanced Architecture of Catalonia (IAAC)
Photo credits:
Adriá Goula
www.adriagoula.com

Additional credits:
Design team:
Rodrigo Rubio, Miguel Guerrero.
Wood engineering:
Fupicsa (MetsöWood);
Photovoltaic engineering:
TFM (Comsa);
Promotion:
Visoren SA.

→ Page: 106

J

John Wardle Architects
Australia
www.johnwardlearchitects.com

The Shearers Quarters
Architect/designer:
John Wardle Architects
Photo credits:
Trevor Mein
www.meinphoto.com

Additional credits:
John Wardle, Andy Wong, Chloe Lanser, Jeff Arnold;
Builder:
Cordwell Lane;
Structural enginee:
Gandy and Roberts;
Building surveyor:
Holdfast Consulting;
Joiners:
Euro Trend Windows & Doors

→ Page: 100

Jun Igarashi Architects
Japan
www.jun-igarashi.com

House O
Architect/designer:
Jun Igarashi Architects
Photo credits:
Iwan Baan
www.iwanbaan.com,
Sergio Pirrone
www.sergiopirrone.com

Additional credits:
Structural Engineer:
Daisuke Hasegawa & Partners

→ Page: 118

Juri Troy Architects
Austria
www.juritroy.com

Sunlighthouse
Architect/designer:
Juri Troy Architects
Photo credits:
Adam Mork
www.adammork.dk

Additional credits:
Competition in collaboration with DI Hein;
Engineering:
Donau Universität Krems;
Timber construction:
Kaspar Greber Bezau.

→ Page: 40

K

Kengo Kuma & Associates
Japan
www.kkaa.co.jp

Meme Meadows Experimental House
Architect/designer:
Kengo Kuma, Takumi Saikawa

Additional credits:
Structural engineering:
Yashushi Moribe (Showa Womden's University)
Mechanical services;
Electrical planning:
Bumpei Magori (Factor M / Institute of Industrial Science, University of Tokyo);
Visualization system of temperature and humidity:
Tomonari Yashiro Laboratory, Institute of Industrial Science, University of Tokyo;
Main constructor:
Takahashi Construction Co., (Katsunori Takahashi, Hideyuki Hirakawa, HiroNori Kiseki);
Membrane:
Kyoritsu Industries Co. (Takashi Noguchi, Kazuhide Horiguschi, Nobuhiro Iizuka)
Ventilation system:
Okuhara Co. (Katsumi Umezu);
Sanitary equipment:
Hokkaido Alfa Co. (Yutaka Yoneyama);
Electrical system:
Kamiyama Electric Co. (Akira Takao).

→ Page: 200

Kjellgren Kaminsky Architecture
Sweden
www.kjellgrenkaminsky.se

Villa Nyberg
Architect/designer:
Kjellgren Kaminsky Architects
Photo credits:
Kalle Sanner
www.kallesanner.se

→ Page: 178

Kraus Schönberg
Germany
www.kraus-schoenberg.com

Haus W
Architect/designer:
Kraus Schönberg
Photo credits:
Ioana Marinescu
www.ioanamarinescu.com

→ Page: 154

L

Lifethings
Republic of Korea
www.lifethings.in

Sosoljip, Net-Zero Energy House
Architect/designer:
Soo-in Yang and Heunjoo Lee
Photo credits:
Kyungsub Shin
www.shinkyungsub.com

Additional credits:
Project manager:
Kyeongjin Jung;
Project designer:
Jaeseok Choi;
Contractor:
Yim, Hyun Chul (Chaeheon Construction);
Structural engineering:
Park, Byung-soon (The Kujo);
Electrical engineering:
Hangil Engineering;
Mechanical engineering:
Joosung MEC.

→ Page: 160

Lode Architecture
France
www.lode-architecture.com

G House
Architect/designer:
Lode Architecture
Photo credits:
Daniel Moulinet
www.danielmoulinet.com

→ Page: 206

P

Parsonson Architects
New Zealand
www.p-a.co.nz

Shoal Bay Bach
Architect/designer:
Gerald Parsonson and Craig Burt
Photo credits:
Paul McCredie

→ Page: 218

Paul Archer Design
United Kingdom
www.paularcherdesign.co.uk

Green Orchard
Architect/designer:
Paul Archer Design
Photo credits:
Will Pryce
www.willpryce.com,
Paul Archer

→ Page: 166

Pitman Tozer Architects
United Kingdom
www.pitmantozer.com

Gap House
Architect/designer:
Pitman Tozer Architects
Photo credits:
Nick Kane
www.nickkane.co.uk

Additional credits:
M&E engineer:
Arup (feasibility only)
Richard Pearce & Associates;
Structural engineer:
Richard Tant Associates;
Party wall surveyor:
Dunphy & Hayes;
Energy consultants:
Briary Energy;
Landscape consultant:
Nurture Nature;
Contractor:
Brownstone.

→ Page: 52

Powerhouse Company

The Netherlands
www.powerhouse-company.com

Village House

Architect/designer:
Powerhouse Company

Photo credits:
Åke E:son Lindman
www.lindmanphotography.com

Additional credits:
Team:
Charles Bessard, Lotte Adolph Bessard, Ted Schauman, Kristina Tegner, Peter Nilsson;
Structural engineering:
Ove Heede Consult;
Energy consultancy:
Ellehauge & Kildemoes.

→ Page: 172

R

Renzo Piano Building Workshop

Italy
www.rpbw.com

"Diogene" Basic Shelter

Architect/designer:
Renzo Piano Building Workshop

Additional credits:
Design team:
S. Scarabicchi, E. Donadel, M. Rossato-Piano, M. Menardo, P. Colonna;
Project mangement and cost control:
Aja Huber (Vitra AG);
Consultants:
Ing. Maurizio Milan (partner in charge), Ing. Andrea Amoretti, TRANSSOLAR Energietechnik, Prof. Matthias Schuler (partner in charge), Ing. Nadir Abdessemed, Favero & Milan Ingegneria (structure).

→ Page: 132

Rural Urban Framework

Hong Kong
www.rufwork.org

A House for All Seasons

Architect/designer:
John Lin

Photo credits:
Rural Urban Framework
www.rufwork.org

Additional credits:
Project collaborators:
Shaanxi Province Women Federation, Shaanxi Volunteers Association of Red Phoenix Project, Linwei District Women Federation, Qiaonan Town Government, Shijia Village Committee;
Project team:
Crystal Kwan (Leader), Huang Zhiyun, Katja Lam, Li Bin, Maggie Ma, Qian Kun, Jane Zhang, Yanchen Liu.

→ Page: 112

Ryall Porter Sheridan Architects

United States
www.ryallporter.com

Orient House IV and Artist Studio

Architect/designer:
William Ryall AIA, PHIUS, LEED

Photo credits:
Ty Cole
www.tycole.com,
Otto Photo Agency
www.ottoarchive.com

Additional credits:
General contractor:
Phil Manuele, Manuele Contracting;
MEP/environmental:
David White, Right Environments.

→ Page: 222

S

Studio 1984

France
www.1984studios.com

The Nest

Architect/designer:
Marina Ramirez, Maria Sarle, Jordi Pimas, Jean Réhault, Romain Gié

Photo credits:
Studio 1984 Architects

Additional credits:
Partners:
Carpenters:
Bois2boo;
Sawyer:
Scierie Friederich;
Joiner:
Braun;
Structure studies:
Fabrice Moreau.

→ Page: 138

T

Tegnestuen Vandkunsten

Denmark
vandkunsten.com

The Modern Seaweed House

Architect/designer:
Søren Nielsen and Katrine West Kristensen

Photo credits:
Helene Høyer Mikkelsen
www.arkitekturfotografi.net

Additional credits:
Jørgen Søndermark, architect, Realdania Byg, Anne Mette Manelius, Jan Schipull Kauchen, LCA consultancy.

→ Page: 148

Tham & Videgård Arkitekter

Sweden
www.tvark.se

Garden House

Architect/designer:
Bolle Tham and Martin Videgård

Photo credits:
Åke E:son Lindman
www.lindmanphotography.com

Additional credits:
Team:
Fredrik Nilsson, Lukas Thiel, Erik Wåhlström, Johan Björkholm, Dennis Suppers;
Landscape consultants:
C-O-M-B-I-N-E, Anders Mårsén, Eveliina Hafvenstein Säteri.

→ Page: 182

U

Unsangdong Architects Cooperation

Republic of Korea
www.usdspace.com

Kolon e+ Green Home

Architect/designer:
Jang Yoon Gyoo and Shin Chang Hoon

Photo credits:
Sergio Pirrone
www.sergiopirrone.com

Additional credits:
Kolon Global.

→ Page: 228

UUfie

Canada
www.uufie.com

Lake Cottage

Architect/designer:
UUfie

Photo credits:
Naho Kubota
www.nahokubota.com;
UUfie.

→ Page: 194

V

Vo Trong Nghia Architects

Vietnam
www.votrongnghia.com

Stacking Green

Architect/designer:
Vo Trong Nghia, Daisuke Sanuki, Shunri Nishizawa.

Photo credits:
Hiroyuki Oki
www.deconphoto.com

Additional credits:
Contractor:
Wind and Water House JSC.

→ Page: 246

Imprint

Building Better: Sustainable Architecture for Family Homes

This book was conceived, edited, and designed by Gestalten.

Edited by
Sven Ehmann, Robert Klanten, and Sofia Borges

Preface by
Hans Drexler

Intro and project texts by
Sofia Borges

Layout and design by
Sven Michel

Cover photographs by
Paul Archer Design, Barton Myers Associates and Uufie

Cover design by
Sven Michel

Typefaces:
Post Grotesk by Josh Finklea,

Academica by Josef Tyfa and František Štorm

Proofreading by
Transparent Language Solutions

Preface translation by
Transparent Language Solutions

Printed by Optimal Media GmbH, Röbel/Müritz

Made in Germany

Published by Gestalten, Berlin 2014
ISBN 978-3-89955-512-7

© Die Gestalten Verlag GmbH & Co. KG, Berlin 2014

All rights reserved. No part of this publication may be reproduced or transmitted in any form or by any means, electronic or mechanical, including photocopy or any storage and retrieval system, without permission in writing from the publisher.

Respect copyrights, encourage creativity!

For more information, please visit www.gestalten.com.

Bibliographic information published by the Deutsche Nationalbibliothek. The Deutsche Nationalbibliothek lists this publication in the Deutsche Nationalbibliografie; detailed bibliographic data are available online at http://dnb.d-nb.de.

None of the content in this book was published in exchange for payment by commercial parties or designers; Gestalten selected all included work based solely on its artistic merit.

This book was printed on paper certified by the FSC®.

MIX Paper from responsible sources FSC® C108521

Gestalten is a climate-neutral company. We collaborate with the non-profit carbon offset provider myclimate (www.myclimate.org) to neutralize the company's carbon footprint produced through our worldwide business activities by investing in projects that reduce CO_2 emissions (www.gestalten.com/myclimate).